Eric

Hope you enjoy this book about our history.

Ruth White

EVERY HIGHWAY OUT OF NASHVILLE

VOLUME 2

RUTH WHITE

WSM Grand Ole Opry cast of 1953.

- *Lettering by Billy Robinson*

According to Howard White, 'There's more cast members in this picture than any other made. They took us out of Mom's Place (later called Tootsie's) to get this picture made.'

EVERY HIGHWAY OUT
OF NASHVILLE
Volume 2
by Ruth B. White

Catalog data:
Author - White, Ruth Bland
Foreword by Green, Lloyd

New Printing: NovaBooksNashville, September 2014

ISBN: 978-0-9632684-1-9 Soft cover
ISBN: 978-0-9632684-4-0 E-book

First Printing: JMP, August 1990
ISBN: 0-939298-88-0
(Picker's Rest Books
349 Sunset Island Trail
Gallatin, TN 37066)

p. cm series (American Arts Culture)

Dedicated to all the Sidemen who have come before
And all the Sidemen who will follow,
Who, along with the Session players,
Created and continue to promote the Nashville Sound.

In Memory of Howard O. White, Jr., 1926 – 2008

Howard White, 1953

AUTHOR ACKNOWLEDGMENTS

An affectionate toast to Howard White: Without his sagacious grasp of the music business, there would have been no book, and a very special nod to daughter Kathleen for her insight on Howard and his many friends. Bless Lloyd Green, one of the finest steel players ever, for his kind words in the Foreword. I'm also grateful to Mike Streissguth, a New Yorker who writes about Nashville's best and had nice thoughts about me.

Cheers to Billy Edd Wheeler for giving permission to use his words over and over again. Thanks, too, to Billy Robinson who lives 780 steps from me and always talks freely of the era he and Howard enjoyed. My gratitude to Spencer Williams, who happened to own a blue Bonneville Pontiac station wagon exactly like Hank Snow's, and to Joe Lee of West Virginia for encouraging this project. Finally, thanks to the many friends who asked for another book - or sequel - to the first "Every Highway Out of Nashville," while encouraging me to add more road stories. Special praise goes out to those who kept telling me their tales, as well.

Meantime, I remain in the debt of those very important persons who provided words of wisdom for the original book, notably Country Music Hall of Famers Eddy Arnold and Chet Atkins, who are no longer with us, and Jean Shepard, yet another Country Music Hall of Fame member.

Ruth White
Gallatin, TN

PUBLISHER ACKNOWLEDGMENTS

In addition to the creativity of Ruth White and the late Howard White, Nova Books is further indebted to the talent and technical skills of Madeline Godwin, Huntsville, AL; Tom Barkoukis, Nashville TN; and Bill Trott, Phoenix, AZ, all of whom have helped make this publication possible.

Early 1970s' Columbia Records' session featuring Lloyd Green (center) on steel guitar, Henry Strzelecki (foreground), unknown guitarist (left), Pete Wade on guitar (right), Buddy Spicher (behind Lloyd) and (standing) Bobby Harden (singer-producer) with unknown vocalist.

Nova titles published in its American Arts Culture Series:

"Kitty Wells: The Honky Tonk Angels" by Walt Trott, 1993

"Sister Sunshine: Martha Carson" by Walt Trott, 1998

"Flight Of The MoonBirds" by Faye Partee, 2004

"The Original Goober – The Life & Times of James Buchanan" by Ruth White, 2004

"Number One Country Hits, 1944-2004" by Arnold Rogers & Jerry Langley, 2005

"Many Tears Ago: The Life & Times of Jenny Lou Carson" by Arnold Rogers & Jerry Langley, 2005

"Little Known Facts About Country Music" by Jack Selover, 2009

"A Place Called Paradise" by Shirley Hutchins, 2009

"My Memories of Jim Reeves . . . And Other Celebrities" by Joyce Jackson, 2010

FOREWORD

There are very few people alive today who know the smaller nuggets, the backstage banter, the heartbeat, the minutia, if you will, of how what later became known as the "Nashville Sound" began its tentative musical journey in the middle of the 20th century.

Ruth White does. She knew all the major actors as well as the bit players who made their cameo appearances on the musical stages of the Friday Night Frolics in the National Life Building on Seventh Avenue, the Grand Ole Opry at the Ryman Auditorium on Fifth Avenue, and as traveling musicians on stages around the United States and Canada, before the usurpation of the name country into the grotesque metamorphism, which today in the 21st century, masquerades as country music.

Ruth knew all the sidemen and some stars whose first Nashville stop was Mom Upchurch's rooming house at 620 Boscobel Street in East Nashville. If Mom's wasn't the heartbeat of the music coming from Nashville in the 1950's and 1960's, then it certainly supplied the lifeblood that kept the heart beating. But, besides knowing all these characters, and eventually marrying one of them, she delved much deeper into what country music was about in that era. In 1960, she became music librarian for WSM Radio, then ground zero of the music airwaves heard around the North American continent.

Later, in the next decade, as the music industry grew, she worked for Henry Strzelecki's October Records. Henry was also one of the major recording bass players of that golden period of country music. From there she got more involved with music publishing by being in charge of a company owned by two prominent songwriters, Carmol Taylor and Norro Wilson, with Norro also becoming a major record producer. As if those credentials were not sufficient, she then worked for a talent agency and a recording studio, until the late Porter Wagoner asked her to join his staff as administrative manager for half a decade.

Ruth's final Music Row position before retirement was, perhaps fittingly, to join her husband Howard White, one of those early settlers, steel guitarists and roomers at Mom Upchurch's, in their publishing company, the eponymous Howard White Music. To simplify; all of the above personal information about Ruth White is to validate that, having been a part of the Nashville country music community from its embryonic early stages through the full flowering of the Nashville Sound, she is one of the few people alive today who, with intelligence, wit and knowledge, is truly qualified to write this book, "Every Highway Out of Nashville, Volume 2."

Lloyd Green
Madison, Tennessee
June 10, 2014

Porter Wagoner in his Nudie cowboy suit, on stage in 1973,
backed by Mack Magaha.

– Photo by Les Leverett

CONTENTS:

Source achievement awards recipients (from left) Ruth White, Sherytha Scaife, Liz Thiels, Frances Preston, Celia Froehlig and Carol Phillips.

– Photo by Denise Fussell

INTRO

SWEET MEMORIES

"My World is like a river
As dark as it is deep
Night after night the past slips in
And gathers all my sleep ......"

Mickey Newbury

Once upon a time, Howard and I were leaving a session at Pete's Place, a recording studio owned by Pete Drake, a steel guitar player. We stood outside reminiscing with musicians Lloyd Green and Pete Wade, retelling old road stories. Lloyd said, "Someone ought to write a book." Pete said. "It wouldn't be funny to anyone but us."

Then Howard and I talked about such a book.

One day I put a tape in Howard's hands and said, "Here, put your life on tape. It just might make an interesting story." When I returned home from work at Porter Wagoner's office, Howard had put his whole life down on six cassette tapes. I know what we needed; a biography, a history, a comedy, a study in characters, an adventure, a music business study, and above all, a true story of characters we had known in over forty years of show business.

So, in 1990, I got started writing a book, a new phase for me. By working with Howard's tapes, his scrapbook and much discussion, I assembled a manuscript. I knew that not everyone lived life to the fullest, from musician to song plugger, or did exactly like they wanted to do as Howard did. Being at the right place, at the right time with a God-given talent, Howard eventually played steel guitar for five stars on the *Grand Ole Opry* (and, incidentally, some of the not-so-greats). When he got too old for the road, he was able to use his knowledge by working for five of the biggest music publishers in Nashville, owned his own company and even produced records. He came along at a time when it was easy to know the great producers, promoters, bookers and stars. Oh, he knew the entertainment world, inside and out.

I had never written a book, so in preparation I read a lot of books about the music business. At that time most books had been written by New York writers, and it seemed to me that their problem was they had no real feel about our business, no soul. I had been in the "song business" for so long I thought, "Why wouldn't the rules for songwriting apply to writing books."

1

With that in mind, I devised the following simple rules:

> Don't dwell on any subject too long. (My idea.)
> Hit hard and move on. (Howard's idea.)
> Repeat the "hook" as often as possible. (Harlan Howard's idea.)
> Keep it short. (Bob Jennings' theory.)

You've all heard about the songs written in ten minutes, "hits" that just fall into place on a paper napkin at Tootsie's. Well, it really doesn't happen that often. Writing a book doesn't happen in minutes either. This book, like the first "Every Highway Out Of Nashville," actually evolved over a period of years. Just like the songs that came over my desk, it was done with a lot of scratching out and starting over. A lot of time passed, to be exact, twenty-five years. I had people telling me to write a book about my life in the music business, which began in 1947, long before Nashville became *Music City, USA*. I thought about it and came up with a combination of mine and Howard's life; and so much happened the last twenty-five years. There was so much more history in recording, publishing and performing. So, here are my last thoughts in "Every Highway Out Of Nashville – Volume 2."

There's so much to tell and so many ways to tell it. I've truthfully tried to blend my story, Howard's and that of the many musicians, artists, DJs, bookers and promoters I've known for fifty-plus years. It's only through living oral histories that we leave an imprint for generations to come. I believe it is essential we hear the voices of those pioneers who forged the way, so that the "new kids on the block" know just how we have arrived at this place and time in this business we are still calling "Country Music."

This second book, of course, expands on the first and I hope will give the reader a better understanding of our fellow musicians and artists, who become family as they spend days and nights with each other. They were each other's support system. Sidemen sometimes became stars. Stars got bigger and sometimes their brightness dimmed. They might have fought over little things, but their love for each other did not dim. Time and distance played no part. When a fellow musician played his last note or an artist sang his last note, time and distance were removed. The good times are always remembered, not the bad. They are all brothers and sisters. The following is the story of friends – and a few who aren't. All of these stories are by now simply *"Sweet Memories, hm-m-m-m-m-m-m-m-m."*

> ## *"The music business is not a business – it's a happening!"*

Howard White

Ruth and Howard partnering at Creative Studios, Nashville.

1 RIGHT PLACE, RIGHT TIME

"If I leave here tomorrow
Would you still remember me
For I must be travelin' on now
'Cause there's too many places I've got to see."

- Allen Collins and Ronnie Van Zant.

It was July 1952, and Howard was playing at WNOX Radio in Knoxville, Tennessee. The phone rang backstage, as he was preparing to leave. No one else was there, so he answered the phone. The fellow on the other end of the line said he was Randy Hughes in Nashville. He was managing Cowboy Copas, and told Howard that Copas was going on the road and needed a fiddle player, and was there one there available?

As Howard said, "Sometimes in one's life, you just happen to be at the right place at the right time. It just so happened that Don Gibson's whole band had just worked their notice and none of them had a job."

Howard told Randy, "Yes, our fiddle player, Marion Sumner, could work and could you use a steel player and a guitar player?" Randy assured Howard he could use all three of them, so Marion Sumner, Luke Brandon and Howard were all hired for Copas' next tour. None of them had a car, but Howard had saved three hundred and fifty dollars, so he bought a 1933 Ford sedan, rented a U-Haul trailer, and they all headed to Nashville. They pulled into Nashville with that Ford "smokin' and a 'boilin'" right to the Sam Davis Hotel, where they checked in. The next day they met with Hughes and left immediately on a seventeen-day tour to the Midwest with Copas.

"At the time, we all thought there had never been such a tour," Howard said, describing their experience. "The first stop between dates was from Salem, Illinois, to North Platte, Nebraska, a distance of nine-hundred miles. We worked seventeen one-night stands with distances between dates about the same. Later, I learned that this was not unusual for country bands. The bookers who booked the show dates didn't really worry about how far apart the dates were. A joke back then was that the bookers stood back and threw darts at the U.S. map to see where they would book next."

Howard came down with strep throat on that tour, but was afraid he would lose his job if anyone knew he was sick. That's how it was – sick or well, you played the date. When they got back to Nashville, the other guys quit, but Howard stayed on. He said, "I thought I had made it! I had, playing in Nashville! My life-long dream had come true. All the hours spent learning to play steel guitar by listening to the Opry and Jerry Byrd records, had finally gotten me to Nashville."

Simply put, Howard was thrilled to be playing on the road with Cowboy Copas. Bob Foster had the job before him, but quit to get off the road. Bob was still playing Opry spots with Copas, but Copas felt since Howard was playing his road dates, it was only fair Howard play his Opry spots with him. Howard said, "Copas let me play his Opry spots with him - the *Grand Ole Opry!*" From that point on, Howard spent the next fifteen years giving of his talent, energies, life, body and soul to the great, sometimes rough and tough, life of a country musician.

The experiences that follow were the way Howard's life in the music business happened, all of it. His life as a dedicated musician had begun. Consequently, my life paralleled his in this business we like to call music.

Autographed sheet music featuring Kathy and Cowboy Copas.

5

2 SNOOKY GROWS UP

"I've laid around and played around
This old town too long
Winter's coming on . . .
And I feel like I gotta travel on."

- Paul Clayton, Pete Seeger, Ronnie Gilbert,
Lee Hays, Fred Hellerman, Dave Lazer & Larry Ehrlich

There's a beginning to every song, every record and every story, and our story begins when Howard Osmond White, Jr., was born March 26, 1926, in Charlotte, Mecklenburg County, North Carolina, the eldest son of Howard and Eula Mae White. His Aunt Edie called him "Snooky" and even today friends and relatives in Charlotte still know him as Snooky.

Howard described his home this way: "Our house was very much like 'The Walton's' house on TV. We didn't have a farm, we had two-and-a-half acres, a cow, a lot of grass to mow and a lot of chores for me and my two brothers to share in during those Great Depression years. My father was a harsh taskmaster. When he left for work and he said, 'Bud, put leaves in the cow stable today.' He didn't mean tomorrow."

Meantime, Dad worked long hours as an aide for Cameron Morrison, a North Carolina Governor and later both a U.S. Congressman and Senator. He earned twenty-five dollars a week, getting small raises as times got better during those Depression years. He managed baseball teams, almost semi-pro. He wanted Howard to grow up and play baseball, but by then Howard had discovered the *Grand Ole Opry*. They had a "Victrola" on which Howard listened to Blue Yodeler Jimmie Rodgers records. Howard's whole life was influenced and altered by the radio and that Victrola.

Howard's father loved the song "Birmingham Jail," so when Howard began to play guitar, he would play it as his dad hummed along. Much later in 2006, Howard recorded that song with Pete Wade on guitar, Buddy Spicher on fiddle, and Millie Kirkham singing her high, sad soprano.

The Whites were justly proud of their ancestors. On May 19, 1775, a group of North Carolina patriots met and drafted a Declaration of Independence, declaring that the people of Mecklenburg County were free and independent of the British Crown. This Declaration was adopted, signed and taken by horseback to the Continental Congress in Philadelphia. The delegates there, however, felt it was premature.

Over a year later, on July 4, 1776, these same delegates voted to declare all thirteen American colonies free and independent of the tyranny of the Crown. The previous North Carolina document became known as the "Mecklenburg Declaration Of Independence." Four of its signers were kin to the Whites. Signers Hezekiah and Abraham Alexander were Howard's fifth great-grandfathers. Howard's Carolina ancestors began fighting the British before the rest of the country. Howard always felt that this fighting heritage was what gave him the courage to be able to stand what life sometimes handed you. It's probably what gave him the courage to fight back physically, like a night at Tootsie's when an usher from the Opry accosted him on the stairway. Howard knocked the guy clear down the steps, on which Tootsie stored cases of beer. As the guy tumbled down, you could hear bottles breaking, and see beer and blood everywhere! Then Randy Hughes came in, picked the guy up, and threw him head first out the door!

All of Howard's people were Presbyterians. Actually, the pioneers in his part of the world were mainly Presbyterian. They were born and raised in the church, married in the church and when they died buried in the churchyard. Most of their activities were centered around church or school. In high school, Howard's love life was limited to only three girls. Much more important to him then was basketball. He learned that you really didn't have to study, if you could play ball well. As Howard exuberantly recalled, "Once at an exciting game, the score was tied! I had the ball and time was running out. Daddy made a bet I'd make the basket, and a friend bet I wouldn't. I made it, and we won the game and Daddy won his bet!"

The eleventh grade was the last grade Sharon High School had in those days, but, after Howard completed the eleventh, a twelfth grade was added. So Howard returned to school, just so he could play basketball another year. As a result, he had two graduations.

In those days, Howard's family and friends didn't have much, and neither did anyone else, so the kids didn't realize they were poor. They loved summers, when they could go barefoot and skinny dip in Little Mike Creek. They would get watermelons from a nearby field, put them in the creek to cool, then bust them open and eat 'em. Typhoid Fever season usually stopped them from swimming, until they all lined up at the Community Center for shots. Howard said: "The only whipping my mama ever gave me, was because I disobeyed her and went swimming before my shot."

Howard and pals played a lot of sandlot baseball. They climbed a lot of trees and swung from limb to limb like Tarzan. Howard's mom would say, "Lawd, they're gonna break their bones." When Howard was fifteen years old, his dad took him to a chicken farm and put him out to work. Howard worked like the men, loading hundred-pound bags of feed for twelve dollars a week. That's when Howard grew up, thinking, "Is this all there is to life?" That job lasted until one day he was delivering eggs in a pick-up truck, hit a rut and broke all the damn eggs.

Then he discovered music, and nothing else mattered, not even girls. He began to hear the most beautiful sounds in the evenings, drifting over the meadows. That's when he found the Jamison family, who gathered every night on their front porch and played string music, that is guitar, banjo, mandolin and fiddle. They played tunes like "Over the Waves" and "I'll Be All Smiles Tonight." According to Howard, " It was the most beautiful music I ever heard, and when they taught me a C, F and G chord on their guitar, I felt like I was in Heaven."

Howard's dad bought him a twelve-dollar and fifty-cent Kalamazoo guitar for Christmas. Howard taught himself to play by listening to records and the radio. In winter they could get the *Grand Ole Opry* without any static, "clear from Nashville." The radio was an important part of life then, as television was not yet on the scene, and if you wanted to see a "picture show," you had to go to downtown Charlotte.

Nobody in Howard's family played an instrument, but he remembered that his Grandpa Porter used to wake everybody up by playing his fiddle. As Howard got a bit older, he discovered another instrument, the steel guitar. He said: "I watched the ads, earned some money at a service station, and bought a steel guitar, and a Sears & Roebuck amplifier. Breaking a string was a disaster to a poor boy, but my cousin came to my rescue. She worked at Burwell & Dunn, and they sold strings, among other things. She brought me Black Diamond strings for twenty-five cents a set. To the uninitiated, they never were the greatest of strings."

Howard kept hearing Jerry Byrd broadcasting from WLW-Cincinnati. Jerry fast became Howard's idol. Howard even wrote him, asking how he got the sounds he produced. Jerry answered him back, giving his tunings and advice on string arrangements and gauges. From that time on, Howard was hooked, and there was no other instrument for him but "The Steel."

He formed a band in high school, playing at barbecues, ice cream suppers, cakewalks and square dances. He learned early on that people were quick to complain. They'd say, "You're not playing loud enough" or "You're playing too loud," but Howard didn't really care. He was doing what he wanted to do, though his dad tried to discourage him, saying, "Why don't you get a real job, Bud?" (Musicians were not thought of highly in those days. Some folks said they drank and wouldn't work.) General opinion was, "What will the neighbors say!" That was the eleventh commandment.

Still, Howard kept on playing music and dreaming sweet dreams of one day going to Nashville. After all, playing music seemed better that hoeing corn or working on a chicken farm and delivering eggs. Whatever Howard's dreams were, or whatever dreams of his generation were, it was all interrupted by the declaration of World War II! No one could really make plans, because as they reached eighteen, they had to give their lives to Uncle Sam for a while. Who knew where they would be or even if they would come back home at all, and a lot of them didn't. At that time, few thought ahead as to how their lives might be affected by the war. From 1941-1945, they were just expected to serve. No one wanted to be called a draft dodger. Nobody thought much about the psychological scars on those who serve. During the war they did their job, no questions asked. And that's what Howard did, no questions asked.

3 THE WORST OF TIMES – THE BEST OF TIMES

*"There is the Winter of Darkness
And the Spring of Hope . . . "*
- Charles Dickens.

In the fall of 1943, when Howard was seventeen, he enrolled in Presbyterian Junior College in Maxton, North Carolina. The White family had moved to Washington, D.C., with then-Congressman Morrison. During the Christmas holidays, Howard went to visit with his family. All his older friends were in the service. He told his father he wanted to enlist in the Navy, but his eyesight was bad and he had been turned down previously.

Mr. White agreed to talk to Congressman Morrison about getting him into the military, regardless of his eyesight. In the meantime, Howard got a job in the House of Representatives' post office. In March, he turned eighteen and indeed Morrison got him into the Navy. Howard attended boot camp at Bainbridge, Maryland. After that, the Navy sent him into Special Services at a Naval Air Force base near Washington, D.C., serving in the chemical warfare branch. There he was to learn about "human guinea pigs." Typically, when the Navy called for volunteers – it was "you, you and you!"

Howard was amongst a thousand sailors selected to test for uniform protection against the use of Mustard and Lewisite gases. Howard recalled their uniforms looked somewhat like what astronauts wear now. What they did was march Howard and the others into gas chambers, and turned on the gas in order to determine if the suits leaked. Some of the guys were burned, and Howard explained what happened to him:

"I developed a nervous condition that grew worse and worse. I went down from one hundred and sixty pounds to one hundred and twenty-nine pounds. I lost touch with reality. I didn't eat or sleep. Then one day, I refused to go back into the chamber. Unacceptable behavior! I was relieved of duty and sent to Bethesda Naval Hospital. I really didn't understand why I was in the hospital. In reality, I was so sick, I didn't care where I was, as long as it wasn't in that gas chamber. After evaluation, they sent me to St. Elizabeth's in Washington, D. C., considered a 'Nut House.' We inmates called it 'Dizzy Lizzy.'"

Howard was so sick he didn't realize what was happening, but the Red Cross filled out papers for him regarding disability compensation. "Bless their hearts," Howard said. He was entitled to compensation, but wasn't told by the military that he could apply. Howard didn't ask questions, he just did as he was told. He knew nothing of his rights. All of those "gas victims" had been sworn to secrecy, and they kept their word for thirty years.

Howard was locked up from May to October. There was no medication offered then, no sophisticated tranquilizers. The only treatment was "rest." Day after weary day wore on, one after another. Reflecting on this, Howard mused, "Time seems to stand still in a mental hospital. I cannot remember much, but it seems to me that for any eighteen-year-old to be kept locked up, just resting and eating, without any protests, they must be sick, or at the very least, out of touch with reality."

Howard was assigned to a locked, non-violent ward. He was impressed by the fact that they took the whole ward to eat, but before they were taken back, they counted the silverware. He made a friend on the ward, Joe Godwin, who had been a second lieutenant in the Marines, a Chaplain, and was a veteran of the Guadalcanal Campaign. There were about a hundred men on the ward, all military.

Howard continued: "I was afraid most of the time. Fear was the most common emotion on the ward. We didn't know what was happening? I was only eighteen and had never been far from my family. But no one harassed me. When I got better, I progressed to a better ward and met Mose Moots, who played a mandolin. I found a guitar and they let us go around to the wards and entertain."

In the whole time Howard was at "Dizzy Lizzy," he talked to doctors only two or three times. The interviews centered on his childhood and how he got along with his folks. Then, after eight months, they told him he was cured, and he could go home and carry on with his life. By that time, Howard's family had moved back to Charlotte, and his father was working for the sheriff's department. Howard went home, hopefully to pick up the threads of his life. Everyone said, "What you need is to go to work."

So, he tried a job at Mill Power Supply Company, and hated it. He fought it every day. Then his mental condition deteriorated little by little. He stopped eating and began standing around in military-like clothes, as though at attention. He rebelled against everything. One day he started out to walk to Charlotte. His dad picked him up and then had him locked up in jail. This was in 1945. Then they got him into Lynwood Hospital in Augusta, Georgia, yet another military mental hospital. Howard weighed in at one hundred and twenty pounds. The same routine was followed as at Dizzy Lizzy's: rest and eat. Up until that time, the military would not admit that Howard's condition was service-connected.

Finally, on May 2, 1945, the Veterans Administration Board decided, thanks to a North Carolina congressman, and the Red Cross at St. Elizabeth, that Howard's condition was incurred in the line of duty during World War II, and that this was the first mental illness on file. Never was there any mention of the gas chamber and Special Services. He finally began to receive a ten per cent disability, which he gave to his parents until 1966. Howard and I were married by that time and we had just bought our first house.

It was always strange to Howard that in the hospital they said, "All you need is to rest." At home they all said, "All you need is to work." And he did try to work, to be "normal." First, he worked at a gas station, until he could wash cars and change tires no longer. He then went to work for Duke Power Company, reading meters. He hated that, too; he burned up in summer and froze in winter. Somehow he controlled himself and then, with the war over, and his friends coming home, he settled down.

Music was still on Howard's mind. He put a little band together and played some at night. About 1947, he auditioned for Arthur "Guitar Boogie" Smith at WBT-Charlotte, to play with The Briar Hoppers. Arthur is given credit for not only writing "Guitar Boogie," but also for "Dueling Banjos." Disappointed, Howard was turned down and they hired Nat Richardson, only a fair player. "That turn-down made me even more determined," said Howard. "Later, after I made it in Nashville, Daddy said that Nashville wouldn't even give Arthur a look-in."

Howard then did a lot of work with Claude Casey, who had gone to WBT in fall 1940. Casey, who stayed at WBT twelve years, said he remembered spending many enjoyable times with Howard and other musicians, pickin' in Howard Simpson's studio. They did a lot of demo (demonstration disc) sessions at Simpson's and some of them stirred up some attention. Howard remembered fondly, "I played on the first demo of the song 'A Fool Such As I.' It was written by Bill Trader and Dewey Price sang the vocal. Both Hank Snow and Elvis Presley later had hits on the song."

An odd thing happened in 2004, many years after that demo session. Howard was told that an unknown steel player in South Carolina had said on the Internet that he had recorded the first demo of "A Fool Such As I." Howard called and confronted him:

Howard: "You did not play on that demo, I did."

Guy: "No, I did."

Howard: "You can check with Bill Trader or Howard Simpson or anyone on that session and they'll back me up."

Guy: "Maybe you were standing outside and watching."

Howard: "If you don't deny that statement, I'm coming to South Carolina and beat the hell out of you."

Guy: "I think you mean that!"

Bill Trader wrote Howard a letter in 1990, which read, "I can never thank you enough for playing on that first demo of 'Fool' and your support from its embryonic stage to its current revival."

It was very important to Howard that no one got credit for what he or anyone else had done. One day as we walked by a certain steel player, we heard a fan ask him, "Did you play on Foley's 'Blues In My Heart'?" The steel player exclaimed, "Sure did!" As we passed by, Howard said, "No you didn't, Jerry Byrd did." We kept walking and nothing else was ever said.

Howard worked with Claude on many occasions. Claude Casey was a good singer and a yodeler. He was a songwriter, who later appeared in

Western movies. Then he owned and operated WJES in Johnston, South Carolina, until he died in 1999.

In 1948, Howard met Shannon Grayson at a demo session in Charlotte. Shannon asked Howard to record with him and The Golden Valley Boys. They went to Cincinnati and cut a gospel session for King Records, with Syd Nathan producing. The band on that session was Millard Pressley (mandolin), Harvey Rayborn (bass), E. C. Beatty (rhythm guitar) and Howard on steel. They recorded two songs, "I Like The Old Time Way" and "I'm Gonna Walk On." Howard said, "The most notable thing that happened to me in Cincinnati was that I got to meet my idol, Jerry Byrd, who was working there at the time."

In 1949, Howard recorded again with Shannon Grayson on RCA. They recorded this session in a hotel room in Atlanta, Georgia. RCA used to record anywhere by bringing in their own equipment and engineer to some hotel room. Steve Sholes produced that session. The same musicians played on that session, as on the previous one. They recorded four songs: "Sunset Of Time," "Someday In Heaven," "If You Don't Love Your Neighbor" and "The Secret Weapon." (Grayson died May 10, 1993, in Matthews, North Carolina.)

Without any plans at all, Howard decided to go to Nashville. He thought maybe he could get a gig playing in a club; however, like so many other musicians in Nashville, without a plan of action, he didn't get a job right away. He had plenty of advice from the folks at home, but like all young musicians, dedicated to their profession, no one could advise him about anything. A real, honest-to-God musician, dedicated to his profession, knows that his first love is his guitar. Howard went to see Big Jeff Bess, who had a program on WLAC, but Jeff didn't need anyone. He had met Jerry Rivers, who had played fiddle with Hank Williams in Charlotte, so he went to see him, but Jerry didn't know of any openings. Howard had to have a job of some kind, so he read the help wanted ads and answered an ad to install venetian blinds. Howard was not blessed with patience or a mechanical mind, but they hired him, gave him a truck, a load of venetian blinds and a city map. Howard said: "I didn't know any more about getting around Nashville than if I had parachuted into Moscow one night. A whole comedy could have been written about me trying to install those blinds. After a week, I quit."

One night, Howard wandered into the *Friday Night Frolics* and met Randy Hughes. Randy said he needed a steel player to work at the Clover Club with his band. Howard asked, "When?" Randy said, "How 'bout tonight?" That began a long friendship between Randy and Howard. The Clover Club was what the musicians called a "Skull Orchard." It was across the street from the Plantation Club at 343 Murfreesboro Road. The elite went to the Plantation to hear the Big Bands play there. The Clover Club was a place for beer drinkers, who liked hardcore country music. Howard remembered that nothing bad happened when they played there. "That is," he added, "Nobody got killed."

By chance, Howard met Tommy "Butterball" Page who had been playing with Ernest Tubb. Butterball told Howard he had a gig in Glen Burnie, Maryland, and wanted Howard to go along and play steel. So Howard went to Maryland with Butterball and played with him a few months.

Howard, who was now beginning to gain needed experience, remembered, "The only good thing that happened was that Tex Ritter came to the Hippodrome Theater in Baltimore, to play for a week. I auditioned and was selected to work with Tex for that week. Tex was a fine man and I enjoyed that week. I valued his friendship all through the years. Minnie Pearl was also on that job."

The steel guitarist recalled a funny story regarding Tex. He and Tex were standing back stage when an ardent fan rushed up saying, "Oh, Mr. Ritter, I've always wanted to meet you." Tex thanked the fan and then, without missing a beat, turned to Howard and said, "And I want you to meet my steel player, *Mr. Fartblossom.*" The fan, never realizing what Tex had said, turned to Howard and said, "Nice to meet you, Mr. Blossom."

There were so many fan stories the musicians told. One night Buddy Emmons, playing steel, had been bugged by a fan standing right in front of him all night, watching as he played. Buddy kept a spray can of insect repellant beside him to spray at bugs the footlights attracted. Finally, frustrated, he picked up the can, sprayed the fan with it and said, "Bug!" The fan, standing there in his bib overalls, had pliers in his back pocket. He got out those pliers, reached over and cut all of the strings on Buddy's steel guitar.

Then there was the time that DJ Tom Perryman, who then was running Jim Reeves' radio station, chanced upon a fan, who said to Tom, "Didn't you use to be Tom Perryman?" Tom answered, "Yes, and who am I now?"

After the Tex Ritter dates, Howard returned to North Carolina. That's when Daddy John Love, retired from Wade Mainer's Mountaineers, entered the scene. Lowell Blanchard of WNOX-Knoxville had hired Daddy John to sing and yodel on the station's Saturday night *Tennessee Barn Dance.* He asked Howard to go along and play steel. They took a Trailways' Bus to Knoxville, traveling free, as Daddy John's brother-in-law was an owner in Trailways.

Well, Don Gibson had heard White play and after Howard returned home to Charlotte, Don called to ask him to come back and play with him. Don's steel player, "Eagle Eye," was going back to school. Don was working the *Tennessee Barn Dance*, as well as WNOX's *Mid-Day Merry-Go-'Round*. At the same time, Howard had an offer from Mel Price in Eastern Shore, Maryland, to go up there and work.

"I quickly reasoned that Knoxville was on the way to Nashville, so I opted for the Knoxville job with Don Gibson." Of course, the big question was how was he going to get there? Just in time, a friend with a chicken truck came along and took Howard with him to Knoxville. That was in 1951. He stayed with Don a year, along with Marion Sumner, Luke Brandon and bass player Billy Kirby. Mel Price and Howard stayed friends all their lives. Mel became a DJ, playing real country music. In later years, he was at WAAI in Easton, Maryland. He kept Howard alive, re-playing his old records. In 2010, Mel sent me a CD copy of his program on which he had played Howard's recording of "The Dove" and Don Gibson's "No Shoulder To Cry On," on which Howard is featured.

Howard and the band were doing great. It wasn't Nashville, but they were playing on the *Mid-Day Merry-Go-'Round*, the popular WNOX show. So many people played there on their way to Nashville, including Bill Carlisle, Martha Carson, Chet Atkins, The Carters, Carl and Pearl Butler, Archie Campbell, and Howard made friends with them all. Howard never forgot that Archie Campbell invited him for Thanksgiving dinner, when Howard would have been all alone, with no place to go. WNOX hired an accordion player on staff, too, Tony Musco, whose parents were from Italy. It seems the whole WNOX crew played square dances at night.

To make extra money, Howard taught steel guitar for a while. Two of his students were a young Ronnie and Larry Light. The siblings had been taking a Wahoo A Music Course from WROL. Howard went to the Light home and worked out a deal to give other paying students lessons and in return offered the Light brothers free lessons. Later, Ronnie and Larry both came to Nashville, attaining some success there, as well.

Don Gibson hailed from Shelby, North Carolina, and began working professionally at about age fourteen. In retrospect, Howard said: "Don was easy to work for, but he was always sick, a real hypochondriac. He was always going to the doctor or getting ready to go to the doctor. As we drove along in a car, he started wearing a football helmet, as he was afraid there might be an accident."

Back then he was married to a nurse named Beth, a real sweet girl, but he left her for a girl he met at The Blue Circle, a hamburger joint. When Don met Arthur Q. Smith, who claimed to have written "Wedding Bells" and "Missing In Action," they began co-writing songs. They turned out some great songs. Arthur Q. Smith then was a hotel desk clerk at a little hotel near WNOX. He once gave up fifty percent of the song, "Missing In Action," recorded by Ernest Tubb, to Leonard Sherski (using the pseudonym Helen Kaye), in exchange for a bar bill owed.

Don and the band recorded a demo session at WBIR Radio, which Don sent to promoter Troy Martin in Nashville. Then Troy set up a session at Castle Studios downtown in the old Tulane Hotel on Church Street, for July 7, 1952, with Don and his band, recording four songs. Released on Columbia, the tracks were: "No Shoulder To Cry On" (co-written by Don Gibson and "Helen Kaye"); "We're Stepping Out Tonight" (written by Billy Wallace); "Sample Kisses" (written by Arthur Q.); and "Let Me Stay In Your Arms" (written by J. D. Miller & Jimmy Newman). Playing also on that session were Grady Martin on guitar, and Marvin Hughes on keyboards. The two singles Columbia released, didn't hit. Don had to wait a few more years before scoring big at RCA, with the likes of "Oh Lonesome Me" and "Blue, Blue Day."

In about 1958, Don came back to Nashville, under the guidance of D. Kilpatrick, WSM program director. Howard, who was by then playing in Nashville, told D. about Don, telling him that Don was a great act. I met Don at the Opry one night in the 1960's. He sang "Where No One Stands Alone" and the audience was so moved, they didn't make a sound. Don was walking away from center stage before the applause brought down the house.

There's no telling how long that band would have stayed with Don. They were doing OK, making about eighty-five dollars a week per man, playing all the shows offered. Then Lowell Blanchard, venerable announcer and emcee at WNOX, talked Don into putting the band on salary. That move cut the band to thirty-five dollars each per week. They all quit. Billy Kirby joined the Army. The rest thought they might go to Florida, but as Howard said: "Our last night, when the call came in from Randy Hughes to go to work for Cowboy Copas in Nashville, my whole life fell into place. All my dreams had been answered. This time, I had a real plan, a real job, working with Copas."

By the early 1960's, Don was having problems with drinking and narcotics. He called Howard at home one night and asked him to bring him a fifth of whiskey to his hotel. Howard and I bought a bottle and went to Don's suite at the old Capitol Park Inn. We spent a little time talking about the old days. Then Don asked me to go in the next room and talk to his wife. When I went in, she was in bed, completely out, and all kinds of bottles with needles were lined up on the dresser. I went right out and told Howard we had better leave, which we did.

Actually, up to that point, Howard had no idea how sick Don was. The next day, Wesley Rose called Howard and told him Don had been hospitalized. We went to see him and he was in bed without his toupee on. He immediately cried, "Howard, I didn't want Ruth to see me without my hair." After that, Howard rarely saw Don, except sometimes at the Opry, and once he took Bill Carlisle to see him. Don married again in 1967, to a wonderful girl, Bobbie Patterson, who took great care of him. Don credited her with adding stability to his life and helping him overcome his problems. Don, in ill health, was depressed and brooded about a career hurt by his addictions. On November 17, 2003, Don died at age seventy-five. He was a great musician, singer and writer. He was buried in the family plot at Shelby and at last Don was at rest, a situation he sought all his life.

4 COWBOY COPAS

"I have roamed this whole world over
Been contented and carefree
When I hear an old time love song
Think I'm down in Nashville, Tennessee."

- Cowboy Copas/Chaw Mank

Opry announcer Ott Devine called him "The best dressed man from the West," his wife Lucille and his friends called him "Cope" and he was known to fans as "Cowboy Copas, The Oklahoma Cowboy." His mother named him Lloyd Estel Copas and taught him to play guitar. The "official" story was that he was born in Muskogee, Oklahoma.

That's the story he told Howard and all the world; however, later research found that he was actually born July 15, 1913 in Adams County, Ohio, near Blue Creek. At age fourteen, he began to appear regularly on local radio, played at fairs and local events. He became a member of WSM's *Grand Ole Opry* in 1946.

Howard came from Knoxville to Nashville to work with Copas as his steel guitar player in 1952. Howard always called him simply "Copas." He continued, "When I came out on the Opry stage that first time with Copas, I could hardly hold my bar, I was so nervous. You can't imagine what it was like for a country boy to be allowed on that stage where all the great pickers had played."

The tours might have been long and hard, but that was and is a part of the business. Howard became a part of that business before the days of Silver Eagle buses, semi-trucks, Interstates and big money. Back then "Country" was still called "Hillbilly." In the 1960's WSM still categorized their records three ways: Classical, Pop or Hillbilly. One didn't speak of just "WSM Radio." We spoke of WSM in reverent tones, calling it "The Station." Everyone knew that *The Station* was WSM.

Copas had a number of hits on King Records, "Filipino Baby" in 1946, "Signed, Sealed and Delivered" in 1947 and "Tennessee Moon" in 1948. In 1960, he recorded "Alabam" on Starday Records, and that was recorded strictly by accident. Copas was at Owen Bradley's Quonset Hut on 16th Avenue South, February 2, 1960, recording an album. Don Pierce wanted him to include an example of old-time flattop picking, so Copas remembered a song he got from his father when he was a boy called "Alabam." His father told him he got the melody from an old tune called "Coney Island Washboard," and the words came from old sayings. Copas played around with the tune, making up words as he went along. The engineer, Tommy Hill, said that they did "Alabam" in one take. Kathy Copas played the tambourine when drummer Buddy Harman handed it to her, saying to hold the beat.

National Home & Life Insurance building headquarters, Nashville, where it all began for WSM.

On that session, too, were "Lightnin" Chance, bass; Grady Martin, guitar; and Benny Martin, fiddle. No one remembers who the steel guitar player really was, but it may have been Roy Wiggins. About all you can hear on the record is Grady on his Martin guitar, Kathy on tambourine, Harman on drums and a steel guitar. Howard reasoned, "On a song like that, a lot of instrumentation is not needed." Upon listening to it on playback, they all knew it was a hit. When Ralph Emery, WSM DJ, played it, he liked it, the listeners loved it, a single was released, and the rest is part of history.

While Copas was still on King, he recorded a version of "Tennessee Waltz." Murray Nash, who had a long career at RCA, Acuff-Rose and Mercury, recalled: "I knew Steve Sholes at RCA and he signed Pee Wee King to RCA. He was looking for a song and we discovered a waltz in Pee Wee's attic. Pee Wee and Redd Stewart had written it and had called it "No Name Waltz." Then they forgot it. We changed the name to "Tennessee Waltz" and had Pee Wee record it on acetate on a disc cutter owned by a dance studio. I sent it to RCA in New York for review. They turned it down saying, 'No more waltzes.' Eventually in 1947, I took Pee Wee and Redd to Chicago to record for RCA and Cowboy Copas went along to play guitar. They had recorded three songs and needed a fourth. Pee Wee remembered the waltz and they cut it as a fill-in."

This was Nash's story (I've heard a lot of them); however, Copas had a session booked in Cincinnati for King and on his way back to Nashville, stopped there to record. It was then he also recorded "Tennessee Waltz"

(March 29, 1947). Howard and I found a 78-rpm record of "Tennessee Waltz" by Copas at a flea market in the 1960's. New to us were the writer credits on the record, given to Pee Wee King, Redd Stewart AND Cowboy Copas. Howard asked Dean May, longtime publishing administrator for Acuff-Rose, about the credits. Her only reply was, "Howard we don't like to talk about that." Then Howard remembered that while working for Copas, Cowboy told him that Pee Wee and Redd had offered him part of the writing for "Tennessee Waltz" for fifteen dollars (there are other sources that say the offer was for twenty-five dollars), but fifteen was what Copas told Howard. Pee Wee and Redd wrote for Acuff-Rose and evidently labels were printed and records pressed before King realized Copas was not one of the writers.

The RCA record by Pee Wee King did well, reportedly selling a half-million records; however, the song really became a mega-hit when Patti Page recorded it in 1950, utilizing the electronic multiple-voice technique. It sold several million. Royalties were huge for Acuff-Rose Publishing, Pee Wee and Redd. Page's Mercury disc became a number one pop record thirteen weeks, crossing over to peak at number two on the country chart. Incidentally, King's original release on his song charted thirty-five weeks, topping out at number three, but following Page's success some two years later, his version was re-released by RCA, giving him another Top Ten charting. So Cowboy lost out on a fortune, but nonetheless had garnered a Top Five single out of the deal.

Howard didn't think Copas ever spent time worrying about what might have been. He liked simple things out of life. Copas swore that dogs laughed and oftentimes a dog's expression made Copas laugh. He liked to hunt and many times Howard would go hunting with him, just to be with him. Actually, Howard hated hunting and he said he would sit under a tree while Copas continued chasing squirrels.

Copas lived in a modest stone house in Nashville's Inglewood neighborhood when Howard worked for him. Howard had reminisced, "I pass it now and think of how many times I pulled into that driveway ready to go on tour." Copas was kind to his musicians, noted Howard, adding, "It was a rarity in those days."

Cowboy liked to sing, pick his guitar and entertain at the Opry. He loved his wife and his children, Kathy Loma, Gary Lee and Michael. Kathy Copas Hughes Hughes (she married two men named Hughes) recalls the time when she was a child and she and her parents stopped to eat out on the road. Times were tough then, but little Kathy ordered chicken. Cowboy and Lucille didn't eat anything. Kathy said, "They didn't tell me anything about not being able to afford it then, but when I was grown, they never let me forget it."

Howard said, "Of all the people I worked for, I liked Copas the best. He was a good man. I went hunting and played golf with him. I went because he wanted me to, not because I liked hunting or golf."

Kathy sang harmonies with her dad and proved a perfect lady on the road. Lazy Jim Day, the show's comic, was a naturally funny man and aptly named. One day on tour, according to Howard, they passed an outstanding, beautiful motel. They tried to get Lazy Jim to turn around and look at it. As they sped by, Jim said, "Oh, well, one of these days, we'll be back and I'll make sure I'm facing the other way." Lazy Jim did an act on stage called "The Singing News," a bit of country rhyming set to music which went something like: *Do you know women's dresses get shorter every year. Pretty soon they won't even be here . . ."* He also played a little short banjo he called his "minnow dipper."

One night, fiddler Dale Potter tuned Jim's banjo in a minor key. Jim could not get his minnow dipper to note right, and had to leave the stage. Naturally, all the boys thought it was funny. Howard said he felt sympathy for Jim, remembering when Shot Jackson "let down" all his strings at the *Friday Night Frolics,* and he couldn't play till he retuned – not a quick job on a steel guitar.

They played with Copas at a drive-in theater in Hazard, Kentucky, where the stage was the top of the concession stand. There were a lot of those type venues in those days in small towns. As they were getting ready to leave, and the movie had just started, they heard a gunshot. They all dropped to the ground, but the manager wasn't disturbed. "Aw," he said, "It was nothing serious. Some guy took both speakers in his car." They looked for Lazy Jim and found him in a dressing room dancing for some guy that requested he dance some more. Jim had heard the gun shot and was afraid *not* to dance as long as the guy wanted. The people of Hazard are known to settle disputes with guns sometimes.

According to Hal Smith, formerly of Pamper Music, Lazy Jim Day was the most underrated comedian out of Nashville. He was one of a kind with his minnow dipper and bib overalls. He was totally unconcerned about events around him. He had been known to walk across a fine hotel lobby with so many beer cans stashed in his overalls, they fell out on the floor. Once they were leaving town, on their way West, when Jim remembered he had left his banjo at home. Copas was disgusted, saying, "If I was your wife, I'd shoot you right between the eyes." Jim retorted, "If I was married to you, I'd shoot myself."

Lazy Jim and Howard chanced to play with Grandpa Jones at one time. They were up north in a bad snowstorm and had been following a snow-plow for some time up the road. Snow was knee deep. Finally, the snowplow stopped and they had to wait behind it. Lazy Jim calmly got out of the car, walked through the knee-deep snow, went up to the snow plow operator and said in his slow country drawl, "It's a tryin' to snow ain't it!"

On March 11, 1953, Howard recorded with Copas, along with Dale Potter and Randy Hughes, for King Records in Cincinnati. Syd Nathan, owner of King, was also the producer. Some of the sides they recorded were: "Tennessee Senorita," "If You Will, Let Me Be Your Love," "Wreath On The Door Of My Heart" and "I Can't Go On." When "Wreath On The Door . . . " was released as a single, radio wouldn't play it. They said it was too sad. All four cuts were later included in an album, "A Heartbreak Ago," on Masterpiece Records.

Another time in Dayton, Ohio, the troupe was playing a date at the Blue Angel, which had just converted from pop to country music. Copas had a few too many drinks when he went on stage. He sang a song, then called on Lazy Jim Day to do his comedy routine. Then Copas sang another song and called again on Jim to do his routine. Copas did this three times and finally Jim said, "Cope, I've done all my routines." Ray Edenton, the guitar player with the band, remembered on that day Copas couldn't think of his songs' lyrics, so Ray stood behind him and fed the words to him.

Hardy Day, who played bass for Copas, played a joke on Howard once. Hardy knew that Howard had eyes for a girl he met on a previous date, so he told Howard this girl had just called and wanted Howard to pick her up at the bus station. It was raining hard, but Howard went to the bus station and, of course, there was no girl. As he drove back to the hotel, he got madder and madder, realizing that Hardy had set him up. He didn't say anything to Hardy just then, but the next day, in the car, Howard hit Hardy in the back of the head. Everybody laughed, but Howard knew that Hardy had really gotten what he intended, to tee him off.

Howard and the band had so much fun touring with Copas. One night, headed home, they were going through Kentucky when one of the bandsmen remembered they would pass Pauline's, a well-known house of ill repute. So they decided to pay Pauline's house a visit. Everyone knew that if a milk can was out, the police were watching. When they arrived, no milk can was out, so they trooped in, dirty and tired from the trip. The price was too high for Howard's budget, so he told Pauline it was highway robbery. She threw him out of her place and as he left he told her to go to hell. Then he sat in the car and waited. When the others came out, Copas laughed and told him, "You are probably the only steel player to ever be thrown out of a house of ill repute."

By far the strangest thing that happened to Howard was while on the road with Copas. It's hard to believe, but Howard said, "Upon my word, it's true." On Friday night they played a show in Michigan, then drove immediately back to Nashville in order to rehearse for the *Prince Albert Show* Saturday morning. They left immediately after the Opry spot Saturday night to play Chain of Rocks Park near St. Louis on Sunday. They started for home after that. Now they had not slept since Thursday night. Copas and Howard were asleep on the back seat. Jackie Phelps was driving and he and Jimmy Self were in the front seat. Jackie decided to stop in Pinckneyville, Illinois, to get coffee for himself and Jimmy. While they were in the café, Howard woke up and decided to go to the rest room. He passed Jackie and Jimmy at the cash register and thought they saw him. However, as he went back out to get in the car, they had driven off and Howard saw their taillights driving out of sight. He went back in the café to see if he could get transportation home, finding out there were no trains or buses.

Howard phoned the Highway Patrol, but there had been a prison break and all the patrolmen were in another area. The café man asked him if he had any money. Luckily, he was carrying all the money from their sales of songbooks. So the guy in the café called a man he knew who had a small private plane. The pilot said he could fly to Herron, Illinois, and from there Howard could catch a commercial flight. Howard talked to the man at the café all night long.

It seems that about daylight, Copas woke up and said, "Where's Howard?" Jackie thought he might be in the trunk (what would he be doing there!). They called back to the café and Howard told them his plans. So they told him they would leave the car at the Nashville airport and Howard could pick it up there. Copas and band would go on to their next date in Georgia, and Howard could drive the car down and meet them. So Howard took a taxi out to the cornfield, where a doctor had a landing strip. Off in the distance, he heard the little plane sounding like a bumblebee. The corn was so high around the landing strip, the plane looked like Cyrus McCormick with his reaper coming through the field. The pilot flew him to Herron, where Howard took an Ozark flight to Nashville. It was Monday when he finally drove the car into Georgia. He had not slept since the previous Thursday night. In Howard's words: "I was dead tired! I almost wrecked the car several times. When I finally connected with Copas, I was a long time out of patience, pills and booze. I was still going on coffee and will power."

Actually, a similar story happened to Kitty Wells. One night, somewhere in Minnesota, her bus made a stop. Miss Kitty decided to get off the bus for a minute. As she rushed back, she saw the bus had left her and was rolling down the highway. There was nothing to do but wait, so she sat down on a bench, knowing she would be missed sooner or later. About an hour later, the bus and crew returned for their missing girl singer.

Copas was known as The Waltz King and Howard said, "My style of playing steel fit right in with his style of music." They used to be regular guests on the *Prince Albert Show* with Red Foley. Howard said, "Years later, I listened to tapes from that show and think how beautiful that music really was, with Jerry Byrd playing steel with Foley." Those were the days before pedal steel came into vogue. Howard said, "The best three minutes I ever spent on the Opry stage was when the producers let Jerry Byrd and I play twin steels on the *Prince Albert Show*. I was with Copas and Jerry was with Foley. Our guitars matched. They were made especially for us by a Nashville jeweler, Ira Trotter and a guitarist, Grady Moore."

The *Prince Albert Show*, sponsored by Prince Albert Smoking Tobacco, was the Opry's NBC network portion. It was the only portion of the Opry that was rehearsed. They rehearsed on Saturdays at ten or eleven a.m. Being a network broadcast, it had to be timed perfectly.

Copas was always ready to help his band members. Howard had written a couple of instrumentals and Copas liked them. He went to Fred Rose, who along with Roy Acuff, owned Hickory Records and Acuff-Rose Music Publishing. In 1951, Murray Nash constructed the first publisher's recording studio in Nashville in Fred's garage at 3621 Rainbow Trail. In 1953, Fred Rose agreed to produce and record Howard there. Luke Brandon and

Grady Martin played guitars and Strolling Tom Pritchard played upright bass. Howard was the featured artist on steel and became Hickory's second artist.

Acuff-Rose published the songs. Two singles were released: "The Dove," backed with "Ensonata"; and "Steel Guitar Swallow," backed with "Rosette." Howard wrote "Ensonata" and "Rosette." It was Fred's idea to do "The Dove" and "Steel Guitar Swallow." They were public domain (PD) songs originally, inspired by "La Paloma" and "La Golondrina." Howard wrote the arrangements. Hickory Records actually sold some records and when they were mailed out to the DJs, and they played them when signing on or off. One day, Fred said to Howard, "You've sold nine hundred records in British Guiana! Do you want to book out there?" That was a joke, of course, how in the world would you ever sell one record in British Guiana! Acuff-Rose was absolutely honest. They paid Howard every cent they owed him in writer royalties. Up until 1980, these old instrumental records still earned a few cents and they paid him in postage stamps.

Howard wrote another song in 1954, to be recorded, "Border Serenade," but Fred died December 1, 1954 and Howard never recorded it. However, renowned steel player, Buddy Emmons did, on Columbia Records, and later on, yet another fine steel player, Russ Hicks recorded it. Copas' heart was in the right place, but what will be, will be.

One night in March 1963, a small plane carrying Copas, Patsy Cline and Hawkshaw Hawkins, piloted by Randy Hughes, crashed, killing all aboard. They had been in Kansas City to play a benefit show honoring the late DJ Jack Call, and were returning home.

Howard said, "I've asked myself over and over, since the fifth of March, 1963, why was Copas taken from us, and of course there never is an answer."

It was said that other entertainers were invited to fly on that plane. Dottie West said she had a prior engagement, Billy Walker cancelled at the last minute to take a commercial flight, and bass player Lightnin' Chance declined, as he had been scheduled to work in Florida. Hawkshaw was the last of the four to agree to fly with them, as fate stepped in to put the four together.

Their last stop on the way home to Nashville was in Dyersburg, Tennessee, and the airport manager asked them to stay there for the night, as it was reported that the weather between Dyersburg and Nashville was

Pickin' & Singing News
Vol II #2

MAY 22, 1954.

Popular Nashville Sideman Has First Record Released

NASHVILLE, Tenn. — Howard White, one of the WSM Grand Ole Opry's leading sidemen, is now a recording artist in his own name, although he has been in hundreds of recording sessions with no recognition in the past.

Under contract to Hickory Records, Nashville, Tenn., White's first release about three weeks ago was "The Dove", and "Ensonata", both of the Mexican variety. With the Grand Ole Opry in Nashville for the past two years, White came here from jobs on stations in Charlotte, N. C., Knoxville, Tenn., and Baltimore, Md.

extremely turbulent. Randy elected to fly on, ninety air miles, to Nashville. He told the manager, "If I can't handle the situation, I'm gonna come back." They taxied off at 6:07 p.m. and Randy headed his green and yellow single engine Comanche onward to Music City. Randy was not an instrument-rated pilot. The winds were high and it was getting darker. Near Camden a farmer saw a plane circling his home a little after 7 p.m. Dick Blake, a promoter and former World War II pilot, told Howard, "Randy probably flew into the clouds and unable to read his instruments, and unable to see out the window, didn't know if he was level, upward or downward" The plane tore into the trees and sawed off their tops. They hit with considerable impact, straight into the ground, crashing about 7 p.m. There were no survivors.

Howard told me: "I lost my friends that night. There was Copas, my first employer in Nashville. Then there was Hawk - I worked with he and Jean Shepard - and Randy, my pal, whom I worked with at the Clover Club and who brought me to Nashville to work with Copas. I had told Randy, 'Be careful, those planes will kill ya!' Randy replied, 'I can take care of it.' I had worked package tours with Patsy, and had joined her many times at the Opry for a drink that she always carried in her pocketbook."

After a moment of silence, the Opry went on the following Saturday night, after the March 5th plane crash and an auto accident two days later (March 7th) that claimed the life of Jack Anglin, half of the famed Johnnie & Jack duo. Howard was with Hank Snow by then, and he bowed his head with the rest of the Opry cast. It seemed impossible to Howard that the Opry went on, never missing a beat, but they did. He said, "I guess we had to go on with this business of music in our various ways."

Many years later, Howard and I saw one of the many plays about Patsy Cline in Reno, Nevada. At the end, they played a tape of a plane crashing. It was terrible to listen to and Howard ran out of the casino crying. The Jordanaires were on that show and we didn't understand how they stood it night after night.

Howard thought so much of Copas and they talked together a lot. However, there were several things that Copas didn't tell him. One was that he had a "love child." The story is that Cowboy and Joella were married when she was only fourteen years old. Her father had the marriage annulled a week later. This was in 1933, before Copas married Lucille. He saw Joella at rare times through the years, and Joella gave birth to a boy they named Randy. She and Copas kept it a secret all through the years, as they were afraid it would ruin his career at that time. Joella later married Dale Potter, the fiddle player. After Copas died, Howard and I met Joella with Dale, while they were in Nashville. They lived in Las Vegas and through the years, Joella called me often.

Then there was always the question about where Copas was born. Copas had everyone believe he was born in Oklahoma, which gave credence to his stage name, "The Oklahoma Cowboy." After all, cowboys were not supposed to come from Ohio (though at least one other did, Leonard Slye, a.k.a. Roy Rogers, cinematic "King of the Cowboys"). It wasn't until after we published the first "Every Highway Out Of Nashville" that we found out from Ed Naylor, of Portsmouth, Ohio, then working for *Steel Guitar World*, that Copas was born in Ohio.

Copas was known for his honesty and Howard and most others believed he was from Oklahoma. Howard asked Kathy if she or Lucille had his birth certificate, but she said they couldn't find it. Howard even called Muskogee and after diligent research, they could not find a record of his birth. That's when Howard knew it had all been an entertainment hoax. John Roger Simon, who wrote the definitive book - "Cowboy Copas: And the Golden Age of Country Music" (2008) - showed us the real birth certificate from Adams County, Ohio.

The place of Copas' birth became a joke as time went on, not unlike today's regarding President Obama's birth certificate. No one but Copas, in all his honesty, could have pulled the wool over almost everyone's eyes. Maybe he didn't tell Howard the truth, as Howard wished he had done, but in Howard's words: "My time allowed with Copas was the best."

Howard views Hawkshaw Hawkins portrait with Hawk's son, Don Hawkins.

5 THE CHRISTENING

"Everyone will have some fun
At the Grand Ole Opry tonight."
- from The Prince Albert theme.

This story has been told time and again, but there are young people that might read this book that are unaware, so maybe it will bear re-telling. The historic *Grand Ole Opry* was born in 1925, the year before Howard was born. That's how he always remembered just how old "she" was. Here is the story of the early days with some of Howard's own antics included.

"Tradition" says that on November 28, 1925, Uncle Jimmy Thompson, a country fiddler, near eighty years old, sat in a comfortable chair before a microphone, and with his niece, Eva Thompson Jones, at the piano, became the first performer on what would become the WSM *Barn Dance*. George D. Hay, who called himself *The Solemn Old Judge,* opened the show by blowing on a wooden steamboat whistle he kept under his arm. That whistle sound became as much a part of the show as a fiddle did. Judge Hay announced that Uncle Jimmy would be pleased to answer requests for old tunes. Immediately, letters and telegrams began pouring in. Broadcasting history was written that night in Nashville. As the program expanded, more and more rural musicians showed up to perform on the *Barn Dance*. Dr. Humphrey Bates' Possum Hunters were the first country band. Then Grandpappy George Wilkerson's Fruit Jar Drinkers, the Crook Brothers, and Sam and Kirk McGee appeared

Nobody got paid. An old-timer said, "Back then we played for nothing. Radio was new and we were just glad we got to play on the radio." Later they began to get five dollars each for a Saturday night. The first individual star to join the broadcast in 1925, was Uncle Dave Macon, The Dixie Dewdrop. He had been a headliner on the Loew's Vaudeville Circuit. He performed up-tempo novelty songs on his banjo, such as "Bile Dem Cabbage Down" and "Cacklin' Hen." He carried three banjos, all tuned to a different key. He was a sight to see, sitting on a cane-bottomed chair, kicking his legs up and playing hell out of his banjo. I remember him, still performing in 1947, when I worked at Strobel's Music Shop in the Arcade. He was an old man then. There was an older lady, Miss Willie Grubbs, who also worked there. Uncle Dave would come in on Saturday mornings, then Miss Willie would run and hide when he came in. Uncle Dave just loved to sneak up on her and pinch her on the butt. She wore a corset; I don't know how he managed to get through it.

The most historic event was the night of December 25, 1928 at the WSM *Barn Dance*. Judge Hay was emceeing *The Music Appreciation Hour*, a very highbrow program conducted by Dr. Walter Damrosch. When it was over, Judge Hay stepped to the microphone to announce *The Barn Dance*. After paying his respects to Dr. Damrosch, he announced, *"Friends, the pro-*

gram which has come to a close was devoted to the classics. For the past hour we have been listening to music from Grand Opera, but now we will present the Grand Ole Opry." He blew his steamboat whistle and the name "WSM Barn Dance" was forever erased from the Saturday night show, as the new name stuck and it became for all time *The Grand Ole Opry.*

The Opry had eight homes: In 1925, it began in WSM's Studio A, on the fifth floor at the home office of the National Life Insurance Company. They quickly outgrew that studio and built Studio B, with a large plate glass window. They now had an audience that watched from the hall outside. In a few years, Studio C was built, an auditorium studio. It had a portable stage and the latest acoustical treatment of walls and ceilings of that time. It could seat five hundred. The audience promptly filled it. This same auditorium was later used for many live shows like *The Friday Night Frolics,* simply called "The Frolics" by the "Hillbillies." Howard worked on *The Frolics* there even in the 1960's. Eventually, the name was changed to *The Friday Night Opry* and was moved to the Ryman Auditorium. Another show originating from Studio C was *Sunday Down South,* which launched the careers of singer Snooky Lanson, The Anita Kerr singers and pianist-producer Owen Bradley.

Then one Saturday night, two top National Life officials were refused admittance to their own offices, because of the crowds. For a time there was talk that National Life might take the Opry off the air. Instead, in 1934, the Opry moved to the Hillsboro Theater, where twenty-four hundred could be seated. Then they outgrew that location. In 1936, the Opry moved again, to Dixie Tabernacle on Fatherland Street in East Nashville. It had rough wooden benches and sawdust on the floors. The crowds ran over three thousand every Saturday night, so in 1939, they moved to the War Memorial Auditorium, across the street from the National Life Building. For the first time, a charge was made to attend – twenty-five cents. In 1943, the Opry moved to the Ryman Auditorium on Fifth Avenue. The Ryman was originally built as the Union Gospel Tabernacle in 1891, by order of riverboat Captain Tom Ryman.

Ryman did so for an evangelist, Sam Jones, who had converted Ryman to Christianity, so he wanted the new auditorium to be used by Jones to convert his followers. Of course, Judge Hay's steamboat whistle fit right in there. The old place still had the old wooden pews and stained glass windows. But it also had no air conditioning and poor dressing room facilities for entertainers. The floors, walls and ceiling support beams were all wooden. An army of fire marshals patrolled every performance, for fire was a real fear. The upper floor rows still supported a sign that read "Confederate Balcony." That is where the Confederate Veterans met for reunions. It was a fact that if you spilled a Coke in the balcony, it ran down between the floorboards onto the people seated below. The Ryman became known as "The Mother Church Of Country Music." Old timers just learned to live with the deficiencies of the old building. Finally, in about 1963, National Life bought the old "Mother Church."

Time has a way of changing everything, and in 1974, the brand new four thousand, four hundred-seat Opry House at the then Opryland, opened its doors and the Opry moved into its new home. The final show on the Ryman stage was a tearful one and many tears of regret were shed in the beer at Tootsie's Orchid Lounge, the notorious "watering hole" across the alley from the Ryman. The beautiful new Opry House was in its location in its new suburban home near Donelson, situated by the Cumberland River. At last, they had air conditioning, modern restrooms and more dressing rooms, as well as a great new stage area. It now appealed to every tourist's taste and obviously the new facilities pleased the performers. Of course, to bring authenticity to the stage of the new Opry House, someone had the foresight to cut a circle out of the old Ryman stage and insert it into the new stage.

Without fail, any new artist that appears on that stage and stands in that circle at the mike, comments: "It's such a thrill to be standing on this stage where all the greats stood."

A lot of stars have been born on the *Grand Ole Opry*. There was Pee Wee King & His Golden West Cowboys who joined in 1937. Roy Acuff, who became known as King of Country Music, came to the Opry in 1938, with his band, The Crazy Tennesseans, renamed the more acceptable Smoky Mountain Boys. Bill Monroe, Father of Bluegrass, arrived in 1939. Sarah Ophelia Colley, "Minnie Pearl," who joined in 1940. There followed people like Ernest Tubb & His Texas Troubadours; Eddy Arnold, The Tennessee Plowboy; Cowboy Copas, Grandpa Jones, Little Jimmy Dickens, Hank Snow, Red Foley, Hank Williams, The Carters and Chet Atkins; Carl Smith, Kitty Wells, Queen of Country Music; Marty Robbins, Jean Shepard, George Jones, Johnny Cash, Porter Wagoner, Patsy Cline, Loretta Lynn, Dolly Parton, Tammy Wynette, and the list goes on and on - and on.

Then there were the laughs by the funny men at the Opry, like Whitey Ford, better known as the Duke of Paducah. He became a member of the Opry shortly after Minnie Pearl, and was a veteran comic from vaudeville days, dating back to 1922. The Opry hired him as a comic on *The Prince Albert Show's* NBC network portion, but he could play tenor banjo and harmonica. The Duke dressed in a too small green suit, high button shoes and a funny green hat. He was famous for his opening line: "If you see anything green, laugh!" He played his own invention called the "Comodeola," made from a toilet seat and guitar strings. His tag line through all the years was: "I'm going back to the wagon, boys, these shoes are killing me."

Other delightful funny men followed, Rod Brasfield, Dr. Lew Childre, Stringbean (David Akeman), and Lonzo & Oscar. There was a time when every member of Roy Acuff's band thought they had to make you laugh, notably Bashful Brother Oswald (Pete Kirby) and Lonnie "Pap" Wilson. Even Roy got laughs by balancing his fiddle bow on his nose or "walking the dog" with his Yo-Yo.

There are legends who have almost been forgotten, but they are part of Opry history. There was DeFord Bailey, black harmonica player whose

"Pan American Blues" was played the night Judge Hay gave the Opry its name. Jamup and Honey were a black-faced act from the minstrel days. Originally, Lee Davis "Honey" Wilds, came to Nashville as a partner of Lee Roy "Lasses" White in 1932, calling themselves Lasses and Honey. They had been a part of the All Stars Minstrel Show on the vaudeville circuit. They had their own show on Friday nights and publicity referred to them as the Deans of the burnt-cork artists. They went on the Opry in 1934 as regulars. They appeared in blackface, wearing tuxedos and white gloves, and were very popular. After, Lasses White moved to Hollywood, Honey Wilds carried on and as time passed, he had three different partners he called Jamup: Tom Woods, Bunny Biggs and Harry LeVan. Once at a tent show, Don Davis and Grady Martin, pranksters, found a King Snake about five feet long outside the tent. They tied string to the snake and put it on one side of the stage. Then they pulled the string to the other side of the stage. They waited until Jamup and Honey came to the microphone.

When they were into their routine, Grady and Don pulled the snake right in front of them. They looked down and Honey made an exit. He just disappeared. Harry LeVan, Jamup at the time, just backed away and continued his act. Don said, "I don't remember how long it took us to find Honey."

The Poe Sisters were the first females to tour with Ernest Tubb. The Old Hickory Singers, Claude Waller, Claude Sharpe, Joe McPherson and Ross Dowden, a quartet, were at the Opry for many years. Asher Sizemore and Little Jimmy used to sing "How Beautiful Heaven Must Be." Then there were bands like The Georgia Peach Pickers and The Arkansas Cotton Pickers. Until about 1939, the Opry placed nearly all their emphasis on bands.

George D. Hay wanted nothing on the Opry but pure country, no electrified instruments, no drums or horns. But then came Pee Wee King, Roy Acuff and Eddy Arnold. The rush was on – Ernest Tubb, Red Foley, Cowboy Copas and Hank Williams. It was hard to get Judge Hay to allow a piano, but someone finally convinced him it was a string instrument, much to the relief of the likes of Moon Mullican and Del Wood.

It's a wonder the Opry survived with the inherent desire of Nashvillians of the time to suppress anything hillbilly. Even in 1963, when I worked at WSM, a Nashvillian buying tickets to the Opry would invariably say, "These aren't for me. They're for friends from out of town." Hillbillies made National Life nervous. They were very cautious. Other similar shows began biting the dust around them: *The Ozark Jubilee, Louisiana Hayride, National Barn Dance, Atlanta Barn Dance, Old Dominion Barn Dance* among others. When WSM radio was founded by Edwin W. Craig, then Nashville Life's vice president, his father was the company's president. So Edwin was allowed to have his very own radio station – WSM – which stood for "We Shield Millions," a neat tie-in to insurance. Craig found out that country people identified strongly with acts like Uncle Dave Macon. When an insurance agent knocked at their door and said, "I'm from the *Grand Ole Opry*," this helped get his foot in the door to sell insurance.

WSM didn't always stay on the air twenty-four hours. According to promoter Murray Nash, he went to see station executive Jack DeWitt and told him they could have CONELRAD (meaning Control Of Electromagnetic Radiation) if they stayed on the air twenty-four hours. CONELRAD was the first early warning system of AM Radio for the public at large. So DeWitt brought Eddie Hill from Memphis to do their first all-night show, which incidentally promoted the Opry.

The Opry was and is the most unique live country show in country music. It is live, unrehearsed and unproduced and the longest-running regular program in radio history. Hopefully, the new breed at the Opry will keep the music genuine, down-to-earth, honest and real. Somehow, I don't think so. A conversation heard between a WSM official and an old artist went like this:

Official: "We're trying to get rid of all the gray hairs."

Artist: "Well, we're dying off as fast as we can."

We are left to wonder what the Solemn Old Judge George D. Hay, would say about the new Opry House, all the electrically-amplified instruments, drums, a stray horn or two, the comfort of the new auditorium, private dressing rooms and above all, air conditioning. Do the new artists even know that there was a time when all the audience members were waving fans back and forth to keep cool in the summertime?

Would Judge Hay still close each show as he used to?

"That's all for now friends, Because the tall pines pine, And the paw paws pause, And the bumble bees bumble all around, The grasshoppers hop, While gently the old cow moves away, George D. Hay saying, so long for now."

Sh-h-h-h . . . Was that a steamboat whistle that's a 'blowin'?

Judge George D. Hay.

6 KEEP IT LOW TO THE GROUND, BOYS

*"It's never going to be the
Same for me, before I was 25."*

-Steven Tyler.

Howard White got to the *Grand Ole Opry* before all the founders passed on. The real flavor of the Opry was still there. On a still night, if you wander into the old Ryman Auditorium, and if you listen real good, the ghosts of the old voices can still be heard. Howard said: "I am glad that when I played at the Opry, Judge Hay was still there, telling us all, 'Keep it low to the ground, boys.' What he meant was keep it simple, keep it real, hang on to the original."

Uncle Dave Macon was there singing, "Hand Me Down My Walking Cane." Dr. Lew Childre, who called Howard "Poncho," was there. So was Robert Lunn, the "Talkin' Blues" boy, Minnie Pearl and her sidekick, Rod Brasfield, Oscar Stone and the Possum Hunters, Sam and Kirk McGee, DeFord Bailey, Fiddlin' Sid Harkreader – they were all there, the real characters of the Opry. As Howard grew older, he began to really appreciate the ground that had been laid for the artists that followed. They were not big moneymakers compared to today's performers, but they played to many a packed schoolhouse auditorium, at tent shows and fairs. Like the Ryman, there was no air conditioning at these venues, but the fans didn't seem to mind. Howard recalled: "When the curtain rose on Saturday nights, the people out there loved us. None of that 'polite' applause you hear these days at the new Opry House. I mean they LOVED us! The fans knew us musicians by name and we had our following, just like the stars. Stars, sidemen, we were all treated alike on Saturday nights."

The slick New Yorkers and Californians that are running things in Nashville don't appreciate the early stars. Money is their main objective. But if it weren't for the old ones, the Tin Pan Alley - *Music Row* - of Nashville would not even exist. When Howard came to the Opry in 1952, drums were not allowed on stage. They came on gradually, at first only a snare drum, played by Harold Weakly. Electric instruments had not been allowed too long. Dobros had been used instead of steel guitars. There was a succession of good program directors that ran things, Jim Denny, Jack Stapp, D. Kilpatrick and Ott Devine. These were the last of the "good ole boys," according to Howard, or as he said, "They really cared about us."

Money was not the main object when Howard played. Total income for a sideman on Saturday night was ten dollars. That was for what they called "two spots," that is for two thirty minute shows. If you were lucky enough to play the *The Frolics* on Friday night, it paid seven dollars. Howard moaned,

"By the time they took the tax and Social Security out, you paid for your cleaning, gas and a 'half-pint,' there wasn't much left." The star made thirty-four dollars. The only exceptions to this pay was the hour network portion, *The Prince Albert Show*, and special arrangements with Roy Acuff, Hank Snow, Ernest Tubb and Minnie Pearl. (Those four happened to be National Life stockholders.)

These wages were all "arranged" for by George Cooper, president of AFM Local 257, and WSM. At one time, WSM aired mostly live shows, but as time moved on and more and more recorded music was programmed, the union became concerned about its pop musicians being put out of work. Mr. Cooper played bass on a morning show with a staff band called *The Waking Crew*. So Cooper struck a deal with WSM – if they would keep *The Waking Crew* on salary, the union would allow WSM to pay their Opry musicians this low figure. Later they did raise the musician pay to fifteen dollars – ten dollars for the first show, and five dollars for the second show. This "deal" continued for years, after Cooper retired and even after he died. Amazing, when you know that every segment of the Opry's broadcasts were paid for by sponsors, and WSM had sponsors waiting in line. After the Opry moved to the new Opry House, WSM began paying so well that the musicians wanted to stay in town and play the Opry.

CHECK NUMBER	SERVICE THROUGH			TOTAL EARNINGS
	MONTH	DAY	YEAR	
9 9 1 9 2	9	1 1	6 5	1 0 0 0

DEDUCTIONS			NET AMOUNT
F.O.A. & S.I.	INCOME TAX	MISC.	
3 6	1 2 0		8 4 4

Howard's Opry pay stub in 1965. He didn't get rich!

Yes, the times changed. Howard, looking back, remarked: "People like Ott Devine seemed to care for us. We took our troubles to him and we called him at home, if we felt like we really needed something. You can't blame the man if he 'hid out' occasionally. He had the power to put you on or take you off the Opry. I have worked more than once with some one like Sam and Kirk McGee, who really didn't need a steel player, but Ott put me there because I needed the money and happened to be between jobs. Or, Hank Snow didn't show up and there I was at the Opry. Ott would put me on with somebody, just so I could make the money. Once I even played 'Sweet Hour Of Prayer' with Fiddlin' Sid Harkreader."

The stage manager was Vito Pellettieri, who put the show together. How he even got a show on and off in all that confusion, both on stage and off, was somehow a miracle, brought off by Vito. He loved a dirty joke and kept everybody laughing. Howard would arrive at the Opry and say, "What time am I on, Vito?" He'd always reply, "Four a.m.!" It was a standing joke. The Opry line-up was posted on Thursdays on the fifth floor of the old National Building, right outside the Men's Rest Room. Vito always drew a picture of a fish to represent George Morgan. (George was Catholic as was Vito.)

Howard looking back said, "Everything used to be so much fun when we were all getting dressed together and sitting in the same dressing room. Today, when I visit the new place, and everybody is hiding out in their own private dressing room, like in Hollywood, I wonder if they have really progressed. One night I ran into Hank Snow, alone in his room, waiting to go on stage. He said, 'Howard, it ain't no more fun like it used to be!'"

Maybe this is what happens when you don't "keep it low to the ground."

Howard visits Hank's grave site.

7 THE COMING OF THE ROADS

"From time to time you
Should sit tall on your
Horse and look back over
The trails you have traveled."

- Old Indian Saying.

Did you ever wonder what might have happened to the music we love, had there been no progress? Just how would we have arrived at "Green, Green Grass Of Home" if we had not preserved "Barbara Allen." How did folk music our forbears sang in their cabins become the country music of today? Country music historians say that the pioneers of our business carried the music to the people in the early days of radio. These pioneers traveled under the most adverse conditions on what was laughingly called the "Kerosene Circuit," there being no electricity in the hill-towns of the South.

Nashville became a center of music, long before the record companies and publishing houses found it. The important factor that the historians leave out of their stories of the beginnings of this thing called music, is the coming of the roads that paved the way for the musicians who followed.

Imagine a time, little more than two hundred years ago, when Middle Tennessee was a raw wilderness. There was not a single permanent resident, Indian or white man, living in this whole area. (Through an agreement of the various Indian tribes, this area was reserved as a hunting ground.) *Music City, USA* was not even a dream.

The first white men to come here were hunters. Settlers followed. In 1779, the James Robertson party walked through what we know now as East Nashville, near where Main Street is today. On Christmas day, the whole company crossed the Cumberland River on foot. The river was frozen completely from bank-to-bank. They stopped and built their cabins at about present-day Church Street, near a spring. (This spot was just above where now the General Jackson Showboat docks at Opryland.) They named this settlement Nashborough. It wasn't until 1874, that the name was changed to Nashville.

Other than drums of Indians, the very first "Nashville Sounds" were the sounds of John Gamble's (Gambil) fiddle, which he carried in a sack of doeskin under his arm, where he always carried it when not in use. He could play such fine music that he kept the pioneers laughing and dancing old-fashioned square dances and the "Virginia Reel." They "cut the pigeon wing" and jogged and jogged. Gamble could make his fiddle laugh and talk. One of the great modern day fiddle players is Johnny Gimble, from Texas. The similarity of names makes one wonder.

33

Music was handed down from one generation to the next. Without radio, or TV, the people made their own music. It is said that Rachel, wife of Andrew Jackson, was a musician. We believe she played Spanish Guitar. In the collection of the Ladies Hermitage Association, is the music that Rachel is said to have played. The collection contains old folk music such as "Farewell, Since We Must Part" and "I'll Never Mention Him." Her guitar is on view at the Hermitage. Some fifteen years ago, Howard and I produced these songs in an album, played the way they would have been played back then. Pianist Beegie Adair was the arranger, and Laney Smallwood Hicks sang.

As the town of Nashville grew, the need for roads became of utmost importance. Early on, travel was by river or by Indian trails on horseback. By 1787, a road was completed through the Cumberland Gap, going through the Southeast Pass (now Emory's Gap.) Then it passed Bledsoe's Lick, following the Old Trace (now Gallatin Pike) to Nashville. By 1831, the Franklin Turnpike was built, followed by the Murfreesboro and Gallatin Turnpikes in 1839. These "Turnpikes" made the people long for more roads, so in quick succession, the Nolensville Turnpike was built in 1841, the Lebanon and Charlotte Turnpikes in 1842 and the White's Creek Pike in 1845. Mudd Tavern was located on Elm Hill Pike, a favorite "watering hole' for Andrew Jackson. There was also the Hillsboro, Harding (Richland), Hydes Ferry, Brick Church and Dickerson Turnpikes. Ferries connected the Pikes at river crossings. The first bridge was built at a cost of eighty-five thousand dollars from the Public Square to Gallatin Pike.

Lucinda White arrived in Tennessee from North Carolina about 1803. At the age of 60, she opened a tavern on land near the Franklin Turnpike and the Natchez Trace. She made her own wine to serve in her tavern. Soon her tavern became the "in" place to be for Nashvillians and travelers alike. She became the "Tootsie" of her day, her admirers calling her "Granny." It's not too hard to imagine Tootsie's Orchid Lounge partakers sitting in Granny White's Tavern, drinking and swapping stories. Granny White died in 1816. The Pike, which runs directly past her property, is named for her: Granny White Pike.

These Turnpikes have continued to serve Nashville from dirt roads to asphalt. Historically, a "turnpike" is a "toll road." The turnpikes out of Nashville were rough, dirty and all were toll roads. At some point, the turnpikes gradually became known as just "pikes." It probably happened when the toll was dropped. Then later the natives began calling the old pikes simply "roads" – Gallatin Road, Franklin Road, etc. With the coming of the Interstates, the big green signs naming the exits have reverted back to designating the roads as pikes. Thusly, the pikes live again!

With the growing popularity of the automobile in the 1920's and the repeal of Prohibition in 1933, life changed, particularly in the South. A thirst for entertainment motivated the people. Radio whetted that thirst. Nashville had WYNY, "The Dynamite of Dixie," owned by Luke Lea in 1929. They shared airtime with WDAD, "Dad's Tire Store On Broad." Life and Casualty established WLAC. WSM, "We Shield Millions," began in the fall of 1925, as a one thousand-watt station and grew to a five-thousand-watt station. Headlines in the newspapers read, "Call letters WSM assigned to National Life." By October 5, 1925, WSM was on the air and on November 28, George D. Hay, coming to Nashville from WLS, Chicago, launched the WSM *Barn Dance* that he later renamed *The Grand Ole Opry*. When WSM was given "clear channel status" in 1929 by the FCC, it was able to reach thousands of farmhouses without interference from other transmitters. In 1932, WSM built the nation's tallest radio tower, eight hundred and seventy-eight feet tall, increasing power to fifty-thousand watts.

Folk singing suddenly became a business. Everybody who could hold a guitar, fiddle or banjo, and had knowledge of old-time tunes, wanted to get into the act. Front porch musicians began attaining fame on radio shows like the *Grand Ole Opry*, WLS *National Barn Dance*, *Boone County Jamboree*, West Virginia's *WWVA Jamboree*, *The Renfro Valley Barn Dance* and Richmond's *The Old Dominion Barn Dance*. To gain wider audiences, they took their shows on the road, out to the people.

Due to those farsighted entertainers, who unknowingly did well for future traveling musicians, Nashville became a natural hub for entertainers to travel in and out of back then. There were none of today's super highways, but for a time, these two-lane pikes served them well. Howard and his generation of musicians would have killed for these interstates of today.

Radio entertainers started out by building their own circuits of one-night stands. Sometimes they made hardly more than money enough to eat on. Fans of these entertainers knew them by name and by traveling, the artists made new fans for future shows. They played schoolhouses, courthouses, tent shows, medicine shows and square dances, wherever a sponsor could be found. Their contracts were pretty much the same, that is, on a given date and time, they would appear at a date for a specified percentage of the gate. Often the gate collected little more than twenty-five or fifty dollars. When the "take" was split with them and when the net was divided between the band, after gas and travel expenses were paid, there was hardly enough left to eat on. Back then, admission was twenty-five cents for adults and ten cents for children.

Personal appearances reached a new high when the Smoky Mountain Boys "packed 'em in" at McFadden School in Murfreesboro, Tennessee, to the tune of a hundred dollar house. When other entertainers found out about this, they also took to the road, feeling times were "looking up" for entertainers. Opry troupes worked the road all week, then would be back for their Opry appearance on Saturday night. They were bone weary tired, playing to audiences until late at night, packing and re-packing their instruments and driving to some small tourist court for a few hours sleep. There were no Holiday Inns back then. Roy Acuff said that in the early days, in the summer, when a trip was long, they had been known to stop and bathe in a creek.

The back-roads they traveled were often old gravel roads. There was ice in the winter and in the spring the creeks rose. Hank Williams used to

35

end his shows by saying, "We'll see you next Saturday night, the Good Lord willing and if the creeks don't rise." There was more truth than fiction in that sign-off. There was usually no time to change clothes or tune up the instruments. Back stage, as a rule, was so primitive there was seldom a room to change into costumes, so they changed in cars and alleys. They played at venues without electricity and in old schoolhouses lit by kerosene lamps. They often ran out of gas and blew-out tires. Sometimes the shows were sparsely attended. They would wait for the cars to begin to arrive before tuning up. Occasionally only three or four would attend and there were times when you couldn't squeeze another person in. For the places with no electricity, a few groups carried a public address system that would work by using a car battery.

When Howard got to Nashville, musicians were still living a transient life. There was a lot of moving from job to job, station to station, and from one record company to another. They didn't worry about money, the job, a place to live or where the next date would be. Their basic philosophy was, "I was looking for a job when I found this one." It was easy to move from one band to another with no trouble. Times and songs were simpler then. They all knew the songs of all the popular stars and could change bands over night without any trouble at all.

Howard said, "The money we made in the old days didn't seem important, as we didn't make enough money to worry about. Union scale was fifteen dollars a day, plus transportation and hotel. Out of that money we paid for our own food, clothing and any other necessities of life." If they worked all thirty days of the month (never), it was possible to make four hundred and fifty dollars a month. The amount of money they worked for didn't seem to be the important factor, it was the "Who they worked for and with." They were so dedicated to playing and entertaining that nothing else mattered. Pete Wade, who became an important session player, worked with Ray Price. He said, "I would have played for nothing, just to work with Price."

Howard explained life on the road this way: "Traveling those old roads was such a trying experience in 'the good old days,' and so boring that it made clowns of nearly all of us. In retrospect, I can only wonder what kept any of us sane. We had to relieve the monotony of it all. That's why the old road stories become legends. And just as legends do, the telling as to who, what, where, when and why, change with the re-telling. Without meaning to, we made ourselves into legendary characters by creating our own diversions. Thus road stories were born."

Probably you can now understand what made musicians be like they were, why they behaved like they did, and how they got on the road in the first place. Now imagine yourself in an old limousine with five or six guys, pulling a U-Haul trailer loaded with guitars, amps, drums and stage clothes. More than likely a bass fiddle may have been carried in the car laying long-ways over the front seat. Maybe there might even be a girl singer or even a girl friend. After ten days of show dates, little or no sleep, except cat naps, while sitting up in the car, and tired, oh so tired, it should be easy to understand that the road stories you will read about are real. They were all experienced by somebody out there. The pioneers of the day paved the way, but when Howard started on the road in the late 1940's before coming to Nashville, conditions had not changed much.

The biggest name at the Opry when Howard was there fifteen years, was Roy Acuff, dubbed the King of Country Music (he got so he believed the "King" part). Some of the great road stories are told about Roy. Roy said that one week he passed through Nashville so many times, he felt like a Trailways' bus driver. Due to the "Turnpike System" (remember, no interstates), it was a sure thing to pass through Nashville many times a week to play shows in different locations. Roy and his Smoky Mountain Boys - and Girls - were booked to play a church basement in Bowling Green, Kentucky, on a Sunday, then drive back through Nashville to get to Lynchburg, Tennessee, on Monday. They next drove on to Birmingham, then back through Nashville to Jackson, Tennessee, on Wednesday. They drove back through Nashville to get to Chattanooga for Thursday's gig, then on to Atlanta. Early Saturday morning, they started back for Nashville, where their luck ran out forty miles out of Nashville. Their white, four-door 1940 Ford sedan, which had been stretched to eight doors, broke down. They managed to make it to the Opry for a Saturday night show, although there had been no time to clean up or change clothes. (Is it any wonder why one would turn to drink!)

Acuff, in the old days (and not so old days), was known to have a few drinks just to get over the rough spots. One year, Christmas Day fell on Saturday. Naturally, the Opry went on as usual. Roy had been celebrating and was wandering around on the stage. He was heard to say in a Seagram-7 Crown voice, "I'll be home in a minute, Mildred." He kept on repeating this and his voice carried out clearly over the airwaves. He was forgiven, due to circumstances. It was on Christmas day in 1936, that he and Mildred Douglas had eloped. It was their anniversary, as well as Christmas, and Saturday night at the Opry. When the show ended, Roy was no doubt "home in a minute."

In the '50's Acuff bought the Dunbar Cave Resort and shows were staged in the Cave. There was a swimming pool on the grounds and shady places for picnicking on the grounds. Howard became a backstage comedian imitating Roy Acuff. He sounded just like Roy saying, "Why don't you come up to the Dunbar and see me and Os and Jimmy Riddle and the lake, with all the ducks on it." One night backstage, Howard was doing his impersonation of Roy for the boys outside of the dressing room. He really had Roy down pat, his mannerisms and sounded just like Roy. Howard was well into his thing about Roy and Oswald at the Dunbar, when Roy walked up behind him. Howard was really on a roll and the boys didn't tell him Roy was listening. When Howard finished his act, Roy said, "That's the best I ever heard." The boys cracked up. Howard took off, but later Roy told Howard, "You can do this act all you want to, but I've already made the money out of it." Actually, Roy loved to hear Howard imitate him, and had him go through his routine one Saturday night on his Opry program, when he introduced Howard as his brother from East Tennessee. Howard also did his Acuff imitation on Ralph Emery's late night DJ show, and it became a regular part of his act at the Acuff-Rose Golf Tournament. Howard kept Dunbar Cave and Roy famous, long after Roy sold it.

Jimmy Riddle, Roy's harmonica and piano player, liked to hear Howard talk like Roy. Back stage at the Opry, he'd ask Howard, "Roy, how about a raise?" Howard would answer, "Hell, no, you're making too much now!" Before Dunbar Cave, Roy tried to buy the Sampson's Mineral Well at Rock City in Smith County near Carthage. The Well had been a health resort and the mineral water had been sold to people near and far. Sampson had been drilling for oil and they hit the artesian mineral water instead. Acuff wanted to turn the old resort into an amusement park. Virgil Sampson, who owned the well until he died at age 102, refused to sell to him. Howard said, "I sure am glad he didn't sell to Roy. It was a lot easier to imitate Roy when talking about the Dunbar, rather than Sampson's Mineral Well."

Roy Claxton Acuff didn't start out to be a paid entertainer. Where he was from, he and his friends didn't get paid for singing or fiddling, they just played for the fun of it. He had no idea he would become known as the King of Country Music. An interesting note is that when Ida Carr and Neil Acuff named their second son "Roy," the name had another meaning. Roy happened to be the shortened version of "Leroy," derived from the French "Le roi" or "the King." It was prophetic that these East Tennessee mountain people proclaimed Roy a King from the beginning, although unaware they were doing so.

Acuff was the first great singing artist on the Opry, but there were a lot of great ones to follow. Traveling was rough in the old day, but all those "rough riders" paved the way for the boys of today in their big entertainer buses that pass you, giving no hint of who's behind those curtained windows. Things have really changed since the coming of good roads and good money, for the stars and their musicians. In the 1950's and '60's the big stars of the day were only making five hundred to a thousand dollars a day, and out of that sum had to pay the musicians and expenses. Some of the stars lived by the rule, kind of like the musicians, "I was looking for a musician when I found this one," kind of like the musicians themselves. Howard insisted, "The simplicity of the times and low pay for the stars and musicians, created the conditions for the seeming lack of stability we enjoyed."

8 THIS JOB FOR HIRE

"The life I love is making
Music with my friends
And I can't wait to get
On the road again."

- Willie Nelson.

Howard loved his job with Copas. Seven of them traveled together in a Cadillac limousine, plus luggage and instruments. They took their turns driving, and then tried to sleep, but there really wasn't a lot of sleep accomplished when one sits upright in a car. Eventually, the long tours and sleepless nights caught up with Howard and his old 1945 problems returned. They were working in Kansas, the last night of a tour, when Howard broke down and started crying on stage.

Kathy Copas was an angel. She talked to Howard and she and Copas sent him home to North Carolina to rest. That was always what the V.A. Hospitals had prescribed. The pressure of life on the road was not good for Howard, but that was just part of show business and he knew it. He wanted to play music, had dreamed of it all his life, so he always pushed on.

That's why, after a few days at home and Minnie Pearl called, Howard went back to Nashville. Minnie and Henry Cannon, her husband, had a State Fair tour lined up. Henry owned a private plane and he was flying them from date to date, "Barnstorming." After all, Charlotte wasn't Nashville and that's where Howard wanted to be. He was afraid of flying and never lost that fear, but it was faster than an automobile.

Howard said, "Working with Minnie was a delight." The band had Howard, Mel Tillis on guitar and Roger Miller on fiddle. Roger was no fiddle player. He could only play "Bile Dem Cabbage Down." Years later, Minnie was on Ralph Emery's TV Show, talking about those dates. She said, "Can you imagine those three together! It was a riot all the time!" Howard, in turn, said, "Minnie was such fun to work with. She'd tell her jokes, do her little dance, sing 'Careless Love,' while I played steel for her. She'd throw her leg up and I would do a glissando up the strings." Henry flew the plane, but he was a cautious flyer, never flying unless the weather was agreeable for flying.

John Kelly, noted tour promoter, booked a "Twin Act" on the shows, Herbert and Howard Smith. They were identical – no one could tell them apart. One day they set Minnie and Henry into gales of laughter when Herbert went to Henry and complained because the printer had put his name under Howard's picture and Howard's name under his picture. Who could tell! On the first half of the show, they were billed as the "Smith Twins." On the second half they were billed as the "Duo From South Of The Border." They put sashes around their waists for this portion and sang Spanish songs. One night someone in the audience threw a prize onion and hit Herbert in the face – (or was it Howard?) - Minnie went out on the stage and told the audience that in her opinion this was very bad manners. Howard said, "I was really impressed with Minnie. It showed what a fine person she was to take up for an unknown act like that."

Red Sovine and the Glaser Brothers were also on that tour. Mel Tillis was once quoted in a Don Cusic book as saying that Roger and Howard were always fighting, but that wasn't true according to Howard. He said, "We only had one altercation and that was in the hall at a motel, over some girls. I don't know why I started that!"

When the fair tour was over, Howard was without a job. "Copas offered me my job back, but my friend, Jack Logan, was playing for him." Jack had a wife and baby and one thing Howard wouldn't do was take another man's job. So he refused to go back with Copas at that time. He stuck to the old Opry adage, "I was looking for a job when I found this one." He did let people know at the Opry that he was out of work.

One night at the Opry, Tommy Jackson, the fiddle player, went to Howard and asked him if he could go down to Louisiana and work for Hank Williams. At this time, Hank had been fired from the Opry. Howard knew of Hank's reputation, an addiction to alcohol and narcotics, but he also knew Hank was a great writer and singer. Hank had real charisma and audiences loved him. His band had all quit as Hank, hurt by the Opry's action, went downhill fast. He had landed back at *The Louisiana Hayride*. After Jackson told Howard the job was open, Dale Potter, another fiddler, called Hank in Bossier City for Howard. Hank hired Howard and Howard went to Louisiana to work for Williams.

Howard recalled: "I didn't know just how downhill Hank was, until I got to Louisiana. Hank was divorced from Audrey at the time and had married Billie Jean Jones Eshliman. Billie Jean seemed to like me, probably because I was kind to her. She did little things for me, like straighten my tie before going on stage. Hank didn't like this one bit. Hank was drunk almost all the time. He was nothing but skin and bones. He was also on morphine and chloralhydrate (medicine) as prescribed to him by his doctor to ease pain in his back. Then one night, I heard him cuss his mother out on a phone backstage. That did it! I lasted two weeks."

Two weeks was all Howard could stand. He returned to Nashville and by then Jack Logan had left Copas, so Howard went back to work with Cowboy. That was only about two months before Hank Williams died on January 1, 1953, traveling to Oak Hill, West Virginia. Howard said, "I remember well the night we heard Hank died. We were on our way to Keokuk, Iowa, for a New Year's date when the news came on the radio. We were all stunned. Hank had become such a legend, the greatest thing ever in country music at that time. We all knew he was in terrible shape, but none of us were prepared to hear he was really dead."

Hank was buried in Montgomery, Alabama. Red Foley sang "Peace In the Valley" to a crowd of twenty-five thousand. Foley's manager, Dub Allbritten, said that Hank had called Red and asked him to sing that song at his funeral only days before he died. That might have been Hank's last request. After Hank died, Billie Jean Williams married Johnny Horton, famous for the song, "The Battle of New Orleans." Horton was killed later in an auto accident in Texas. Shortly after his death, she briefly attempted to record for 20th Century Fox Records as Billie Jean Horton, charting a single song, "Ocean of Tears," which stalled at number twenty-nine after three weeks in August 1961.

Merle Kilgore, who once was into the occult, told me an eerie story one day. He said that he and Johnny Horton had a pact. They both believed you could talk to the dead. So if one of them died first, he would get in touch with the other, using the code words, "The drummer is a rummer and cannot keep a beat." Then the one alive would know the deceased one was trying to talk to him. Merle said he heard nothing from Johnny, until one day a psychic from New York called him and said a spirit was trying to reach him. She said, "I don't know who it was, but the spirit said to tell Merle Kilgore in Nashville that the drummer is a rummer and cannot keep a beat."

Copas was being booked by Hoot Gilliam from Arkansas, and was working smaller venues, schoolhouses, little theaters, all one-nighters. Then Dick Blake booked them at the Lyric Theater in Indianapolis for a week's engagement. Howard thought that was the living end, just to stay in one place for a week. Then Copas confided to Howard that he lost fifteen thousand dollars in one year by having a band. Howard knew then that the handwriting was on the wall. That was a lot of money in those days. Copas was working a lot of percentage dates. If Copas lost money, he still paid the band. After Copas told Howard how much the band was costing him, not too much time elapsed before he decided to disband.

So, Howard was without a job again, but he had made up his mind. He was in Nashville to stay. He said, "I've never done without a full meal or a bed to sleep in and I was a veteran hillbilly now, so I figured somehow I would hang in there." Howard didn't have the responsibility of a wife or child. Living was a lot simpler in the '50's. Gas was thirty-five cents cent a gallon, cigarettes were twenty-five cents a pack and a half-pint was only a dollar and a quarter. A bed at Mom's boarding house was only five dollars a week (later raised to seven dollars). Breakfast was seventy-five cents and supper was eighty-five cents. All he had to worry about was his next job. As long as he could play the Opry and stay in Nashville, he had everything he wanted.

After Copas disbanded, Howard's old friend Randy Hughes again came to his rescue. Randy was managing Patsy Cline and Ferlin Husky. Ferlin had just had a big hit, "Gone," and needed a steel player, so Randy got Howard the job. Thus began a succession of many jobs with many artists, which took Howard to all fifty states and five countries.

By the time Howard began working for Ferlin, he considered himself a veteran musician. Bud Isaacs had played a new-fangled steel guitar on the record "Slowly" by Webb Pierce. He wanted one of those pedal guitars, so he went to Shot Jackson, who told him he could build him one. Shot and Buddy Emmons had not yet formed Sho-Bud, so Shot built the first "Sho-Bud" in Jack Anglin's chicken house, according to Shot. (Sometimes Shot was known for stretching the truth just a little.) Howard said, "That was the finest guitar I ever owned."

When Sho-Bud Guitar Company became a real business, it soon became a huge business. Howard said, "I wish I had that guitar back. Shot kept it when he made me a new one about 1965." Howard and I had taken the well-used old Sho-Bud guitar in for repairs. Shot said, "Howard, that's the ugliest guitar I've ever seen. It embarrasses me. I'll make you a new one." Maybe it was ugly but Howard opined that the new guitar was never the same as the old one. They both had six pedals and two necks, but Shot shortened the necks on the new one. He did it for a reason, they had added a high string and it kept breaking on the old length. The shortened length of the strings didn't give Howard the sound that he wanted. He sold the new guitar to Carl Knight in about 1969. That first Sho-Bud would surely belong in the Hall of Fame if anyone knew what Shot did with it.

Ferlin Husky was from Hickory Grove, Missouri. After working in California and touring with Smiley Burnette, he landed a record contract with Capitol Records. After two name changes, he chose Ferlin Huskey. He later changed the spelling of "Huskey" to "Husky." He developed the "Simon Crum" comedy routine. He came to the Opry in 1954. Ferlin was one of a kind. He was probably the greatest country music showman ever. His comedy character, Simon, came alive any time Ferlin wanted him to, on stage or off stage. Ferlin and Simon were two people into one. No one ever knew what Ferlin would do next. People swore that there really were two people in one body. He was known to get off the bus and have a one-man fight with Simon. One night they checked in at a fine hotel. Ferlin went in using a set of deer antlers as a walking cane. Another time they went into a café and Ferlin went in dressed like an Indian.

He sat down and kept the corners of his mouth turned down. The fans loved him and his song "Gone," not only hit on the country charts, it crossed over to the pop charts as well. Other entertainers lamented that you never wanted to follow Ferlin on stage. At this time, after "Gone" had hit, Ferlin's band was made up of Randy Hughes (rhythm guitar), Ike Inman (bass), Sammy Pruett (lead guitar) and Howard on steel. Millie Kirkham, who had sung the high part on the record, went along with them, and also on that package show was Martha Carson. Millie, in later years, said she was warned to look out for Howard, but she found out it was Ferlin she needed to watch out for.

They all arrived for a show date on New Year's Eve in St. Paul, Minnesota, to find out that Millie's luggage had been left behind at the previous date. Howard said, "It was four below zero, but it felt more like it was twenty-four below." It had been dark when the boys had loaded all the luggage and instruments. In the confusion and bitter cold, someone just overlooked Millie's gear. There they were in St. Paul and Millie's show clothes were hundreds of miles down the road. The show must go on, so at show time, Millie appeared on stage in a borrowed knit dress from Martha Carson, that was so big on Millie, she had to tuck it way up at the waist, and a pair of shoes hurriedly bought at a nearby store. Martha sang her hit, "Satisfied" that night, but I suspect in Millie's heart she was singing, "Nobody Knows The Trouble I've Seen." When she sang "Gone" with Ferlin, that song was probably more appropriate for that occasion.

In 1956, Howard recorded two sides with Simon Crum on Capitol, "Little Red Webb" and "Don't Be Mad." They recorded at Columbia Studios with Ken Nelson producing. Randy Hughes played rhythm guitar, Sammy Pruett lead guitar, Ike Inman bass and Tommy Vaden was on fiddle. Howard also did a TV Show with Ferlin, *Country Style, USA*. Ferlin sang a duet with Kathy Copas, "Hey, Good Lookin'." Ferlin did his Simon Crum act, vocally imitating Webb Pierce and Kitty Wells. Ike Inman played bass, Tommy Vaden fiddled, while Randy Hughes played guitar and Marvin Hughes (no relation) was on piano (ironically, Kathy was then wed to Randy, and after he died, married Marvin). Incidentally, the *Country Style, USA* shows can now be bought via Bear Family Records.

During 1956, Chet Atkins produced a session on Dave Rich and the Echoes Of Calvary Quartet on RCA. Howard played on this session, along with Floyd Cramer (organ) and Spider Rich (lead guitar), recording "Where Else Would I Want To Be" and "Brand New Feeling."

After a year, Ferlin disbanded and Howard went to work for Wilma Lee and Stoney Cooper. The Coopers played for years in West Virginia before coming to Nashville. Wilma Lee came from a famous family singing gospel songs, The Leary Family. Stoney joined the family band as a singer and fiddle player. He and Wilma Lee soon fell in love, married and later became members of the *Grand Ole Opry*. They were real country, playing authentic traditional country sounds. The Clinch Mountain Clan, as their band was called, were fun to work with for Howard. Jimmy Elrod played banjo and George McCormick played guitar. Howard remained friends with them through the years. George later became a member of Porter Wagoner's Wagon Masters, though Elrod eventually abandoned the business for a well-paying job at Peterbilt Trucks.

In 1957, Howard and the Clan recorded two songs with the Coopers, "Heartbreak Street" and "This Ole House." Johnny Erdelyan was producer and the musicians besides Howard were George McCormick, Jimmy Elrod, Benny Martin (fiddle) and Joe "Flapjack" Phillips (bass). Everyone thought that "Heartbreak Street" would be a hit but, alas, it wasn't.

Howard also played on a radio show that was recorded and released as *Radio Gems #3*. It was released on Hickory Records, the same label as the Coopers' "Heartbreak Street." Radio Gems included the standards "We Live In Two Different Worlds," "Poor Ellen Smith," "Wildwood Flower" and "Is It Right"

"We musicians sold artist songbooks and pictures for a commission. That was the custom. Back then there weren't any concession managers following in a semi truck. Our daily pay wasn't much and we depended on the concession money to eat. Then Wilma Lee and Stoney cut our concession fee, so I quit. Maybe, I was just tired of playing 'Big Midnight Special.'"

Howard learned Wilma Lee was very superstitious. If something like a black cat crossed in front of the car, she would always make the sign of the cross on the windshield. They were all tired one night when Stoney was driving, and Stoney went to sleep and ran off the road into a cornfield. That mishap woke him up, but all he said was, "Upon my word, Wilma!" Regarding quitting the Clan, Howard mused, "They needed a steel guitar like a hole in the head. In reality, what they needed was a Dobro."

In 1954, Howard went to work for Audrey Williams, Hank Williams' first wife, who billed herself as "Mrs. Hank Williams." On the show, too, were Ken (Loosh) Marvin, guitar and front man; Goober Buchanan, bass and comedian; and Buddy Spicher, fiddle. Dale Potter was supposed to have played fiddle, but gave the job to Buddy. Then Buddy left in the middle of the tour and Benny Williams replaced him. In 1959, Hank Jr., then about ten years old, was featured artist. Junior sang daddy's songs and crowds loved him. Howard surmised, "Audrey may not have been the greatest singer in the world, but she was fair to her band and shows went over well." They always traveled first class, riding in Cadillacs and stretch limos, and staying at the finest hotels. Howard added, "Audrey never interfered with the musicians or tried to tell us how to play."

Audrey's show was billed as the "Hank Williams Memorial Show." First, they did a Southern tour, playing Memphis, New Orleans, Jackson (Mississippi), and KWKH's *Louisiana Hayride*. The "Big Bopper" was on their Southern tour. Then came a three-week tour of Alaska in late January and early February (not the warmest time in that clime). Vic Lewis was the show's promoter. He was a good booker, but Goober Buchanan claimed, "Vic had been a pitchman for the Gaiety Theater in Detroit, a burlesque house. He had a habit of advertising a lot of names on the show, whether they were booked or not. I don't know how he stayed out of trouble. He was mighty careless with the truth."

As Howard noted, "If the artist Vic claimed was booked didn't appear, Vic claimed he was ill. Then he would read a telegram from the artist to the audience. He even made up names for the bill like Little Lennie Ford and Uncle Grady Moss."

Even today, Hank Jr. gives Howard credit for giving him his first drink. Howard reasoned, "I don't remember that, but I probably did." When Junior grew up, he didn't become famous for singing his father's songs, but did things his own way. He didn't stay long in the shadow of his father, like Audrey wanted him to do. His fans think they discovered him, Hank Jr., the authentic rebel!

After the Southern tour, they all drove to Seattle and then flew to Anchorage. Next they played Fairbanks, doing twenty shows there at the American air base. Then flying to Juneau, they played a theater two nights and performed for two dances at a country club. Howard and Goober visited the famed Red Dog Saloon in Juneau. That was also the year Alaska became a State and The Red Dog Saloon gave Goober a certificate certifying he was there that historic year. Howard was one of his "Drinking Witnesses." Then they flew on a "Flying Goose" to Ketchikan. Lycrecia, Audrey's daughter, appeared on some of the shows and sang "Hey, Good Lookin'" with half-brother Hank, Jr.

The Red Dog Saloon

Certifies That

J. L. "Goober" Buchanan

was in Juneau the Capital City of Alaska
the Year it became the 49th State of the Union

Drinking Witnesses

Melvin Hollis   Ruby Fansy
Donald Brown   KATHY FRAQNER
Violet F. Brown   Frances Finger (Mrs.)
Elizabeth Ahsook   * Howard A. White Jr.

Further Attested To By;
Gordon Kanouse
GORDON KANOUSE
Proprietor
Juneau Alaska   1959

Howard remembered a particularly fine hotel they stayed in: "I walked in and Goober was sitting there like an English nobleman. He was dressed all in black with white gloves. I asked him why he was so dressed up. Goober said that Miss Audrey had said, 'Goober, honey, we're staying at the finest hotels. You're gonna have to dress better.' So, as a joke Goober overdressed."

Somewhere between the Southern tour and Alaska, Audrey and Howard began an affair that lasted throughout the Alaskan trek. Goober said,

"Loosh and I were rooming together and Audrey and Howard were in the next room. Loosh kept me awake all night, looking through the keyhole, trying to see what Audrey and Howard were doing." When the tour ended and they left for home, Audrey and Howard flew back from Seattle, while others picked up the car she had left there. It was the middle of the snow season in February, and they drove across the northern states. They said it was the worst trip they were ever on.

In August 1957, Audrey and Eddie Crandall had opened an office at 2508 Franklin Road, Nashville - the Williams-Crandall Agency. He and Audrey had a romantic relationship going; however, Audrey ended that relationship as soon as she got back to Nashville. When Howard saw Eddie on Broad Street, Eddie's only words were, "Oh, no, not you!" Howard spent a lot of time at Audrey's home on Franklin Road, when they first came home. Then they went on tour to New York. After the tour, they all crowded into one car heading back to the hotel. Lycrecia, who was Audrey's teen-aged daughter from her first marriage, sat on Howard's lap. Upon getting back to Nashville, Howard called Lycrecia, asking her to go to the Melrose Theater with him. They met there and Mrs. Raglan, the nanny at Audrey's house, found out about it and told Audrey. She was very angry and called Howard to cuss him out. They never saw each other as a "thing" again, but as Howard said: "Our relationship wasn't that intense, nor did it last long. She bought Eddie a pink Cadillac, clothes and jewelry. She never bought me anything!"

Vic Lewis and Howard became great friends through the years. In later years, they did some business together. In 1963, Audrey's money and Vic's know-how combined to put together a film for a company they designated Marathon Pictures. They actually filmed at Trafco Studios, owned by the Methodist Church and located behind a Cadillac dealership in Nashville. They titled their movie "Country Music On Broadway." Premiering it at the Tennessee Theater, there was a glittering array of country music stars, some of whom appeared in the film. Howard, who by that time was playing with Hank Snow, is in the movie with Hank, performing "A Fool Such As I." It featured Audrey and Hank, Jr.

The next year, Audrey and Vic produced another movie, "Second Fiddle To A Steel Guitar," and thanks to Audrey, Howard was in the cinematic staff band this time. Again, every country music star available at the time, was in it, too, along with Hollywood players Arnold Stang, Leo Gorcey and Huntz Hall, professional thespians. Stang was a comedian, while Leo and Huntz had made a long career of playing original Dead End Kids, utilizing additional tags along the way, such as the East Side Kids and The Bowery Boys in a series of low-budget movies.

Howard and Leo Gorcey hit it off right away, and on an off-day of shooting, Howard and I went to Leo's hotel room to visit him. I expected everybody to be there, but he was alone. He obviously expected a party, as his dresser was filled with every type of alcoholic beverage. Afterwards, we got him a date with a young blonde named Charlene, double dating every night while Leo was in town. Leo, Howard and I stayed friends as long as he lived. Sadly, he died in June 1969, a day before his fifty-second birthday.

I think Leo Gorcey would get the prize for being the most outlandish character I have ever known. He was noted for being the toughest of the Dead End Kids. Once arrested in Los Angeles for going ninety-two miles an hour down Wilshire Boulevard, he sported a belt buckle that bore the names of four ex-wives and spaces for two more (he had one more, his fifth, who survived him). In the middle were the initials LBG, meaning *Love Broke Gorcey.* We thought Charlene might fill one of those spaces. He bought her a ticket to California, but they didn't marry. Leo called me "The Boss" and his letters came to us as "The Boss and Howard White, Jr." He sent us tapes with songs he had written, all bad. For instance, one began: *"He was soaked to the skin / With lots and lots of gin / But couldn't find a girl to tuck him in. He traveled far and wide / With his bottle at his side / And could never find a gal to stem the tide . . ."*

All his letters were signed "Rover." He signed a picture to us which said, "To Howard and the Boss; About That International Disease . . . Love, Leo." Leo lived at the Brandy Lee Ranch, Los Molinos, California.

About 1963, Audrey brought Buddy Lee, an ex-professional wrestler, to Nashville. Buddy had been promoting shows in Columbia, South Carolina. Buddy started a little booking agency in town and began working with Audrey and Hank, Jr. Then Audrey bought into the agency and they opened offices at 812 16th Avenue South in 1964. They named it the Aud-Lee Agency. Audrey lived fast and hard for the next ten years. Time ran out on her in 1975. The Buddy Lee Agency went on and at one time booked some great acts like George Jones and Tammy Wynette.

Howard worked some show dates with Jim Reeves, when Jim was new in town and had not brought his own band with him. Ralph Emery said, "The first time I saw Howard, he was working with Jim Reeves in the '50's at the old and original Maxwell House on Church Street, at a DJ Convention breakfast." Howard knew Jim wanted to bring in his old steel player, Jimmy Day. In those days, you had to have a job playing to join the musicians' union. Howard said, "So when Jim was ready to bring in his old band and I knew Jim wanted Day and not me, I stepped aside and Jimmy Day came to Nashville and joined the union."

Between jobs, the musicians hung out at a place next door to the old National Life Building, the coffee shop in the Clarkston Hotel. It was a good place to pick up news about all kinds of things relating to the music business. Johnny Johnson, a guitar picker, told Howard there that Judy

Lynn's manager, John Kelly, was putting a band together for Judy. Judy, a singer from Idaho, was Miss Idaho 1955. He landed the job, along with the fiddle player Don "Suds" Slayman, Joel Price and Luke Brandon, guitars, and Willie Ackerman, drums. Don was named "Suds" because he drank so much beer. Willie Ackerman said Suds gave him his very first "pill" – only a half. He said he stayed up all night. Willie was pulled right out of high school for this gig. Later, he played on the *Hee Haw* TV show twenty years.

Suds was Howard's roommate, and good friend throughout their lives. They shared many years and beers together. One afternoon, somewhere in Wyoming, they had nothing to do, so they went to the movies. They had seen an ad in the paper for a "Mr. Magoo" cartoon showing at the local movie house. Well, Howard loved Magoo, so he and Suds went, arriving in the middle of the feature film. It finished and the house lights came on. They waited for the show to begin again, so they could see Magoo. Some guy began sweeping the floor. Howard asked him when the next show would begin. He said, "There won't be another show tonight." Howard said, "Damn! Such a theater! Hell, man!" He stomped out with Suds following. It was bitter cold and the streets were lined with ice. Howard was wearing boots and was so angry, he hauled off, kicked a chunk of ice – and broke his toe!

One night in Idaho, a drunk wannabe steel player, who called himself Bob White (a.k.a. as Bob Hershey) tried to pick a fight with Little Jimmy Dickens, who was on the same show with Judy. They were outside and Howard was standing behind Dickens, who only stood as tall as Howard's chest. Bob White wrapped his belt around his fist and struck out at Dickens. Instead, he hit Howard right in the mouth. Howard said, "He ran and when I came to, he was gone." In later years, Bob White was murdered in a bizarre Mafia killing, his body dumped out on the Interstate.

Howard was with Judy in New York City at the same time Joel Price was in the band. Poor old Joel was noted for being the biggest "worry-wart" in the business. He over-planned everything. The bandsmen were all mad at Joel, because he insisted they leave too early for the show date. As Howard said, "We would have had time to see a nine-inning ball game with the time he allowed to get to a date only sixty miles away." They were on the Expressway when Joel, who was driving, said, "Howard, hand me that map in the glove compartment." Howard handed him the first map he saw. Joel said, "That's the wrong map." Howard handed him another, saying, "Is this the right one?" Then Howard tore up the map in little pieces and threw it out the window. The band rolled with laughter until they all found out they didn't know what exit to use. They managed to find the right exit, arriving a long time before show time. Howard said, "We still had five-and-a-half hours before time to go on." (That could have been an exaggeration.)

Finally, Judy decided to go to Las Vegas permanently. The band all went their separate ways. She continued to work in the Vegas area for twenty-five years. None of the band wanted Vegas as a home base, so they quit working for Judy. In later years, Howard talked to Judy regularly. She told him she was "saved" in 1972, and in 1980 left show business. She became an Evangelist. Howard was not surprised. He remembered she always carried her Bible with her on the road. Howard said, "I was gratified to hear her say that I was always kind to her. Certainly, she was always kind to me."

Again, Howard was at the Clarkston Coffee Shop when Jackie Phelps asked him if he wanted to go to work for Hawkshaw Hawkins and Jean Shepard. Howard said, "It sounded good to me. Hawk had a 1950 Flex bus, the first that I knew about in Nashville." When Howard went with them, Hawk and Jean were not yet married. Hawk was from West Virginia, Jean from Oklahoma, and both joined the Opry in 1955. Hawk, an expert with the bullwhip, worked rodeos and Wild West shows. Jean, at one time, had her own all-girl band, the Melody Ranch Girls. Hawk, a trained horseman, bought a "high school" horse in Kansas and used it on his shows. That horse could kneel down, count and darn near up-staged Hawk and Jean.

During that time, Howard made one of a series of filmed appearances with Hawk and Jean called "Classic Country" as produced by (Al) Gannaway Films. They were shot at the old Bradley's Barn on Sixteenth Avenue South, before Bradley built the now famous Quonset Hut, which later CBS purchased. This Barn is not to be confused with the later Bradley's Barn that Owen built in Mt. Juliet. Little Rita Fay was also on that portion, along with her mother and father, Kitty and Smiley Wilson. Whenever the "Big Boys" came to town, they always thought the set had to have hay bales and wagon wheels on it. The Gannaway sets were no different. There were lots of hay bales for the cast to sit on. The next step was to hire folks just to sit on the bales. The musicians called them "hay-sitters." Hawk and Jean were a great act, but argued a lot. Howard remembered Jean saying to Hawk, "You are going to marry me," as she punched him in the stomach. Their touring was constant and so were the arguments. It grated on Howard's nerves, so eventually he left this job, too.

After a period of ten years, it occurred to Howard that he had played with a lot of artists and not getting any younger, and suddenly here he was out of work again. He began hitting the road with various artists including Red Sovine, Grandpa Jones and The Duke of Paducah. When fans would ask why he played with so many people, his standard reply was, "I just got tired of playing the same songs over and over."

While Howard was working the Indiana State Fair with Red Sovine, it happened that Hank Snow was also on the bill, backed only by fiddler Chubby Wise. Hank, about to form a new band, asked Howard if he wanted to join him. Howard took the offer and thus began his longest period playing with an artist. Between 1960 and 1965, they went everywhere, akin to Hank's number one song "I've Been Everywhere."

This gig offered by Hank Snow came at the right moment. It was an exciting offer, after all the years drifting from artist to artist. *"Hold back, because then when you do something, it will really sound exciting. Wait for the right moment, instead of being Mr. Busy."* - Jason Bonham, son of Bonzo Bonham, Led Zeppelin drummer.

9 THE LITTLE GENERAL

"I've been everywhere, boys....
'We know some place you haven't been....'
No, I've been everywhere."

Geoff Mack.

"Hank," Howard said, when he started working for him in 1960, "I hear you drink a lot and I'll be glad to drink with you – if you pay for it." That began almost five years as a "Rainbow Ranch Boy" with Hank Snow, The Singing Ranger. Around the Opry they called him *The Little General*. The band fell right in, a pretty good four-piece group: Chubby Wise, fiddle; Tommy Floyd, bass; Ed Hyde, guitar; and Howard on steel guitar. Later on, Ralph Jernigan replaced Tommy Floyd on bass. Hank was very particular about the band's sound. For instance, once Howard recorded the song "Poor Little Jimmie" with Hank, using a muted sound, the Little General liked that sound and wanted his subsequent steel-players to use it on that song (not that they always did).

Hank, Clarence Eugene Snow, was born May 9, 1914, in Nova Scotia, Canada. When he first came to the United States he wanted to be a singing cowboy. That was not to be, but in 1950 his record of "I'm Movin' On" catapulted him into stardom. Hank wrote both the words and the music. It stayed on the charts forty-four weeks and at number one twenty-one weeks. (The only others to remain in top spot twenty-one weeks were Eddy Arnold in 1947, with "I'll Hold You In My Heart," and Webb Pierce's "In the Jailhouse Now" in 1955 - until 2013, when Florida Georgia Line & Nelly topped them with "Cruise," tallying twenty-two weeks at number one.)

Steve Sholes, who signed Hank to RCA in the States, loved telling how Hank kept bringing him the same railroad song over and over. Sholes kept rejecting it until finally, out of desperation, he let Hank cut it. "I'm Movin' On" became one of the longest running records in the history of country. Snow's very first American charting, however, was "Marriage Vow," a 1949 Top Ten single written by Jenny Lou Carson.

Hank was still a superstar in the 1960's, and also a big stockholder in National Life Insurance Company, original owners of WSM's *Grand Ole Opry*. Louie Buck, a WSM announcer, advised Hank to buy this stock and the advice paid off. Hank's band used to try to figure out how much Hank's stock was really worth. Whatever anyone says about Hank, he knew how to handle money, and he took everything seriously, his performances and his business dealings.

Hank made few mistakes, and was a clever man with money most of the time. While other "hillbillies" seemed to spend more than they made, Hank was frugal and held on to his money. He confided to Howard that he did make one mistake. Apparently he met his match in "Colonel" Tom Parker, who at one time or another managed Hank, Eddy Arnold and Elvis Presley. One Christmas, Parker gave Hank a huge RCA color television set. Hank was really proud about that, until he found out Parker had somehow negotiated the TV through Hank's recording contract with RCA. Initially thinking Parker had "given" it to him, in actuality, Hank was paying for that set himself, out of his own royalties.

'I'm Movin' On' sheet music.

One night on a show in Virginia, Parker booked Elvis Presley as a closing act. Hank was singing and the girls were screaming, "We want Elvis! We want Elvis!" Finally, a fed-up Hank told them, "I'll bring the little son-of-a-bitch on, if you'll shut up!" None of the band had ever seen anything like Elvis. He was indeed a sight to behold. Steel player Bobbe

Seymour was a boy attending that show. Years later, as Bobbe told Howard, "The first time I ever saw you play was at a Hank Snow-Elvis Presley show in Virginia."

Colonel Parker was general manager of Hank Snow Attractions and Jamboree Attractions. They represented Eddy Arnold, Faron Young, Slim Whitman and Hank's son Jimmie Rodgers Snow. Hank was touring in Texas when he called Hill and Range Publishing and said, "I found this kid in Memphis and put him on my show at the end, a mistake. When he finished, everybody got up and looked for him backstage and I'm left sitting there strumming my guitar." That "kid" was Elvis. Parker led Hank to believe that Jamboree Attractions was making a bid to manage Elvis, but once again Parker got the best of Hank. He signed Elvis to himself and cut Hank out. When Parker and Hank had a phone conversation, Hank asked, "Have we signed the damn kid or not?" Parker said, "No, WE haven't, I have signed him!"

That dissolved their partnership, though the assets of the company amounted to nothing more than a few boxes of stationery. Hill and Range started two publishing companies with Elvis - Presley Music and Gladys Music - and Parker became the most famous of promoters, thanks to Elvis. Parker was once a dogcatcher in Tampa, Florida, and performed a circus act with chickens on a hot plate. By becoming sole manager of Elvis Presley, his fame and fortune was secured forever.

As Hank and Howard rode the highways, Hank told him many stories of how he was abused as a child, of being put out to sea as a cabin boy at only ten years old. People said Hank was a controlled, arrogant little man. He stood only five foot, four inches tall. Hank was God fearing, but others thought he was a cold prude. He always seemed like an outsider to the Opry gang. Being Canadian was enough to make the country world of the '50's distrust him. At the time Howard was working for Hank, he really felt close to Hank, and thought that life had just turned Hank the way he was. Hank had a tough life during the Great Depression. Canada had food coupons then and he told Howard about trading coupons for cash money, so he could have ferry fare to go across the lake to the place he took guitar lessons. He later gave guitar lessons himself. He married Minnie Blanche Aalders, a fine, understanding woman. "Min" put up with Hank for a lifetime. They began their life together by living in a barn, and in the winter the snow blew in around the cracks. They had to tie their bed up to the wall to hold it up. Their son Jimmie Rodgers Snow, was born in a charity ward in a Salvation Army Hospital in 1935, and was named for Hank's idol, the "Singing Brakeman," Jimmie Rodgers (who died of tuberculosis in 1933). At some point in later life, Jimmie began using the spelling "Jimmy."

When Hank discovered Jimmie Rodgers, who also recorded for RCA, he became a life long fan. Hank began his professional career at a Canadian radio, and became a featured act on *The Canadian Farm Hour.* Hank first recorded for RCA-Canada. After Hank came to California, hoping to become a singing cowboy and failed, Ernest Tubb brought him to Nashville.

Hank wasn't doing well at the Opry, and was ready to leave when he hit with "I'm Movin' On." He stayed with the WSM program until his death forty-nine years later.

In 1950, Hank bought a house with three acres of land on Marthona Drive in suburban Madison. He called it the Rainbow Ranch and built a barn for his trick horse, Shawnee. Even though only a small amount of land, he designated it a ranch. He designed an iron archway over the entry of his drive, inscribed with "Rainbow Ranch." He hired a caretaker, Willie Fred Carter, who nearly everyone knew as "Squirlie." Squirlie put managing Rainbow Ranch above everything else, though he also played a little steel guitar and could sing a bit. Hank's bands, dating from the first one in Canada, were always called "Rainbow Ranch Boys."

Sometimes Hank would call Howard late at night, even after Howard was asleep, to ask him to come out to the ranch. Howard always went, and he and Hank would play guitars and sing until Howard could no longer stay awake. Then Hank would have Min put Howard to bed and the next morning she would fix Howard breakfast. There are people now who can hardly believe this, but it's true: Hank was a very private person, a real introvert. Hank had a Myna Bird and when he would cough, the bird would cough just like Hank. Hank would whistle the first line of "Indian Love Call," whistling *When I'm calling you . . . ,* and that bird would sing back the last half of the line, *"Ooh, ooh, ooh, ooh, ooh, ooh . . . "*

Hank also had that horse, which he'd acquired back when he yearned to be a singing cowboy. One night, after he and Howard had consumed a fair amount of booze, they ambled down to the barn, where Hank wanted to show Howard tricks Shawnee could do. Hank laid down in the stall beside the horse, amongst horse manure, and Shawnee pulled a handkerchief out of Hank's pocket. Although Hank had hoped to be a singing cowboy, he just never looked the part, being so short. Howard reasoned, "Maybe he should have been a jockey!"

Hank had two main quirks on the road. One, he absolutely refused to stay in a motel that didn't have carpeting, said Howard, "In those days a lot of motel rooms had linoleum, particularly in the West." Two, whenever he left a motel room, every little thing had to be put back in order just as it was when he entered it. Just once, they had checked out of a motel and were driving along the highway, when Hank said, "Where's the bag of money?" Venues usually paid in cash after the shows. In fact, back then, the contracts always read, "To be paid in cash, in U.S. Currency." Hank would put the money in a bag, and always placed it under the bed. And that's where that bag was! Still under the bed! They doubled back, went to Hank's room and luckily the moneybag was still there. Howard said, "Why don't we just leave it there as a tip for the maid?" Everybody laughed except Hank.

Hank loved the ladies, which sometimes presented problems for the boys in the band. They were playing in Canada once when Hank spotted a beautiful Indian girl. He told Howard he wanted to meet her, so Howard went out into the audience to tell her Hank wanted to meet her. Once backstage, a very quick friendship developed between the girl and Hank. He christened her "Red Wing" and she even began singing with the band. She couldn't sing very well, but Hank never let a little thing like that bother him. He even took her to Europe once on tour. One night after a show in Kentucky, some guy cursed in front of her and the always-chivalrous Hank, tried to sue the poor fellow. As a result, all the band members had to go back to Kentucky and appear as witnesses. Naturally, the case was thrown out of court. Hank brought Red Wing to Nashville and put her up in an apartment; however, their relationship was not to last. Red Wing brought her mother from Canada to live with her, prompting Hank to send them both back to Canada.

Howard didn't think that Hank ever met the movie star Ava Gardner, but every time they played or drove through North Carolina, Hank would sigh, "Oh, Ava!" (He pronounced Ava A-h-hva.) Ava was from North Carolina and had married the likes of Mickey Rooney, Artie Shaw and Frank Sinatra. Hank and Howard saw her movie, "The Night Of the Iguana," in 1964. Hank thought Ava was the most beautiful of all women, and Howard said, "If he could have met her, he probably would have died from excitement." Oh, A-h-hva!

There were always a lot of stories about Hank. One that's been around was about Hank and Sleepy McDaniel who, at one time, played with Hank. On one date, after they had all been drinking, Hank fell off the stage. Hank, angrily took it out on Sleepy for his own misstep. He scowled, "Sleepy, from now on, watch where I'm walking!"

Hank was working a lot of days on the road while Howard was in the band. One trip that Howard remembered well was a 1961 tour of forty-two one-nighters in Canada, starting at Glace Bay, Nova Scotia and ending at Victoria Island, British Columbia. Little Jimmy Dickens and Wilf Carter (Montana Slim) were on those dates. There was also a new duo on the tour, Bob Regan and Lucille Starr, The Canadian Sweethearts. Marty Landau, in California, booked the Sweethearts on this tour, though Hank had just vaguely heard of them. Bob and Lucille drove from California to Nashville to meet up with Hank and the Rainbow Ranch Boys at Rainbow Ranch to start on the tour. Jimmy Dickens rode with the Sweethearts and the band rode in their customary vehicle, a Pontiac Station Wagon. They departed on the tour at midnight; Hank never left until midnight (like they were sneaking out of town?). Actually, it saved him a night's room cost.

At that time the band consisted of Chubby Wise, Ed Hyde, Ralph Jernigan and Howard. Traveling in that motorcade was Hank, his band, Bob and Lucille, Little Jimmy Dickens, Wilf Carter and his family, and sometimes the comic duo Homer and Jethro. They had to travel so hard each day, they were lucky to get three hours sleep in a motel. Most of the time they slept in their cars if they could, playing in a different town each day. Because of the long drives between dates and very little sleep, the boys all partook of diet pills, or as they called them "Uppers" (Amphetamines). Consequently, none of them cared very much about eating. Merle Kilgore, later Hank Williams, Jr.'s manager, once said, "Nashville wouldn't even be on the map, if it wasn't for those little white pills."

They all knew each other very well by the time this tour was over and they had so much fun it was unbelievable. Bob Regan particularly liked to play tricks on poor Little Jimmy Dickens. When Jimmy was ready to go out on stage, Bob would grab him and roll him in the stage curtains. Jimmy then couldn't get himself unrolled to get on stage on time when he was announced. Of course, Howard was a willing partner in all these shenanigans. One time they were all in the parking lot after the show and Howard held Jimmy by the neck, pretending Jimmy's head was a microphone. Lucille added to the fun by singing over the "microphone." People stood around, not knowing whether to laugh or walk away.

One night Howard, Bob and Lucille and Jimmy had been drinking. Jimmy decided to go to bed. The others decided they didn't feel like going to bed, so, after some time had elapsed, Bob said, "Lets go wake up Jimmy." They knocked on Dickens' door and he answered wearing only his shorts, which reached down to his knees and had little red hearts all over them. They went in and Jimmy got in bed. Then Howard, Bob and Lucille, took the blanket and wrapped Jimmy in it from his head to his fee. They finished by wrapping the sheets around him, too. He looked like a mummy. Then Bob called the hotel desk and asked them to send up fourteen buckets of ice and ten bottles of 7-Up. Then the three instigators took off and watched secretly from the hall. When the bellboy knocked on the door, Jimmy got up, hopped to the door, still wrapped like a mummy, and that bellboy took one look and ran. The next day, a sober Dickens told them that he had lost his pajamas. Howard didn't tell him that Lucille had hidden them under the mattress.

There were so many tricks played on Dickens that he finally went to Hank to ask for help. The next day, after they all checked in at the hotel, Hank called all the guys into his room. He told them, "No more pranks. It's gone far enough." Howard said, "Well we stopped making Jimmy's life miserable, but as to the others, well, we figured, what Hank didn't know wouldn't hurt him."

One night Bob was driving, Lucille was in the middle and Howard was in the rider's seat. Hank was sitting on Lucille's lap. This arrangement could have been questioned except they had all been drinking. Bob decided to make life more interesting, so he drove all the way down the main street of town over the curb, around a pole and down the curb; over the next curb, around the pole and down the curb. They went all the way down the street in this manner. Every time they hit the curb, they bounced and Hank's head would bounce up and hit the mirror. On the bounce up, Hank's toupee would stick to the mirror, on the second bounce, it would stick to his head, off and on, off and on. Howard watched the toupee with fascination. Hank only murmured, "Bob, do you think you might take it easier on the curbs?"

Hank's drink of choice then was Smirnoff Vodka. One of his peculiar habits was that he would drink a year and then quit drinking for a year. Howard said, "Hank would drink until midnight of December 31st. Then at 12:01 a.m. on January 1st, he would absolutely stop drinking. The year he was sober, he was easy to get along with, but the year he was drinking, one had better not cross him. At least this was his pattern, when I worked for him." (Howard learned to drink Vodka with Hank, but he didn't quit the year Hank did.)

Lucille and Howard developed a close friendship on that tour. Bob did not treat Lucille very well. On stage, he stomped on her feet. She told Howard that when they were alone, he sometimes beat her. Howard said nothing to Bob about it. They finally reached Calgary, Alberta, and were playing the famous Calgary Stampede. Hank told Bob that sometimes the cowboys got rowdy, and would even ride their horses through the corridors of the hotel. So he advised Bob not to let Lucille go down the hallways alone. Instead, Bob locked Lucille out of their room. She was scared and embarrassed, and didn't want to be seen, so she hid behind a palm tree in the lobby. Howard, leaving the bar, spotted her in hiding. He said, "I felt sorry for her and let her sleep in my room for what was left of the night."

Wilf Carter was an older, easy-going, nice guy. He was a beloved Canadian pioneer, recalled Howard, "When Wilf sang, the audience would get so quiet you could hear a pin drop." One time after playing a show, the newspaper had a music column called, "Win, Place Or Show." The next day, in that column they printed, "Win: Wilf Carter; Place: Canadian Sweethearts; Show: Hank Snow.

Wow! Hank hated that. He called the newspaper and demanded a retraction. He was really angry, but, of course the newspaper ignored Hank, and the cast thought it all very funny. Hank Snow fans loved Howard White, too. He entertained them off stage with his jokes. They would ask Lucille Starr, "What is that sound Hank gets?" Lucille told them, "It's Howard!" "Well, then," they asked, "What is that sound Howard gets on steel?" Steel guitar lovers and fans kept up with Howard, long after he left Hank. He always answered their letters and talked to them whenever they called.

Another time when they were working in Lethbridge, in Alberta, Canada, they had driven all night, then checked into a hotel. Howard decided to get a beer. While at the bar, he spied a cute little Mennonite in his black outfit. Howard found out he had come into town with other Mennonites to sell sheep. Howard called out to him and told him to come have a drink with him. He warned Howard to be quiet, as he didn't want the man in charge to know he was there. Then Howard persuaded the little guy to go up to Chubby's room with him. He wanted Wise to see this cute little guy in black. Howard added, "Chubby wasn't as enthused as I was, probably because he had just fallen asleep after driving all night. After we left, I never saw this little guy again and I didn't know his name."

Their last show on that tour was at a theater in Vancouver, British Columbia. Hank and the Rainbow Ranch Boys went home for two days and then had to leave for a three-week tour in Germany, Italy and France.

They picked up their passports and left for Europe to play military bases. Hank and Howard called Lucille to wish her a fond farewell. Both Hank and Howard remained close to Lucille Starr throughout their lives.

When Howard and the band landed in Germany, Hank said, "Pick up my luggage and carry it, Howard." Now poor Howard had his own luggage, his steel guitar and amp to carry. He looked at Hank and told him, "Carry your own bag, you S.O.B." Nashville promoter "Lucky" Moeller booked Hank in Europe through the Gisela Gunther Agency located in Frankfurt, Germany. They stayed at the Klee Hotel in Wiesbaden, Germany, and flew to Italy and France from Frankfurt. They did two shows a night: one for the enlisted and one for the NCO clubs.

Chubby Wise, who played fiddle for Hank for many years, was the true character of all characters. No story would be complete leaving Chubby out. Howard's fondest memory was when Chubby got religion. He liked to drink and gamble, but with his new found religion, had to give up both. One day Chubby asked Howard, "Do you think it would be a sin to gamble if I didn't bet over a quarter." One night Hank and Howard ran out of soap, so they went to Chubby's room and found Chubby on his knees in prayer, in his little bikini underwear. They apologized for interrupting. Chubby never raised his head. He just informed Hank and Howard, "I'll continue with my prayers after y'all get the soap."

The fiddler was deathly afraid of flying. When Hank and the band had to fly to Europe on a 11 p.m. Pan American flight, Chubby had to get drunk to get on the plane. Then the flight was cancelled until the next day, as they were fogged in. The airline gave them a hotel room. Poor Chubby had to get drunk again the next day. After they arrived in Europe, the whole tour made Chubby very nervous. He was so nervous in Italy that while they were in Naples, he paid a man to follow him with a bucket of champagne. Of course, it was Chubby who was attacked by a band of kids who stole his wallet, his cigarette lighter and a shaker of false teeth powder. (The kids probably thought it was cocaine.)

According to Howard, "We had all been told not to go out on the streets alone at night. Chubby did and ended up at the Italian Police Station looking at mug shots to try to identify the kids. The police didn't speak English and Chubby couldn't speak Italian."

One night after a show, the band loaded up to drive to their next date. Chubby drove for a while then said to Howard, "Hoss, you're going to have to drive. Ol' Chubb's about to fall asleep. Wake me up when daylight comes." So Howard took over the driving, then the boys decided to play a joke on Chubby. They ran Chubb's watch up until it showed 4 a.m., then they woke him up saying, "Wake up Chubby, it's time to drive." Of course, he had only been asleep a few minutes. He woke up, looked at his watch and said, "Oh, boy, 4 a.m. sure comes quick." Then he and Howard changed places. Howard and Chubby were the only drivers in Hank's band then, as Ed Hyde was almost blind. In fact, he once hit a horse while driving. Howard said Ralph Jernigan was too young to be trusted.

I feel honor-bound to tell the truth about one story that has been wrongfully told over and over by fans and performers alike concerning Chubby. The myth persists that Wise got so carried away playing "Orange Blossom Special" one night on stage that he caught Hank's toupee with his fiddle bow and knocked it off. Howard lamented, "When anybody finds out I worked with Hank Snow, they always tell me that story. Ralph Emery even perpetuated the story in his book. Well, friends and neighbors and fellow musicians, I'm here to tell you this story simply ain't true." Howard and I checked with Chubby himself, and he absolutely denied it. Chubby said he thought the story stemmed from a time that Mack Magaha, fiddler for Porter Wagoner, knocked Dolly Parton's wig askew when playing "Orange Blossom Special." Mack played and danced to that tune regularly. That does seem logical. Dolly's wigs only stayed there with the aid of a few hairpins. Magaha was always very active, dancing as he fiddled, while Chubby always just stood there playing great fiddle.

Indeed Chubby got a rich tone on that fiddle. He talked all the time about retiring, but it never dawned on him how he would survive, if he retired. Howard had said, "Of all the boys, I miss Chubby the most. He provided us all with so many laughs. (He died January 6, 1996.)"

Howard was with Hank when he made a tour up the coast of California. It seems Hank had made prior arrangements to visit Spade Cooley, who was in prison at Vacaville in northern California, and to play a free show for the inmates there. Prior to prison, Spade Cooley had one of the greatest Western Swing Bands ever, with hits such as "Shame On You" and "You Can't Break My Heart," both of which he wrote. He was an accomplished violinist, but his career stopped when he was found guilty of slaying his wife Ella Mae Evans. The prison guards let Hank and Howard spend time alone with Cooley in his cell, and Hank promised Cooley he would do everything he could to get him paroled.

Vacaville had hardened criminals, but they applauded Hank wildly and the band played extra well. Hank kept his promise to Spade. He contacted the Governor of California and two governors that were friends of his in the South, and wrote letters to the correctional officials in California. He even composed a petition that was signed by over three hundred people in the music industry who knew Cooley or were familiar with his music. Probably Hank's influence had a lot to do with Cooley's release from prison. The release turned into a tragedy, however, for on the same day as his release, November 23, 1969, he was booked to do a show in Oakland, California. Being on stage for the first time in years, probably was too much pressure. After he was introduced, Spade came out on stage and launched into his signature number on his violin. Almost immediately, he fell backward into someone's arms and died a short time later, apparently from a heart attack (at age fifty-eight).

Howard was playing with Hank in Vancouver, British Columbia, when they got the news. Hank had known Spade Cooley for a long time. Before Hank came to Nashville, he had visited the famed ballroom, The Casino

Gardens, at Santa Monica, California. Cooley was playing there and when Hank was introduced to him, he let Hank sing a number. Hank sang "Molly Darling." They became special friends after that. Hank was very distressed when Cooley died, but he knew he had done his best for his old friend.

Fun kept the boys on the road sane. The night that Howard had the most fun as a Rainbow Ranch Boy was after performing at The Flame Club in Minneapolis, Minnesota. It was just before the end of the baseball season, and some of the Baltimore Orioles - Boog Powell, Jackie Brandt and five others - were in town to play Minnesota, and were at the show. Hank didn't like baseball, but he gave Howard eight dollars to buy drinks and they took the Orioles up to Hank's room at the Maryland Hotel, where they all partied until dawn. They then all went over to the Lemington Hotel, where the rest of the Orioles were and woke them up. As Howard recalled, "They weren't as excited about it all as we were. Maybe this was because the Orioles were playing Minnesota at 11 a.m. I can't prove it now, but I think the Orioles lost. We were probably Minnesota's secret weapon."

Howard was on tour with Hank in Texas, when "Blue Suede Shoes" hit-maker Carl Perkins and his brother Clayton were also on the bill. At break time, Howard went out to Carl's car to speak to him. Talk about drinking! The floor in the back seat was filled with beer cans up to the seat. The band members in the back were resting their feet on top of the cans. Howard said, "I suppose the idea was like trying to see how many cans you can stack up. They were trying to see how many cans you can stack up to get level with the back seat." Just one idea of fun!

Chet Atkins, Hank's producer, always used Howard and Chubby on Hank's RCA sessions, along with studio musicians, while Howard worked with Snow. Howard recorded an album with him, "Big Country Hits – Songs I Hadn't Recorded Till Now." He also played on the singles, "Beggar To A King," "Poor Little Jimmie," "I Know," "The Restless One," and "You Take The Future." Howard was with Hank and George Jones in a hotel room in Canada, when George told Hank he might have a song that would be good for Hank. The Big Bopper (J.P. Richardson) had pitched his tune "Beggar To A King" to Jones. George said, "Hank, I've got a song here that was pitched to me by the writer, The Big Bopper. It isn't for me, but you might like it." Hank listened and when he got back to Nashville, cut it. Well, "Beggar To A King," released in May 1961, went to Number five in *Billboard* and stayed on the charts twenty weeks.

A year later, "You Take The Future" only hit number fifteen, staying on the chart ten weeks. As Hank's records seemed to be showing a chart decline, Chet decided to do something different. In 1962, they recorded "I've Been Everywhere" without a steel guitar. Howard said, "I've always regretted that since it became the biggest record Hank had while I was with him, but I sure played it on stage countless times." It was the first number one record Hank had in seven years since "Let Me Go, Lover." Howard also played on a duet that Hank and Anita Carter recorded, "Together Again." Howard and the band were in a 1963 movie with Snow: Audrey and Vic's

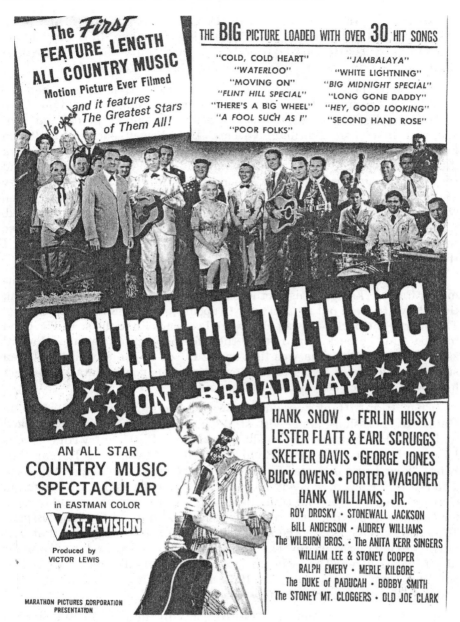

The First FEATURE LENGTH ALL COUNTRY MUSIC Motion Picture Ever Filmed and it features The Greatest Stars of Them All!

THE BIG PICTURE LOADED WITH OVER 30 HIT SONGS

"COLD, COLD HEART"
"WATERLOO"
"MOVING ON"
"FLINT HILL SPECIAL"
"THERE'S A BIG WHEEL"
"A FOOL SUCH AS I"
"POOR FOLKS"

"JAMBALAYA"
"WHITE LIGHTNING"
"BIG MIDNIGHT SPECIAL"
"LONG GONE DADDY"
"HEY, GOOD LOOKING"
"SECOND HAND ROSE"

Country Music ON BROADWAY

AN ALL STAR COUNTRY MUSIC SPECTACULAR in EASTMAN COLOR
VAST-A-VISION
Produced by VICTOR LEWIS

MARATHON PICTURES CORPORATION PRESENTATION

HANK SNOW · FERLIN HUSKY
LESTER FLATT & EARL SCRUGGS
SKEETER DAVIS · GEORGE JONES
BUCK OWENS · PORTER WAGONER
HANK WILLIAMS, JR.
ROY DROSKY · STONEWALL JACKSON
BILL ANDERSON · AUDREY WILLIAMS
The WILBURN BROS. · The ANITA KERR SINGERS
WILLIAM LEE & STONEY COOPER
RALPH EMERY · MERLE KILGORE
The DUKE of PADUCAH · BOBBY SMITH
The STONEY MT. CLOGGERS · OLD JOE CLARK

"Country Music On Broadway," released in July.

After "I've Been Everywhere" went number one, Hank didn't have another chart-topper until 1974. That song was "Hello Love" on RCA, long after Howard departed. It was Lloyd Green who played steel on that successful single. It was Hank's last hit, though he would chart sixteen more songs on *Billboard*.

When the publishers and songwriters in Nashville hear that a certain artist is going to record, they flood the producer with songs. When an artist like Hank Snow was going to record, he'd haul out all the songs that had been sent in for consideration. Hank would bring in some songs of his own, and Chet and Hank would meet to go through it all, deciding which three or four songs they would do on the session. Then they would determine the musicians for their studio session. Sometimes it would be after the session before they decided on singers to overdub. Occasionally Chet would even record a track himself. Then Chet and Hank would play the whole session over and over again, to decide what the single release was going to be. Before Chet Atkins, Steve Sholes had produced Hank. After Sholes started devoting his studio time to Presley, Chet took over. Hank was cautious at first, but when he saw that Chet was all for him and he became more aware of Chet's talents, he accepted him wholeheartedly.

Sometimes Hank had absolutely no finesse, but he was funny to the musicians. Once when Howard was playing a session with Hank, Chet had booked a session banjo player on the session, thinking it would add something to a song they were about to record. Hank went in, looked over the musicians and spotted the banjo. He asked Chet, "What is that banjo player doing on my session?" Chet explained that he thought it would enhance the recording. Hank replied, "Get rid of him. I don't like banjos and I don't like banjo players." The banjo player, Bobby Thompson (familiar to fans of *Hee Haw*), got up to leave, but told Hank, "That's all right, I don't like toupees and I don't like the men who wear them." Thompson was not your ordinary bluegrass banjo picker. He once said, "Steve Martin is known for his fast banjo playing, but I play melancholy."

Another famous line of Hank's was one day at the Glaser Brothers Studio, after he'd been dropped by RCA. Songwriter Gary Gentry was waiting to do a demo session when Hank walked in. Hank turned to Gary and asked, "Do you have a cigarette I could bum?" Gary said, "Yes, but I heard you gave up smoking." Hank casually replied, "No I had to give up sex, I can't give up everything."

The Rainbow Ranch Boys were busy and worked hard. Hank and the boys had few problems, but they were becoming unhappy because they hadn't received a raise in five years. Howard had been with Hank for five years, but Chubby had been with him fourteen years. They were still making seventy-five dollars a week. Hank took to heart what Ernest Tubb said, "They aren't worth any more." Well, he and the boys were playing in Angola, Indiana, when the whole band asked him for a raise and were turned down. The band then gave Hank two weeks notice, as required by the Musicians Union. Hank was furious. When they got back to Nashville, he used every means available to get them to go back to work. He went to see Ott Devine, the Opry manager, and tried to to have them barred from the Opry. When Ott refused, Hank sent a note up to me, at the WSM Library, where I was working, which said: "There is never anything so bad it cannot be worked out, and I would like to offer my apologies for anything that was said while I was drinking and believe me I am through with drinking for a hell of a long time, and maybe never again. Thanks, Hank."

61

After that, Hank even hired a detective to speak with Howard and threatened him if he didn't go back to work for him. The band did meet with Hank at his music store on Church Street, but they all had agreed that probably nothing would ever be the same again, if they did go back to work. Hank never did offer any more money. Howard said, "Knowing how vindictive Hank could be, we figured he would fire us after the next tour, after he had time to hire a new band. None of us accepted his offer to go back again. Later on, Chubby did go back for a while. When Chubby again quit, Hank told him he'd never play in Nashville again. How little Hank knew! Chubby began playing Bluegrass festivals and made a lot more money than if he had stayed with Hank."

By Hank's next tour, he had hired a new band with no trouble at all. He paid them more money, had new sequined outfits made for them and bought a bus for them to travel on. The old Rainbow Ranch Boys had dressed in white shirts with a bolo tie and they rode in a station wagon. Howard said, "Maybe Hank had learned a lesson!"

Many years later in 1990, when Howard and I wrote our first book Hank threatened to sue us. The following is a letter from Hank's attorney, W.P. Ortale:

LAW OFFICES

ORTALE, KELLEY, HERBERT & CRAWFORD

THIRD FLOOR NOEL PLACE

200 FOURTH AVENUE NORTH

P. O. BOX 3375

NASHVILLE, TENNESSEE 37219-0375

(615) 256-9999

WILLIAM P. ORTALE
DAVID B. HERBERT
WILLIAM H. CRAWFORD, JR.
THOMAS C. CORTS
DOUGLAS A. BRACE
WILLIAM M. BILLIPS
WILLIAM A. CRAGG
JOSEPH B. KLOCKENKEMPER, II*
PAUL M. BUCHANAN
JOE I. MAJORS
MICHAEL GIGANDET
DAVID B. SCOTT
WENDY LYNNE LONGMIRE
GERALD C. WIGGER
JOSEPH D. JOHNSON, JR.
JOYCE M. GRIMES
JOSEPH M. HUFFAKER

JOHN W. KELLEY, JR.
(1931-1985)

FACSIMILE
(615) 726-1494

* ALSO ADMITTED IN FLORIDA

August 7, 1991

Mr. Howard White, Jr.
2731 New-Halls Road
Greenbrier, TN 37073

Re: "Every Highway Out of Nashville" by Howard White

Dear Mr. White:

I am Hank Snow's attorney. I recently had a conference with Hank concerning your book and statements in your book about Hank Snow that were untrue. The statements were not only untrue, they were insulting and defaming of Hank Snow's character.

Hank is not only disappointed in the inaccuracies, he is personally offended and many statements are character destructive. We have discussed a defamation of character lawsuit.

If a public apology by you is not placed upon the A.F. of M. bulletin board, on the Grand Ole Opry bulletin board and printed in the Nashville newspapers, I have been instructed to prepare and file a lawsuit. Please let me hear from you immediately.

Very truly yours,

ORTALE, KELLEY, HERBERT & CRAWFORD

W. P. Ortale

Of course, in that book and this one, every word Howard and I wrote is true. We certainly did not mean to defame Hank, just to write a story about Hank that maybe his fans didn't know. In retrospect, I wish we had put Attorney Ortale's letter on the AFM bulletin board and on the Opry bulletin board, and at the bottom added: "Dear Hank, we are heartily sorry for having offended Thee."

We probably would have sold a lot more books that way!

However, we went to our lawyer, Joe P. Binkley, Sr. He read every passage about Hank while we were in his office and said, "There is not a word in here that is a defamation of character." He sent the following letter to Hank's attorney and guess what, we never heard from Hank or his attorney again. The following is the letter Joe Binklely, our attorney, wrote to W.P. Ortale, Hank's attorney:

October 31, 1991

Mr. W. P. Ortale
Attorney-at-Law
Post Office Box 3375
Nashville, Tennessee 37219-0375

        RE: Snow v. White

Dear Bill:

Please be advised that Mr. and Mrs. Howard White were in my office on October 24, 1991, to discuss Mr. Snow's complaint about statements made about him that were contained in the book written by Mr. Howard White with Mrs. Ruth White. We have gone over every sentence in the book that pertains to your client, and we find nothing whatsoever that is derogatory or slanderous.

                        Yours very truly,

                        [signature]
                        JOE P. BINKLEY

JPB/ksr

cc: Mr. and Mrs. Howard White

Hank just loved the idea of suing somebody, anybody. When he and the band got back from their European tour, and Howard was with the band, Hank tried to sue the Gisela Gunther Agency in Germany. Hank was angry because the booker was booking other talent besides him. Nobody would expect any booker to book just one act, but Hank thought he was so important that the booker couldn't book anyone else. Of course, that lawsuit got nowhere.

Hank never really forgave Howard for leaving him. We thought maybe that Hank believed Howard was the ringleader when the band quit. However, in 1994, when Hank had a signing for his book, "The Hank Snow Story," he autographed the book to Howard saying, "To Howard White, your old friend, Hank Snow." In this five hundred and fifty-five page book, he only made one mention of Howard White and that was to name him as an "additional player."

63

One day in 1991 Hank called Lucille Starr, then living in Nashville. He asked her to come by the Rainbow Ranch as he had something to give her. When she got there, he gave her a copy of the VHS he had made from the 8-mm movie he had made when he, Lucille, Howard and the others were on that forty-two-day tour in Canada. He made one stipulation, "Do not ever give or show this tape to Howard White." He was still angry because Howard had left the band thirty-five years earlier. He held that grudge all those years. Lucille promised him she wouldn't and she kept that promise until Hank died. Then she gave a copy to Howard. Real tears rolled down Howard's cheeks. To see them all again, so young, so energetic, brought back so many memories, and after all, like Lucille, he loved old Hank. Howard didn't usually hold grudges.

Hank died in 1999 at age eighty-five. Howard said, "I hope that he, like myself, forgot all the bad times and remembered all the good times we had. After all, we got along great for a long time. Bands come and go, for whatever reason. We had a million and one laughs together. And, friends and neighbors, we drank enough to float us from Nashville to London, England – and he paid for it all."

Howard visited Hank's grave at Springhill Cemetery in Madison. His tombstone had a train on it and read, "Still Movin' On." A North Carolina quarter was on top of the stone. Howard knew that his greatest fan, Peggy Roberts, from Lumberton, North Carolina, had been in town and she had probably left it there. Howard, always the joker, picked up the quarter and left fifteen cents behind.

Howard wrote the following take-off on Hank's "Movin' On," calling it "Movin' On, Number Three": *"Now I'm a little older but I don't care / Cause me and Chubby have been everywhere / I'm movin' on, still movin' on / I ain't quite as fast, but I think I can last / I'm movin' on, still movin' on . . . Now me and Chubby and two or three more / Play every week on the Opry floor / We're movin on, still movin' on / And we love what we do, when we play for you / We're movin' on, still movin'on / And we hope at the end, we'll have a big grin / When we move on . . ."*

- Howard White (with apologies to Hank Snow)

10 THE ROADS MOST TRAVELED

"Some people come into our lives
And quietly go.
Others stay for a while and leave
Footprints on our hearts....
And we are never, ever the same."

- Louis (Grandpa) Jones.

Every "picker" has stories to tell about the good old days. They just love to swap "war stories." Some have changed through the years to fit a person and some have been exaggerated. Truth, however can be stranger than fiction. The "war stories" told in this chapter are still being told over and over.

Louis M. Jones, "Everybody's Favorite Grandpa," known as Grandpa Jones, has been the source of more laughs than anyone else of Opry fame. It was his temper that got him into hot water most of the time. In the '50's he was doing the only network show out of Nashville, *The Prince Albert Show*. They rehearsed for this show, the only Opry portion to be rehearsed, being a network broadcast it had to be perfectly timed. On one show, Howard remembered that Grandpa was supposed to play his banjo until they cut for a commercial. Jack Stapp, then Opry manager, was timing the show. He told Grandpa to cut down some, as they were close on time. Grandpa did and Jack came back and said to cut it down more. Grandpa cut it down some more, and Jack again asked that he cut it down further. That's when Grandpa went into his act, he hit one lick on the banjo, glared at Jack and asked, "Is that short enough!"

Grandpa lived at Mom Upchurch's boarding house for a while. Once his car was parked out back and it got stuck in the snow. Frustrated, he picked up a shovel and beat the heck out of the car! Then there was the time a rat got into his banjo case, backstage in South Carolina. He took his banjo and killed the rat, ruining the banjo in the process. Howard said, "I guess, according to his thinking, he showed the car and the rat."

Howard was with Grandpa in Columbia, South Carolina, when it was raining hard and they got stuck in traffic. Grandpa was driving, and when he tried to back up, got so upset, he stripped the reverse out of the car. They couldn't back up for the rest of the tour. Grandpa just didn't get along well with automobiles. Howard was driving one night in the rain, when the windshield wipers stopped working. Grandpa got out in the pouring rain, grabbed hold of the wipers, moved them manually back and forth, saying, "That'll show ya! Now, work, damn ya!"

Joe Allison said that when Grandpa moved on top of a hill in Ridgetop, Tennessee, his well had to be dug unusually deep. Every week he'd arrive

65

at the Opry for his program and folks would ask, "Have you hit water yet?" Grandpa would say, disgustedly, "No, not yet, but we're still a'drillin'!" Finally, after a month, Grandpa reached the end of his patience, and said, "No! We got down to where we smelled rice and we quit!"

Joe also remembered once when Grandpa started missing chickens. He suspected his dog, but couldn't catch the dog in the act, until one day he spotted the dog going under the fence and headed directly to a chicken and killed it. Grandpa said, "I beat the hell out of that dog." When Allison told him the dog would just get out and do the same thing again, Grandpa replied, "Not 'til the swellin' goes down!"

Grandpa told Howard that he went out to The Nashville Network, to make a commercial for his video, "The Christmas Guest." He noted the background music was so loud, they were doing a drum solo on "Silent Night," so Grandpa told the producer, "Cut down that noise or I'm a'leavin'." At that point, the producer asked Grandpa, "How about just taking the drums off?" Appeased, Grandpa said, "That's fine! Thank ye." Things proceeded with a quieter "Silent Night" backing.

Once when Howard first worked with Grandpa, he realized that without make-up, Grandpa looked exactly like Big Bandleader Tommy Dorsey. Sure enough, one day they stopped at a gas station, and when Howard got out of the car, the attendant stopped him, asking, "Pardon me, but isn't that guy Tommy Dorsey?" Howard assured him that it was not Dorsey, but Grandpa Jones from the *Grand Ole Opry*. As they pulled out, the guy was still standing there, scratching his head, and looking doubtful. No matter how honest you are, said Howard, "people out there" never believe you when their mind is already made up.

Grandpa Jones saw a lot of road time, Opry time and *Hee Haw* time. Howard said, "He's the only man I ever knew who grew naturally into his act (of Grandpa)." In turn, Grandpa remarked, "I don't have to apply much make-up these days." Grandpa didn't retire or slow down before his death in 1998.

Another interesting character was George Morgan of "Candy Kisses" fame. One night, backstage, George was shaking hands with his fans, who would say anything to get backstage to see their favorite star. Howard stood outside the dressing room when a fan told him he was George's cousin, and grew up with him in Cleveland, Ohio. He informed Howard that "ol' George" would be glad to see him. Howard usually didn't argue with 'em, but that night he said, "I thought George grew up around Waverly, Tennessee." (Though George later moved to Ohio.) One thing led to another and the fan kept backing down. Finally, he admitted that his only claim to kinship was that his grandmother and George's grandmother were buried in the same cemetery.

George Morgan was a champion practical joker and while guitarist Don Davis was working with him, the two of them couldn't be stopped. They would go to all lengths to build up a gag for days. George and Don worked poor, meek Don "Suds" Slayman into a frenzy one time. They brought the other bandsmen into the gag. Don spent days telling poor Suds that George was really depressed. George spent the time around Suds with the corners of his mouth turned down. When they knew that Suds was really concerned about George's condition, Don summoned Suds to come to George's room on the double. It appeared George had committed suicide. George laid down in the bathtub nude, and Don poured Mercurochrome (an antibacterial medicine) on his face and throat. When Suds came in the room, Davis was crying, "Poor Whitey (George's nickname), look what he's done to himself!" Suds saw all the "blood" and almost had a heart attack. He started crying and said, "Whitey, you poor son of a bitch!" All the bandsmen had been hiding, but began laughing hysterically. Suds then realized he'd been "had." In his book "Nashville Steeler," Don stressed, "This is the only story about this incident that is true. There are all kinds of variations of this story, like we used catsup, but I did it and it was Mercurochrome."

Another gag that George and Don pulled was on Buddy Killen, then playing bass with George and who later became president of Tree International Music Publishing. George and Don began talking about the world's fastest runner as they drove along. Of course, the band all knew what was going on. Finally, Buddy said, "Well, just how fast can he run?" They told him about eight miles an hour. Buddy said that he could beat that, so, to prove what he said, Buddy got out and ran along side of the car while they clocked him with the speedometer. All the time the boys were saying, "Keep on running, prove you can run faster than eight miles an hour!" Of course, as he ran, George kept telling him he still hadn't beat the record, but was almost up to it. They would let Buddy rest, then started him running again, time after time. Did Buddy ever catch on? Yeah, he finally figured out he had been "had."

Suds told Howard about a trick he and his brother, Bill, pulled in Maryland. It was 1945 when Suds was still in the Army. He and Bill and two other musicians were on their way to bring Suds back to camp. Bill said, "Let's stop at this bar and pick a little and pass the hat." They called it "Busking" (an old English term applied to those performing in a public place, usually to solicit money). They did just that, but didn't collect much. "Suds said, 'We decided to move on to another joint and do a little buskin', you know, pull a slick one.' Suds went in first, in full uniform, sat at the bar and bought a beer. The other boys came in, asked the bartender if they could pick a few songs and pass the hat. It was agreed and after playing a few tunes, they passed the hat, first to Suds. He made sure everybody saw him throw in a five-dollar bill. The word passed, 'Look this poor soldier put in five dollars.' Consequently, the good old boys at the bar didn't want to be outdone by Uncle Sam's finest, so the folding money really flew."

Don Helms, Jerry Rivers, Sammy Pruett, Hillous Butrum and "Cedric Rainwater" (Howard Watts) were in Fayetteville, North Carolina, for a show with Hank Williams. Depending on whom you talk to, this is a great story about a "road happy" band that decided to "put on" Cedric Rainwater. The version here seems to be the accepted one. The band spent quite a while setting Cedric up, telling him they had a great gal stashed in a hotel room. They told Cedric that he could go in with her, but the girl was real shy and he should not turn on any lights. All the while they had Billy Byrd, who was working shows with Ernest Tubb, in the bed, dressed as a girl. They finally let Cedric go into the room. By this time, he was very excited. Cedric got in bed with the "girl," really Billy, and his hand went higher and higher up "her" leg. Then it dawned on him that he had been had! The most famous line to ever hit the Opry was Cedric's: "Ah-h-h Lordy, is zat you, Billy?" That line was repeated over and over backstage at the Opry.

There was the time Norro Wilson was producing a session, which Cedric Rainwater was on, and Harold Bradley was playing guitar. Somehow, Harold hit a really way-out chord that Norro described as "a diminished, suspended chord." Cedric said, "A-a-ah Lordy, Harold, ya got a'hold of a mumblin' somethin' I don't even know what 'tis." Cedric, an original member of Hank Williams' band, was one of Music City's characters. One day he told George Morgan he had to do something he really hated doing. George asked him what and Cedric said he had to sell his gun. George asked why he had to sell it. Cedric answered, "A-a-ah Lordy! Everything I shoot at I hit." George said, "Well, that's the kind of gun I'd like." Cedric replied, "Hoss, I think everything ought to have a sportin' chance."

Emotions can often run high on stage, which causes strange outbursts. Bun Wilson, a drummer, was playing with Carl Smith one night when Carl got on him about the tempo. Bun knew that Carl was the one having trouble with the tempo, even as Carl said, "Can't you get it right!" Bun retorted, "Yeah, I can get it right. I can go to the house!" And he laid down his sticks and walked off the stage. Kitty Wilson was playing standup bass with Rose Maddox one time when Rose turned to Kitty, saying, "Play 4/4 instead of cut time." Kitty, never wrong regarding time, and knowing Rose was wrong, laid down her big bass and walked off stage.

There's an old favorite story about Uncle Dave Macon. Uncle Dave and his boys always carried a bottle in the car that they all sipped on. As they started down a very steep mountain road out West, Uncle Dave looked down the mountain and was frightened. He began to pray and promised the Lord that he and the boys would never drink again if He would just let them get off that mountain safely. When they reached the bottom, Uncle Dave cleared his throat, smacked his lips and said, "Well, boys, the Lord got us through this one. I don't think He'd mind if we have a little sip to calm our nerves. Pass the bottle, boys!"

Howard left home with The Duke of Paducah (comic Whitey Ford) late one night. By the next morning they had gotten as far as Ohio and parked Duke's blue station wagon to go into a bar for a couple of beers "to help along the way." They came out, got into the station wagon and Howard said, "Duke, the key doesn't fit into the ignition." Just then a woman came screaming out of a beauty shop next door to the bar, "They are stealing my car!" Lo and behold, they had parked right next to a station wagon identical to Duke's, same color, same model, same everything. It took a lot of explaining to get that poor little lady settled down. Howard explained, "I always drove when I was with the Duke. He just couldn't drive. I've awakened many a time as I bounced while he drove over a curb."

Howard always said The Duke was great fun to work with. One night Paducah picked Howard up and for some reason Howard was angry at someone. He got into the car and immediately launched into a long tirade about how mad he was. They rode on for awhile and then The Duke showed Howard a small tape recorder, turned it on, and Howard heard himself and his tirade. Paducah had taped it all.

Singer Mel Tillis and Howard were on the road in Rhinelander, Wisconsin, when Mel informed Howard he was feeling very constipated. Mel, who stuttered, said, "H-H-Howard, I'm in bad s-s-shape, I can't s-s-shit." This went on and on. Finally Howard called a local hospital and asked if they could give a man an enema. So Howard scheduled Mel in for treatment, but as soon as he hung up the phone, Mel yelled, "H-H-Howard, c-c-cancel the enema! I'm a's-s-shittin'."

There were almost professional practical jokers in the old days. For instance, Robert Lunn almost had a Ph.D in the field of pranksters. Robert, who toured with Roy Acuff a long time, was known best for a song he wrote called "Talking Blues," a pioneering form of rap music: *Out in the wild woods sitting on a tree / I sat down on a bumble bee / Thought it was a bug or a snake you see / But second thought, I knew it was a bee / Kept stinging, aching too / No relief, uh huh!"* And there were eight more verses! Robert was known for "putting on" new band members. Once they had a new picker with them and they had been traveling all night. The new guy was still asleep when they pulled into a town early in the morning. Robert had their driver pull in front of a theater, then woke up the new guy and told him to go find the theater manager, and ask him if they had a P.A. system? An unsuspecting Kenny Martin did as he was told, as he was so anxious to please. When Kenny found the manager and asked him, the manager said, "Why do you want to know?" "'Cause we're playing here tonight," Kenny said. The manager bellowed, "You're not playing here anytime!" And they weren't! One embarrassed new band member got back in the car wondering what happened, but more "Robert Lunn-wise" than he had been. Of course, Robert had taken him to the wrong theater just for the fun of it.

Robert retired and went to work for the Tennessee State Museum. One day Howard was just outside of the Clarkston Hotel, when Robert approached him. Howard asked Robert how he was feeling. Robert said, "Not too good. I've just come from the doctor and my kidneys are in bad shape. I can't control them at all." Howard remembered, "He looked me right in the eye and as he enlarged on the story, he began trickling sand from his hand onto my shoes. Naturally, thinking his kidneys had failed him, I jumped clear up on the window sill of the building to get out of the way." Just another day with Robert Lunn!

Roy Acuff and Robert were going through a dry county on the train in Texas and asked the conductor how they could get a drink? The conductor told them only doctors could get whiskey in that county for medicinal purposes. Roy looked at Robert and said, "Mr. Lunn, you have just become Doctor Lunn."

Howard vowed, "I'll take an oath that it always rains on Saturday night in Nashville, if I'm playing at the Opry at the Ryman." One of those rainy Saturday nights, Howard was coming down the Ryman's backstage steps carrying his steel guitar in one hand and his amp in the other. Every musician that played there can tell you how slippery those steps could be. On this night, his feet flew out from under him and Howard, guitar and amp, all went flying down the steps. Howard landed on his stomach. After he landed, he looked up right into the sweet face of Kitty Wells. Howard explained, "That was the most embarrassing moment I ever had. Kitty is so religious and most importantly, never took a drink in her life. I did the only thing a Southern gentleman (with a few drinks) could do. I stood up, brushed myself off and said, "S'cuse me."

L. E. White, a songwriter, who managed Conway Twitty's Twitty Bird Music, was visiting Loretta Lynn at Hurricane Mills, one time. He asked, "How much land do you have here?" Loretta replied, "Oh, Lord, I don't know. Doo (her husband) said that we own as far as you can see." L. E. looked up inside the house and saw the ceilings were some twenty feet high. Loretta said, "See that wallpaper up there, I hung it myself." L. E. was at the session when Conway and Loretta recorded his song "After the Fire Is Gone." Right in the middle of a take, Loretta said, "By God, stop it!" She looked at Conway and said, "You ain't singin' that right. You ain't puttin' that wrinkle in it. L. E., come over here and show Conway how to sing it." He was leery of "showing" Conway anything, but he did it. Conway then sang it like L. E., but he never quite got "the wrinkle" that Loretta wanted.

L. E. and Lola Jean Dillon wrote "You're the Reason Our Kids Are Ugly," which Conway and Loretta cut. Just as an aside, John Riggs gave L. E. the idea. John was in England performing, when he first heard the song and was surprised his idea had been taken for a song. One day L. E. and Lola Jean were listening to a German version of that song. L. E. said, "You know it's funny, Lola, when they sing in German, you can't understand them, but when they laugh, they laugh in English." There was a pause and Lola said, "You know, you're right."

George Jones was truly a legend in his own time, but in the old days before he was known as "No Show Jones," and was drinking, he could really make things interesting. Once Howard was driving and George was in the back seat. All of a sudden, George threw a beer can at the windshield in front of Howard. Howard stopped the car, jerked open the door, pulled George out and told him, "If you ever do that again, you little S.O.B., I'll beat the shit out of you." George quietly got back in the car and he never threw another can, at least while Howard was driving.

Another time when Howard was driving with Jones and singer Ernest Ashworth in the car, they were in South Dakota, driving along between snow banks, as Howard recalled, "George was in the back seat and I guess he got bored. He picked up a thermos bottle and asked who it belonged to? Ernest said, 'That's Ol' Ern's.' George promptly threw the thermos out into a snow bank." Everything got quiet, and Howard kept driving. After a few miles, Ol' Ern said, "You shouldn't oughta have done that, George." Howard added, "Nothing else was ever said, but George ignored Ernest the whole tour."

They all knew that George had a good heart. They were in Montana when Jones bought a dog from a guy in a bar, and carried that dog all the way to South Dakota. Webb Pierce was riding beside George and the dog licked Webb in the face all the way. Webb was furious and said he would never ride with George Jones again! Somewhere in South Dakota, George gave the dog away to a service station attendant.

Before Eddy Arnold became a slick "pop" singer, with slicker back-up bands, Little Roy Wiggins was the steel guitar player in Eddy's band. Roy, best known for his unique steel guitar sound called "Ting-a-ling," played on successes like "Molly Darling" and "Bouquet Of Roses." That was back when we knew Eddie as the "Tennessee Plowboy." Roy said their most embarrassing moment was when they were playing in a small town in North Carolina. As Eddy was singing his biggest hit of the day, the entire audience got up and walked out. Eddy and the band were all stunned, until the show sponsor explained. Never had they seen an entire audience just get up and walk out. Eddy felt he must have done something to cause such a mass exit, however, the sponsor apologized and explained, "I'm sorry Mr. Arnold. This is a mill town and everybody that was here had to be at work in fifteen minutes when the shift changed. The auditorium will fill up again when the next shift workers finish their shift." Sure enough, in about twenty minutes, they had an audience full of enthusiastic workers who had just finished their shift.

Red Sovine, Stonewall Jackson and George McCormick were riding together in a car, speeding, when a cop stopped them. Red was driving and the cop asked Red his name. Red said, "Woodrow Wilson Sovine" (his real name.) The cop said, "Who's that sitting beside you?" Red said, "George Washington McCormick" (real name). Of course, the cop thought they were being smart aleck and said, "I guess that's Abraham Lincoln sitting in the back." Red said, "No, sir, that's Stonewall Jackson." The cop said, "Well boys, I guess I'll have to let the Judge find out who you all are." The Judge didn't take long to find out that Red, George and Stonewall were really who they said they were.

Ernest Tubb traveled on a bus, which was eventually dubbed The Green Hornet. He and the boys played Poker to pass the time on long trips. Back at the Opry, someone had coined a word to describe what happened when a person "broke wind." They called it "Free Jax." Once when his Troubadours and Ernest were playing Poker on the bus, someone broke wind. Immediately one of the musicians near said, "Free Jax!" Ernest immediately threw in his cards saying, "That beats my two pair!" (thinking he had heard "three jacks").

Billy Byrd was probably the most famous of Tubb's guitar players. Ernest made his name known on shows and record sessions by saying, "Ah, come in Billy Byrd." In reality, Billy had aspired to become a jazz guitarist, but by eighteen years old, he was playing with Paul Howard and The Arkansas Cotton Pickers at the Dixie Tabernacle on Fatherland Street. There came a time when he needed work, so he asked Tubb for a job. Ernest asked Jack Drake what he thought of Billy? Jack told Ernest he felt Billy was a good jazz player, but might not be good for Ernest. In spite of this, Billy got the job and lasted longer with Tubb than most other guitar players did. Billy needed the work, he said, "By this time, I was married with a family." When Ernest hired Billy he said, "Son, have you got a Western hat or pants and boots?" When Billy said, "No Sir," Ernest got him Western clothes – pants that were too long, plus boots and a hat that were too big. So Billy's first night as a Texas Troubadour was spent trying to fit into his oversize Western duds.

Billy's first night with Tubb and the band happened on the Opry. Ernest had just recorded "Women Make A Fool Out Of Me" right before Billy joined. Billy was afraid they would do that song, but since he was a new band member and a lead guitar player, he asked Ernest not to because he wasn't sure he could do it right. "Please do something simple," Billy pleaded. Ernest agreed, but once on stage, he immediately called for that song. Billy remembered, "I did the intro perfectly, but when my break time came, and Ernest stepped back, and I stepped forward, I started way down on the neck to play double string and started on the wrong notes. I never found the right ones. Ernest stepped forward and said, 'Son, keep hunting it, it's on there somewhere, you'll find it." Billy added, "When we got off stage, to add insult to injury, Ernest said, 'Damn, Son, you really re-wrote that one.'"

Ernest Tubb did have a temper. Jim Denny had been a controversial Opry manager. Once Ernest was so mad at him that he called Denny on the phone and threatened to shoot him. Then he arrived at the WSM downstairs lobby toting a .357 Magnum, leaving his car in the street with the door open. Denny hid out on the fifth floor. The guards detained Ernest in the lobby, but not before he managed to get off a couple of shots before the police arrived, and they took him to a cell until he cooled off.

Sometimes when special occasion song dedications are announced by artists, it just comes out all wrong. For instance, when Howard was with Hank Snow, Hank dedicated a song for a couple's wedding anniversary. The song? "Conscience, I'm Guilty." Somehow that didn't quite fit. One night, before *The Friday Night Frolics* at WSM, Grandpa Jones met a newly married couple at the Clarkston Coffee Shop. He promised to dedicate a song to them when he went on the air, and did. The song? "Wasn't It a Big One, Boys." Perfect for newlyweds?

While Howard was in Knoxville on WNOX's *Mid-Day Merry-Go-'Round*, bandleader Jack Shelton said, "Now we are going to do a little Father's Day Song for all the fathers out there." The song they sang was "Farther Along." Howard said, "I guess there isn't much difference between 'Father' and 'Farther,' is there?" The best one to date was done by Wilma Lee Cooper. Bill Carlisle just had by-pass surgery and so on the Opry, Wilma Lee dedicated a song to him. She sang, "Bury Me Beneath The Willow" (Bill, then eighty-four years old, survived that dedication).

Webb Pierce had trouble at times staying on key. Bud Isaacs played steel for him. Bud is given credit for inventing the pedal steel guitar's sliding harmony sound, imitating the harmony he heard on The Davis Sisters recording of "I Forgot More Than You'll Ever Know." He was the first to use steel in that way on record, specifically on Pierce's "Slowly." Webb and the band were in the dressing room rehearsing, backstage at the Opry, when Webb said, "Bud you're out of tune. Hit me an E." Bud hit the E on his guitar. Pierce said, "That's flat!" Bud replied, "All right, hum me an E."

Radio Dot (Dorothy Marie Henderson) and Smoky Swan were an early Opry act. Once they were playing a tent show with Bill Monroe and Bessie (The Carolina Songbird), featuring Bobby Hicks and Charlie Cline on fiddles. The act called for Dot to hit Smoky over the head with a rolled up newspaper as they sang, "You're No Good." Charlie and Bobby secretly put a stick of wood inside that newspaper. Dot hit Smoky with it and knocked him down, leaving Smoky and Dot both wondering what happened?

In the 1950's Suds Slayman was playing fiddle on a Minnie Pearl recording session at Starday Studios, while Gene Martin played guitar and Junior Huskey was on bass. There was a live audience and the engineers had provided big tubs of beer to keep everybody happy as Minnie recorded. Junior got into the beer and was grinning from ear-to-ear, weaving with his standup bass. The audience was in hysterics, laughing at Junior, while all the time Minnie thought she was getting the laughs. That may be the only time Minnie Pearl ever let anyone upstage her.

Out in the flatlands of the West, you could see way off in the distance. Without fail, there would always be a pick-up truck out in a field. Howard said, "Two to one, you could be sure, that sooner or later that truck would head out for the road we were on. Seemingly to purposefully come out right in front of our car, causing the driver to slam on the brakes. We had a name for these pick-ups, we called them 'Winchester forty-fives' they were so deadly."

Ray Edenton, who became an in-demand A-Team rhythm guitarist, started out in small venues, like most everybody. In 1948, he was working with two other guys in the Virginia area. At that time, Lash LaRue had made a couple of movies and was working stage shows. He was a hot act, doing bullwhip tricks. One day, Craven Edwards, who had been working for Lash, went by Ray's house near Mineral, Virginia, saying they needed Ray and another picker to form a trio with Craven for *The Lash LaRue Show*. So Craven, Ray and Curly Butler formed the trio. They were promised so much a day, including food, hotel and transportation. After a few weeks, they ended up in Hershey, Pennsylvania. Lash said he would pay them at the end of the tour. That last day, Curly and Ray went down to eat breakfast, and the desk clerk told them that Mr. LaRue had left them a message. It read: "Sorry boys. Have been called back to L.A. to film a movie. Nice working with you." No money! Snow was a foot deep. They worked their way home by playing beer joints through Pennsylvania, Maryland and Virginia.

Lloyd Green, one of Nashville's top steel guitar session musicians, said, "I had a truck-driving fan who wanted to learn to play steel guitar. But, he kept having trouble with his high string breaking. When it did, he would call me to come to his house and fix it. He lived about ten miles away, but I just couldn't refuse him. After a few times of this, he realized he was imposing on me. He called one day and said, 'I hate to ask you again, but if we can't get this string situation fixed, I'll be out of business.' Business, what business?"

Velma Williams Smith, the finest rhythm player ever, traveled with Roy Acuff in the early days. On one tour, she remembered that Uncle Dave Macon traveled with them, carrying a country ham in a crate along the way. Everywhere they unpacked, they had to put that crate in and out, and Acuff said he would sure be glad when that ham was gone and they wouldn't have to fool with that crate. Uncle Dave would carve off a piece of the ham and have the restaurant cook it for him every morning. When the ham was finally gone, Uncle Dave said, "I'll just take that crate back home with me. It will make a mighty good nest for my chickens."

Velma also recalled a time that she was still with Roy and they were driving from Nashville to Memphis. She continued, "The fiddle player was driving and the rest of us were asleep." Now you have to know that in most Southern towns there is a square in the middle and the road goes around the square on all sides. Velma said, "When we woke up we were going back the way we had come toward Nashville." The driver had made a complete circle around the square and away from Memphis back toward Nashville. As Howard said, "We always left home at night and the driver would sometimes ask, 'Are we on the right road?' Someone would always answer. 'I'm not sure, but it's a good road, so let's keep it till daylight.'"

Howard said, "Early in my career on the road, when I was with Copas, Randy Hughes woke me up and told me it was my time to drive. I was so tired, but so was everyone else. Randy had something to help me, a 'Bennie,' short for Benzedrine tablets. I learned they could keep you going. Housewives called them diet pills. They picked you up." There were all kinds of pills that kept your eyes open wide. There were "old yellers," officially Oberdrine; the term "black beauties" specifically referred to Biphetamine; and there were "Speckled Birds" and numerous others. There was a black capsule called "California Turn-Arounds," because two of them and a cup of coffee would get you all the way to California and back, and after you got back, they'd have to take the car keys away from you. Such so-called "uppers" have been outlawed now. Anyway, they made one extremely nervous.

Back then anyone could get diet pills from the best doctors by legal prescriptions. A lot of the musicians knew the "right" druggist or the "right" doctor where they obtained them in gross quantities. There was also a "Little Buddy" they could obtain pills from down at the Opry, known unofficially as *the old pill peddler*. Howard and I ran into Little Buddy one night and he lamented, "Howard, they haven't written a good country song since all the old yellers have been taken away." The songwriters of that day should have given Little Buddy an award for "Helping Co-write More Songs Than Anyone In Nashville." Our Little Buddy Jennison died in April 2014.

There was a Dr. Snapp at 627 Woodland Street, conveniently situated around the corner from Mom Upchurch's boarding house, and he was so free with his prescriptions, some of the boys awarded him a plaque for "Helping the Pickers Beyond The Call Of Duty." His prescriptions could be filled, no questions asked, at Consumers Drug Store at 700 Main Street. Long after Howard quit pickin' and using little white pills, a disgruntled patient in 1977, turned states evidence and the musicians' most beloved doctor spent three years in prison on twenty-three counts of illegal drug prescriptions. According to the local newspapers, he'd earned one hundred thousand dollars per year.

In the 1950's and '60's, alcohol was generally the drug of choice among musicians in Music City, but musicians of that era also liked prescription amphetamines to keep them awake during long night drives in the pre-Interstate, pre-Silver Eagles days. Some few abused them. They were prone to talk to each other backstage at the Opry about whatever the latest eye opener was, traded pills, and tried out new ones. On one particular night one of the pickers standing in the wings beside Kitty Wells turned to her out of habit and asked, "What are you on, Miss Kitty?" This Christian lady, who never drank, smoke or took anything – ever - was unsuspecting of the real meaning to his question, simply drawled in all her innocence, "D-E-C-C-A!," meaning her record label.

There was a time when pills and beer caused strange things to happen right on 16th Avenue South (Music Square East, these days). Once, someone put catfish in the replica of Webb Pierce's guitar-shaped swimming pool next to Spence Manor. And there was a time when Cowboy Jack Clement and Joe Talbot put liquid soap detergent in the Country Music Hall of Fame's fountains (back when it was on 16th Avenue South). Someone facetiously stated the suds went down the street and engulfed BMI and CBS. When I got to work, they were sitting in the fountains pouring the suds on their heads with Mason Jars.

Ah, yes, things were more fun in those days. Occasionally remnants of the past come to life. When I was still working on 16th Avenue in 1990, Billy Nelson, Willie's son, then living at Spence Manor, parked his truck in the parking lot there. By morning light, Bob Bean and I arriving at work could see that Billy's truck had been wrecked on all sides and one tire was off. He had come all the way down 16th Avenue on the rim of that wheel. That rim mark stayed on the asphalt a long time. The strangest thing I ever saw was, one day in 1998, when looking out the window at Porter Wagoner's office on 18th Avenue South: About 5 p.m., much to my wondering eye, appeared a little Volkswagen "bug" with a white grand piano on top. A man was running alongside the car, keeping it balanced. Where is a camera when you need one? Well, Music City goes on, but we don't often hear antics to rival these anymore. Is all our "creativity" gone?

When Howard was working with Judy Lynn, they played a date at the White Sands Proving Grounds in New Mexico for the scientists there. The troupe stayed in an old hotel in nearby Las Cruces. The hotel was typical of the old West, made from adobe, with a long front porch, where the cowboys used to tether their horses. An old lady was the innkeeper. She showed Suds and Howard to a room, then exclaimed, "John Dillinger (*America's Number One Public Enemy* of his day) and his pals had their car break down here! A garage across the street kept their car overnight and Dillinger and his gang stayed at this very hotel. In fact, he slept in this very bed you're sleeping in tonight."

Howard said he had always heard, up and down the East coast, that George Washington had slept there, but never had he been enticed by the lure of John Dillinger having slept there. He said, "Just think, I slept in the same bed as Dillinger in Las Cruces, New Mexico! Can the Holiday Inn compete with that?" Dillinger was so famous, there was even a song written about him in 1934, by H. Robinson Vaughan and Dorothy Hardy. One of its verses goes: *"In Chicago he was found / At the show he was shot down, by Purvis and his men all there in line / They hunted day and night, hoping just to get in sight / Of the country's great outlaw of his time . . . His gang*

robbed many a bank / Thousands of dollars they yanked / To him the banks of all cities looked the same / They were not like men of old, who went out to rob of gold / John was said to be much worse than Jesse James."

John Dillinger was the last of the great storied outlaw heroes. He was the first so-named Public Enemy Number One. Reportedly, his last heist was in South Bend, Indiana, in 1934. That's when Anna Sage, a so-called Madam, came forward, wearing orange, I.D.'ing him for Melvin Purvis of the FBI, as Dillinger exited a theater in Chicago (the "Lady's" orange appeared red in the marquee lights).

Jimmy Lott, the drummer with Judy Lynn, guitarist Leon Richardson and bassist Joel "Cuz" Price, stayed up all night, playing cards with the Innkeeper, but Suds Slayman and Howard slept well all night in the bed that John Dillinger had once slept in.

The Canadians are great country music fans and Howard worked a lot there. One tour was with Wilf Carter, Red and Beverly Garrett, and Stacy Culbreth, a dwarf they called Shorty, who played fiddle. Red stayed high on bennies the whole seventy-day tour. One night he put Shorty in the trunk of his car. Another night he locked Shorty outside his room wearing only his shorts. Howard said, "We spent a lot of time just rescuing Shorty." The Canadians looked on Wilf as kind of an evangelist, a real legend. Canadian fiddler Ward Allen, who was with Wilf, told Howard that Queen Elizabeth had one of his albums, the only fiddle album she owned.

Howard was noted for doing outrageous things. For instance, he said, "Once I was in Canada and couldn't find a one-day service laundry. So, at a poor Chinaman's laundry, I told him if he didn't wash my clothes and get them back to me that day, I was going to jump up and down on my laundry. The Chinaman said, 'No, No!' So, right then, I threw my (clothes) on the floor and jumped up and down on them." They were only in town for the one day, so as the Chinaman continued saying, "no, no, no," Howard continued to the next town with his dirty clothes.

Then there was a time in Louisiana with Copas when Howard wanted Gumbo. All the way up the state everyone was "fresh out." When they got to Arkansas Howard said, "Thank God, we're in Arkansas! I can at least get grits." Would you believe the waitress said, "We're out of grits!" Howard, short on patience, said, "I'll turn this table over, if the cook doesn't fix me grits!" One look at Howard told her he would do just that. He got his grits! There was a joke among the musicians that Copas never got anything he ordered, so maybe Howard's problems was Karma.

Many people walked into Howard's life and then were suddenly gone. There was Ira Louvin, one of the most talented people he ever knew, though Ira was always on the edge. He was married to Faye, when she and Ira had a party at their house. Roy Acuff and Shot Jackson were two of the guests. Somehow a fight began and Faye shot Ira five times! He lived, with a bullet so near his heart that they couldn't operate. The next day, Faye's brother, Johnny Johnson, asked Howard and I to help him clean the house. We couldn't believe the condition of the house. There were records all over the floor, a wastebasket full of empty whiskey bottles, food spilled all over the kitchen, and worst of all, blood all up and down the hall. We left, not touching anything, as we felt the police should see it. The next day, Roy and Shot denied being there. They said they left the party before the shooting to get more whiskey. Faye and Ira were divorced after that. Howard was called as a witness, but being a friend of both, he was glad he wasn't called to testify. Aferwards, at a DJ Convention, Ira hugged Howard and I, telling us how much he loved us. A short time later, Ira died in a June 20, 1965 auto accident, along with his fourth wife, the former Anne Young, near Williamsburg, Missouri. He was forty-one.

Early in his career, Buck Owens from Bakersfield, California, appeared at the Opry during a DJ Convention. We were backstage and Howard asked him why he didn't move to Nashville? Buck said, "I don't want Nashville and I don't need Nashville." (I guess he proved he didn't.)

One day Howard was riding with Doyle Wilburn down Gallatin Road, and they pulled in at Corn Brothers Cleaners near Sharpe Road. Doyle asked Howard to go in and pick up his cleaning for him. Howard did and was surprised to find out that with his ticket, Doyle had won a car. What Luck!

One of the people Howard loved was Jumpin' Bill Carlisle. One day Bill told Howard he had been to the Country Music Hall of Fame and saw his picture with brother Cliff Carlisle there on display. "However," Bill pointed out, "Cliff's name was under my picture and under my picture was 'Unknown.'" Carlisle said that he left without calling attention to it, but the next day had somebody go down and steal the picture out of there. That was just like the man, who famously said, as he grew older, "I still jump, but not as high." Howard missed the fun he and Jumpin' Bill had before Bill left us all on March 17, 2003, at age ninety-four.

Odd things happened as the years went by. Howard's first steel guitar was a Rickenbacker that he bought out of a pawnshop in Charlotte, North Carolina. He played that guitar with Don Gibson, Shannon Grayson and Cowboy Copas. He owned other guitars, but he always kept the Rickenbacker for sentimental reasons. In about 2001, for the very first time, he noticed a name etched in the back of the neck: "Slim Swift." He tried to find him, but it was impossible, as all he had to go on was "Slim." Then one day, I spotted a death notice for Harold "Slim" Swift. I called his wife, Frances, and sure enough this was THE Slim Swift that once owned Howard's guitar. His wife said, "Slim once played with Bob Eaton." We knew Eaton, a well-known singer in Nashville in the 1950's. Howard and I were able to pay our respects at the Harpeth Hills Funeral Home for the man who first owned Howard's guitar. Guess no one will ever know how it got into a pawnshop in Charlotte, North Carolina.

Speaking of odd happenings, one night Howard woke me up to tell me he dreamed that Marie, his ex-wife, was in a bad accident. She and a guy were in a car rolling over and over down a hill and he saw they were thrown out of the car. The next morning, Marie's brother, Rex Jenkins, called to tell Howard that Marie had been killed in a car accident in Alabama. She was in the car with songwriter Bobby Rice from Smackover, Arkansas. Witnesses said they were driving at a high rate of speed. A bartender on Music Row said they had left his bar, drinking, on their way to a club in Huntsville. Howard called the police in Alabama and they said the car left the road, went down an embankment, rolling over and over, and both parties were thrown out of the car and killed. Was that Howard's ESP working? Only a few weeks earlier, Howard and I had bumped into Marie at Tootsie's, and she apologized for any hurt she had caused Howard. Another dream Howard had was of Shorty Lavender, a friend who played fiddle for Ray Price, lived at Mom Upchurch's, and in later years became a successful booking agent. He dreamed that he and Shorty were driving on a mountain road and Shorty kept driving closer and closer to the edge. Howard was afraid they were going to go over the mountainside and woke up just as they went over. Soon after this, Shorty died, suffering from cancer. Howard didn't even know he was sick, until he received word of his death.

Luke Brandon, who left Knoxville with Howard to come to Nashville, was one hulluva guitar player. He could play rhythm and lead at the same time. He was so talented, but very elusive. Once, he was waiting for a bus and looked down and saw some ants. One had a big crumb of bread, then another ant took it away. Luke stomped that ant stealing the bread and said, "You dirty little bastard!" That was total justice in Luke's mind. He could have been the most in-demand guitar player in Nashville, but Luke wouldn't stay here. He was always going home to Rockwood, Tennessee.

Howard's best friend, Suds Slayman, left show business after former boss man George Morgan died in 1975, to become a fiddle pickin' mail carrier. Howard remembered that while Suds was living, he was always there when Howard needed him. "I hope that I was there when he needed me," said Howard.

Howard had been in Nashville a long time, but Don Helms, steel guitar player with Hank Williams' Drifting Cowboys, had been here longer. Don was naturally funny, dry and cryptic. One day Howard said to him, "Don you got here before I did." Don answered, "Hoss, when I got here, Uncle Dave Macon was too young to go in Tootsie's." Don also told Howard, "My dog is so old, he can't bark, so when he hears another dog bark, he nods his head." Both Don and Howard were pallbearers at a funeral, and when they got to the grave, Howard said, "Don, do you mind if I stand here?" Don replied, "Not if they're paying Union Scale."

Shot Jackson, who worked for Roy Acuff, designed the Sho-Bud steel guitar, along with Buddy Emmons. Howard said, "It was the best damned pedal steel guitar ever built." Shot's business was on Broad Street. He helped everybody. If you needed credit, you got it. If you were broke and had hocked your guitar or amp, he would loan you one for a job. The steel guitar players hung out there, talking about tunings, gauges, who was working with who, and who was not working. And girls! Shot was also a practical joker. One night at the *Friday Night Frolics*, he unplugged Howard's guitar. Well, Howard didn't realize what Shot had done, until he started to play. "I could've cheerfully shot Shot!" Though Shot never said a kind work about anyone, all the musicians loved him and they all knew Shot loved them. Howard visited Shot in the hospital just to let him know how much he meant to all of them. Howard recalled, "Shot and I cried together. He did more for steel guitar players than anyone before or since."

Howard said that he missed his golfing buddy, Smiley Wilson and his wife, Kitty; but he could still hear them sing "When the White Azaleas Bloom" in his heart. He also missed Carmol Taylor, who never let success spoil a friendship. They had a drink every day together at 4 p.m. Howard said, "I wish we could party down just one more time."

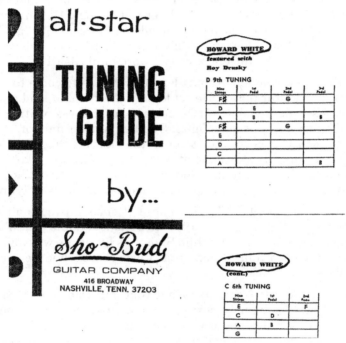

When the old pickers who are still with us get together, there's a lot of laughing about the "good old days." Most of the time they were just tired. They drove to the date, set up, had sound check, played and were "up" for the show, drove to the next date and repeated the whole scene again. Like the song says, they were never promised a rose garden. If old pickers get together, you can bet somebody will always say, *Remember when ...* and the memories get told over and over and like a legend, sound bigger and better every time. One day Howard was laughing with some old timers about the real characters in the music business, the ones they called "Squirrels." The other guys all looked at each other, laughed and said, "Why Howard, you're the biggest character of them all!"

There are a lot of stories to be told in Music City – but maybe you really had to be there.

"*... And that's the way it was.*" – courtesy Walter Cronkite.

11 THEM GIRLS

"If you knew Susie
Like I know Susie
Oh, oh, oh, what a girl
There's none so classy
As this fair lassie . . . "

- B. G. DeSylva and Joseph Meyer.

There are a lot of stories about the guys, but I wouldn't want to neglect "Them Girls." The ones I am talking about here are the girls that just love country pickers. Howard confided, "We've all had our share and at the risk of y'all thinking I'm a 'Tyrone Bitterweed,' there have been a few that liked me too."

Plenty of girls hung out backstage or out at the stage door and at the hotels. Of course, the stars were their main objective, but some of them weren't so particular. The guys used to say, "If they couldn't get a star, they would settle for a musician, if they couldn't get him, they would settle for the bus driver or a roadie."

The girls talked about here are the girls that wouldn't have anything to do with any guy but a picker. They were even crazy about the ones that played certain instruments. That was all they would go out with. There are two happily married gals now that Howard used to date, that later married steel players. Howard didn't marry them, but they did marry steel players. Woe to the fiddle player that liked a girl, who would only go out with steel players. There was one girl, Carolyn, that hung around the *Friday Night Frolics*, who swore she would marry a banjo player, and she did. There were always a lot of gals just waiting for a guy after a show, or the Opry or Tootsie's, only too willing to show you a good time. If they really liked you, they would take a bus and follow you to the next date. This was true in Canada, as well as in the States.

In the 1950's, Howard was working dates in Canada. They were in Quebec where the main language is French. Howard met this girl who was there with her father and brothers, who were surveying land. They happened to be staying at the same hotel with all the musicians. She was real pretty, according to Howard. They went out together and got along fine even with a language barrier. Howard said, "I don't recall her name, if I ever knew it."

On a tour in Germany with Hank Snow, the band had five or six girls all lined up to ride the bus with them, but Hank refused to allow them to go along. Needless to say this was a big disappointment to the boys and the girls. After talking it over, the band decided Hank refused to let the girls aboard because one of them wasn't appointed to be with Hank. Of course, things weren't always that good. In fact, Don Helms, whose wife was bugging him about girls, told her, "I'll tell you one thing, it's a helluva lot harder to get than you think it is."

Howard said, "Maybe I'm prejudiced, but the real beauties seemed to like steel players the best. Each of us had our following in each town. They wrote us letters and came to see us when we played their town again." One gal, Peggy Steelman, who hung around Sho-Bud Guitar Company a lot, even published a steel guitar magazine at her own expense. Several of the steel players got birthday and Christmas cards from her as long as she lived.

Some of the guys called them "snuff queens" years ago, and, snuff queens they've remained all theses years. Howard remembered that Jimmy Day named one of them, who hung out around Tootsie's and The Wagon Wheel, "Suckin' Susie." Suds said he remembered one girl who hung around the Opry boys was called only "Oh Boy." When she made love, she said over and over, "Oh boy! Oh Boy!"

Jack Greene, then a drummer, later a singing star, said a girl followed him down to Texas and he ignored her all the way. He was on stage when she finally gave up and said, "Well, if I can't have your body, just give me your yellow bandana." He did!

Another type of "them girls" was what the boys called "Show Dogs." These were the gals who really put on the dog. They hung around anyone who could get them into show business. They were the wannabe singers or songwriters or whatever. Every little bleached hair was always in place, every little fingernail manicured just right. They dressed in the latest fashions and wore heavy perfumes. Mostly they were untouchable, unless you could do something for them. But, as Howard said, "They were sweet gals and should be allowed space in this history of the girls that hung on the outskirts of the music business."

One steel player, turned businessman, got so tired of the Show Dogs, and after three broken marriages, put an ad in the newspaper for a girl who didn't want to be a singer, a songwriter or get in a part of show business. He got a bag full of mail. He picked one letter out of the pile from a girl that had never been out of her county – and married her.

The best song for the musicians so far is the one recorded by Willie Nelson and Julio Iglesias: *To all the girls we've loved before / Who've gone in and out our doors . . . "* Howard said, "Like Willie and Julio, I want to drink a toast to all those girls we've loved before. Ah, yes, life was sweet when them girls went in and out our doors."

12 MOM! WHICH ONE WAS THE ORIGINAL

"Put them both together they spell M-O-M,
A word that means the world to me . . ."

- With apologies to Howard Johnson and Theodore Morse

Be it ever so humble, there's no place like home. For a lot of the years that Howard played at the Opry, home was at Mom Upchurch's at 620 Boscobel Street. Mom, Delia Upchurch, must have boarded more hillbillies than anyone before or since. She was a good Christian woman, a member of Shelby Avenue Church of Christ, but a bunch of fun-loving musicians must have tried her patience at times. Through her portals passed the Carters, Pee Wee King's band, Grandpa Jones, Carl Smith, Johnny Paycheck, Darrell McCall, Don Davis, Faron Young, Stonewall Jackson, Hank Garland, Buddy Emmons, Buddy Spicher, Pete Wade, Lloyd Green, Shorty Lavender and other various, assorted and sundry musicians. She kept them all, stars, sidemen, bookers, promoters, whatever. Your only credentials were that you be involved in Country Music.

Shorty Boyd and Don Davis, both members of Pee Wee King's band, were Mom's first boarders. It was Don who talked Mom into boarding other musicians. An attraction was her good cooking. The price for supper was eighty-five cents and breakfast was seventy-five cents. Weekly rent was seven dollars. There were three bedrooms downstairs and two upstairs. There was only one shared bath. Amazing, but there wasn't much arguing over the bath, although, on Saturday nights, a dozen hillbillies were all getting ready for the Opry. They all had the run of the house. There was only one phone, one line and no call-waiting. Mail was stacked on a table in the downstairs hall by the phone. Howard, the longest resident, lived there fourteen years, until he and I married.

Mom didn't allow drinking. However, once Howard secretly made Orange Brandy in her basement. He had gotten the recipe in Canada. Mom found it while it was fermenting and made him pour it out, saying, "Honey, we can't have none of that. They might get me for Bootlegging." Howard said, "It wasn't any good anyway. I tasted it and realized I forgot to peel the oranges." Mom dipped snuff, but she hid that fact, and you can bet no one from her church knew it. She also drank a little Mogen David Wine. Once she asked Howard to get her a bottle of *"Morgan David."* Howard said, "Don't you mean 'Mogen David'?" Testily, she replied, "That's what I said, *'Morgan David'!"*

Mom's house was located in East Nashville, but just a stone's throw from the Shelby Bridge and Downtown, near the Ryman and the Opry. It didn't take much gas to get there. Howard claimed that on many Saturday nights, he was broke and would get a gallon of gas costing twenty-five cents just to get to the Opry. Mom's house was built of yellow stone with big tall trees all around, a real homey atmosphere.

Mom's place was also a kind of "booking agency." When an act needed a musician, all they had to do was call Mom's. There was always one there they could use, either living there or visiting. Tours started there because of the central location and everybody knew where Mom's was. When Lloyd Green first came to town and was jobless, Howard heard him play, and got Lloyd his first job by simply calling Faron Young, as Howard knew Faron was looking for a steel player.

Mom knew how long you were going to be out on tour and if someone showed up while you were on the road, she sometimes rented your bed out. Now and then you'd come home to find that person's head on your pillow. Then you yell so loud, the person in your bed would wake up and run off. When one of the boys was down on his luck, Mom fed them anyway, and he didn't pay rent until he found another job. Never has so much credit been given! No books were kept. Mom trusted her boys and they trusted her. She knew all their secrets about their girl friends, ex-wives, who got drunk and who took pills. They all brought their girls around for Mom's judgment. And judge them she did! She might not tell the person involved, but she told all the other boys what she thought. That way word got around. If she didn't like the girl, they didn't last long. Pete Wade, a fine guitar player who probably played on as many sessions as any other picker, brought his girl, Jean, to meet Mom. Mom was crazy about her. They got married and are still married today. And, thank God, Mom really liked me!

The guys cussed around the house, as guys will, and sometimes when Mom had enough, she would cuss back. Mom was always a good sport. Once Dale Potter rode her around the block on a motorcycle. He told her to just sit there and see how comfortable it was, then he just took off with Mom's legs and hair flying. She suffered with the boy's troubles and gloried in their joys. If word of a death needed to be passed, Mom got the word to the right people.

Howard figured that none of them had ever done enough for Mom, so after a number of years had passed, he and Don Davis gave her a party. Nearly all her former roomers came and paid their respects. Howard put her picture in the paper. She was so proud and all her neighbors thought she was really something. Knowing that Mom didn't drink, Howard and I made two different kinds of punch, one with Vodka and one without. Of course, we didn't tell her. All evening we tried to steer her to the punch without the vodka, but she didn't like that batch. She liked the punch with the vodka. Mom had more fun than anyone else there.

Mom has passed on to her just reward now, but her boys will never forget her. Some of them may be up there with her to talk about the old days. Howard and I went down Boscobel Street one day and stopped at 620. An elderly lady was on the front steps. We stopped and she said her name was Alveda

Newman. The bushes and trees were overgrown, but the house was still standing just like always. "Come and see me again," Mrs. Newman called after us. It could have been Mom's voice, as one of her boys left on tour.

Then there was the "other Mom," Louise Hackler, the one who owned a little beer joint on Lower Broad Street, which boasted a back door that opened up on the alley behind the Opry stage door. This place was called "Mom's." Later, Tootsie Bess bought the business and so it became known as Tootsie's Orchid Lounge. Mom Hackler opened the original establishment with her husband, John Hackler. Now Mom had a *shillelagh* (a walking stick) and if you misbehaved, she chased you out with it. (Tootsie had a hat-pin.) Mom catered to her "Opry Boys." No one was allowed in, if they bothered her boys. If the place was full and there wasn't a seat for an Opry Boy, she made the outsider get up and give her boy the seat.

One day Mom asked, "Howard, who is that other woman across the river who calls herself 'Mom'?" Howard told her just who Mom Upchurch was. She replied, "I'm the original Mom, Howard!" She turned to Buddy Emmons, who was sitting next to Howard, and said, "Ain't that right, Buddy! I'm the original Mom!" Forty years later, when Howard and Buddy got together, one of them would say, "Ain't that right, Buddy!"

The boys all drank beer between shows at Mom's, stars, pickers, announcers, whoever. They continued to do so when Mom sold to Tootsie. It was a long time between their first and second shows. Between shows, Grant Turner, long-time Opry announcer, used to drink beer there like the rest. One night, Howard asked him, "Grant, how do you know when you've had enough to drink, you being an announcer?" Turner replied, "Well, I have a couple of key words that I say to myself. If I can still say them, I have another beer, if I can't, I stop drinking."

A lot of beer was uncapped there. Mom stacked it by the case all up and down the steps from the first floor to the second. One time when Howard was passing through, he ran into Rita (Robbins) Edenton. While they were talking, two smart-ass guys who sold concessions at the Opry, asked Rita if Howard was bothering her. She said no, but they were itching for a fight. One guy looked at Howard and said, "We think you are." Howard turned to get John, Mom's husband, to throw the bums out, but when he turned, one of them hit Howard behind his ear. Howard fell down the stairs, but he got up and went up the stairs. Then he hit the guy that had hit him. The guy fell down the stairs, hitting the beer cases as he fell. Howard said, "The last I saw of him, he was falling ass-hole over appetite down the stairs breaking bottles as he fell. There was broken glass and blood all over." Randy Hughes came to Howard's rescue. He had just walked in, saw the problem and threw the guy out on the street. A couple of girls drove Howard back to Mom Upchurch's, but he said he worried all night that maybe he had killed the guy. Neither Howard nor Randy ever heard anything else about him, so they guessed he lived.

In the 1950's and '60's there were two characters who liked to hang around musicians. The boys nicknamed them Junior and Muscles. Junior was six-foot-four and weighed two hundred and seventy pounds. Muscles was about five-foot-four, and weighed ninety to a hundred pounds. Muscles would get drunk and laugh all the time. He talked real fast and his job was selling newspapers on the street. Junior drove a milk-truck and spoke slowly. His favorite expression was "God dog right!" They all kind of adopted them, because they made them laugh. One night Dale Potter and Howard were spending a quiet evening in that "lovely atmosphere," drinking beer when Junior and Muscles approached Dale. Junior said, "Hey Dale, I might wanna borrow some money from you." Dale asked him how much he needed. Junior said, "Well, I may need a five. I'll pay you back." Muscles said, "That's right, Dale. He'll pay you. If he don't, I will" (as he patted his back pocket). Dale said, "Now there's security for you!"

It was against the law to bring whiskey into Mom's, but Junior kept a half-pint in his back pocket. While Junior was talking to them, Muscles would slip his hand into Junior's back pocket, slip out the bottle, take a sip, then put the bottle back into Junior's back pocket. Junior never knew and the boys never told him. One night, Howard asked Junior what he had been doing. Junior said, "Got me a job driving the bus for Lester and Earl." (Flatt and Scruggs). "Really?" Howard asked. "Where y'all going?" Junior said, "England!" Howard asked him, "You driving all the way to England?" Junior said, "You've got that God dog right."

Junior and Muscle stories are still talked about today, even after no one knows what happened to them. I've sat in offices and heard people tell Junior and Muscle stories that never knew them. The ones told herein are absolutely true, not made up to be funny.

Tootsie Bess bought Mom's from the Hacklers and now the tourists that frequent there think it was always Tootsie's Orchid Lounge. They don't know about the "original Mom." And, my how it has changed! The big round table in the front corner, that hit writers used to write songs at, is now a stage where entertainers play for "the door." People dance where we used to drink longnecks. There used to be a jukebox, but no live music. There is a band downstairs, upstairs and in a newly added third floor. On a Saturday night, the Opry boys cannot get in for the tourists. The name of the ones that used to hang out there are now only memories, like Willie Nelson, who with Hank Cochran, wrote hits there. Then there was "Radar," so called because he couldn't see well.

"Scoopie" Bruce Harper was there, always with a story. He was a sometimes writer for country music magazines and a DJ at a small radio station. Big writers from New York used to interview him and repeat his stories in their books. There was Jack Toombs, a taxicab driver who co-wrote a George Morgan song hit, "Almost" (with Vic McAlpin). The musicians who drank there are too numerous to name. So are the songwriters, who jotted their ideas down on paper napkins.

The Opry has moved on. You don't need a shillelagh or hat pin to let the boys sit down anymore. It's all tourists and nobody sits down. However, you can bet that if either Mom or Tootsie were still living, they would still be taking care of their Opry boys, giving them credit when they needed it and listening to their tales of woe as the juke box played another sad song. ... *"Who'll buy my memories / Of things that used to be . . ."* - Willie Nelson.

13 THE BYRD

"That's the Hawaiian in Me"

– "Byrd in Hawaii," Maple, 1973

When Howard's era of steel guitar players think of the sweetest music this side of Heaven, they all agree that the one man who played steel like the angels sing was the Byrd, Jerry, that is. Jerry was Howard's idol and in later years, Jerry told Howard, "You played more like me than any other steel player." Howard said, "Like singers unconsciously sing like other singers, in looking for my own identity, I guess I adopted a kind of Byrd sound."

Howard bought a Rickenbacker steel guitar out of a pawnshop in North Carolina. It had white plastic plates on it, Jerry Byrd's had stainless steel. Howard went to a machine shop and had them cut silver-colored metal plates like Byrd's. Howard said, "It didn't make the guitar sound better, but it did look exactly like Jerry's. I had his tunings and string gauges, so how could I miss!"

Theron Gooslin, early musician, remembered a conversation between Howard and Jerry at the Clarkston Hotel. He told me that Jerry came in and said to Howard, "I can't believe they let pickers like Howard White eat here." Howard then said, "If you don't stop talking about me like that, I'm going to stop playing like you." Theron said, "That was the most beautiful, appropriate, witty tribute I ever heard."

When we originally started writing this chapter, Howard talked to Jerry and tried to get him to tell him some Music City "War Stories." Jerry only said, "I don't believe you could print what I could tell you. Don't spend a lot of space on me. You know my background as a musician and what, if anything, I contributed to this business. That's really all I care about."

A modest man, Jerry! What has he contributed? Well, twenty-five plus albums, over two-hundred and sixty sides, composed thirty-five steel guitar solos, was the first to use steel guitar in a wide variety of musical arrangements as (1) violin and orchestra, (2) with a blues brass section, (3) Japanese songs with a Japanese orchestra, (4) recorded on Monument with a fifty-eight piece Mexico City Symphony. He has a large catalog of Country, Pop and Hawaiian music. He has played in every major hotel in Waikiki. He authored an indepth three hundred and fifty-page instruction book printed in English and Japanese. The Byrd has accomplished more in a lifetime than most in several. A lover of genuine Hawaiian music, he moved there and taught Hawaiian kids to play Hawaiian music.

Howard and I went to the Country Music Foundation's Library to get some facts, as Jerry told us they had seven cassette tapes he had made for them. In fact, it took seven months for them to allow us in to "the sacred catacombs." Finally John Rumble gave us permission to listen to Byrd's tapes he had made for them. This was the only time we had to use the Library, but determination wins out.

Byrd was born in 1920 in Lima, Ohio. He was of English, German and Dutch descent. When he was in the sixth grade, a Hawaiian tent show came through his town, charging one dollar admission. In those depression years, that was a lot of money. But he went and what he saw and heard changed his direction forever. He saw a man with his guitar on his lap, an acoustic Hawaiian steel guitar. Jerry said, "That sound paralyzed me." When electric guitars came in, Jerry ordered an all-metal guitar and amp out of a Spiegel catalog. The cost was sixty-five dollars. In order to buy it, he worked two summers for a house painter for twenty-five cents an hour the first summer and thirty cents an hour the second summer. He bought his own clothes, his schoolbooks and paid his parents five dollars a week board. He borrowed a bicycle and rode to the Railway Express office to pick up his guitar. He played it constantly for two years. He listened to "Hawaii Calls" on the radio, direct from Hawaii on the Mutual Network, then played the songs. He knew immediately what tunings they used and how they were doing it. Howard said, "Steel guitar players are born, not made."

One day a guitar teacher in Lima, Ron Dearth, drove to Jerry's house, took him to his studio and showed him a shiny new black Rickenbacker with plates of chrome. Jerry sat down, played it and started crying. It cost one hundred and fifty dollars. He worked out a deal with Dearth then and there. Dearth gave him forty dollars for his old guitar and Jerry agreed to make Dearth diagram arrangements for all the songs he played. Dearth would give him two dollars apiece until the guitar was paid up.

Jerry's German parents were upset that their son had decided to become a musician. They said, "You don't play music, you go to work!" That made Jerry even more determined. Jerry and his two brothers, who played guitar and ukulele, formed a trio called The Jay Byrd Trio. They played on WBLY in Lima, a one-hundred-watt station. During Jerry's senior year in high school, he took a job, playing with the *Renfro Valley Barn Dance*. At that time the show originated from Dayton, Ohio. Later the show moved to Kentucky.

After high school, Jerry left home. He worked at Renfro from about 1939 to 1942. Then he went to Detroit to work at WJR. He stayed there during the war years. A bout with pneumonia and six months in bed kept him out of service. Then Jerry went with Ernest Tubb. After being with Tubb a year-and-a-half, Red Foley hired him for the *Prince Albert Show*, NBC's network broadcast from the *Grand Ole Opry*. Then Red's band went to Cincinnati and played on the *Midwestern* Hayride for two years. While there, Jerry made his first recordings in 1949, for Mercury Records, cutting some fifty sides, all released as 78-rpm records. Byrd also played sessions for Red Foley, Ernest Tubb, Cowboy Copas, Hank Williams, Jimmy Wakely, Guy Mitchell and Patti Page.

Jerry couldn't remember all the hits he played on by Foley, but recalled being on "Blues In My Heart," "Tennessee Saturday Night" and "Ruby Red

Lips." When Foley wanted something different, Jerry came up with the idea of playing three-part harmony using steel and electric guitars. Zeke Turner would play melody and Jerry played the tenor and baritone parts. It sounded like three guitars. Farris Coursey was playing drums and they decided to use drums to try outside styles of blues and boogie.

Jerry moved to Nashville in 1951, and continued working with Foley. He and the band each made fifty dollars a week with Foley, then they were offered one hundred and sixty dollars weekly to go to Cincinnati. They asked Foley for more money, but even though he promised them more, he never followed through with that promise. The band then gave notice. Foley actually cried when the boys left but, as Jerry said, "Within thirty minutes, he was rehearsing a new band." The new steel player was Billy Robinson, who had been playing at WSIX in Nashville. Jerry and the band became the staff band in Cincinnati and replaced *The Milton Berle Show* for the summer.

Byrd recorded "I Wish I Had A Nickel" with Jimmy Wakely, and "I Love You Because" with Clyde Moody. He was making forty-one dollars and twenty-five cents for a three-hour session, the union scale. Wakely asked Jerry if he was getting leader scale? Jerry wasn't. It was Wakely that told Jerry that leader scale is double rate. Wakely asked, "Who's getting it? You're crazy, why don't you ask for it!" Byrd then asked for leader's fee and got it from then on, but he was hurt that he had been taken advantage of.

Jerry Byrd recorded with Hank Williams when Fred Rose was producing. They had done three songs and had ten minutes left. Hank said, "I kinda have a song in my guitar case." He took out "Lovesick Blues." Rose listened and said, "That's the worst song I ever heard in my life." It was so out of meter that Rose left the studio. They made two cuts. Rose came back in the studio, listened and said, "My God, this is the worst song I ever heard." As things turned out, this song made Hank's career.

Jerry's recording work continued into the "pedal age of steel." He said he thought a lot about playing pedals, but he had his own style, his own sound and in typical Byrd fashion, he refused to compromise. He never changed to pedals as Howard did. When steel players changed to two necks, some even to three or four, Jerry said, "When I master one neck, I'll change to two." He never did. That was "Byrd logic."

Actually times changed and session producers began using pedal steel. Lloyd Green said his most embarrassing moment was when he was booked on a session, playing pedal steel, and Jerry Byrd was booked, playing bass. Jerry said, "We worked hard. We were interested in the singer. That's what made the Nashville Sound, this interesting." There was no pension plan when he was working (or when Howard was working), but Jerry said, "That's life. I have no regrets. I am the luckiest guy in the world. I still play. I have good memories. These are the golden days." And that's The Byrd.

Jerry was sixty-eight years old when this chapter was first written. He died on April 12, 2005, at age eighty-five. The following is a letter from him in 1996. Typical Byrd.

Jerry Byrd

P.O. Box 15026
Honolulu, Hawaii 96830   1-8-'96

Hi there, "Hard"

The tape just arrived + duly played. Interesting. Those things I did with Copas were done at King Studios when I was in Cincinnati - '50-'51- no reverb; -dry as hell. I am reminded again by hearing these how much Copas copied Pete Cassell. But alot of them did: Clyde Moody was one -. Pete was blind - but great. He did recitations better than anyone ever did! I recorded with him in a small studio at WSM - before there were any studios in Nashville. It was on a label called Majestic. about 1946 or so -. He was the idol of many singers and never reached the heights he should have, sadly.

Anyhow -it was good to hear them again - and know what ?? neither one of us could play -!!

Happy New -

JB

14 WHEN YOU HANG UP THE GUITAR

"When these fingers can strum no longer,
Hand the old guitar to young ones stronger."

- Pete Seeger.

Howard White and I met in 1962. He was working with Hank Snow and I had just moved back to Nashville after nine years at Strobel's Music Shop in the Arcade. I had worked there before in 1947, selling sheet music and playing the piano for those who wanted to know what a song sounded like before they bought it. Strobel's also carried instruments and instrument accessories.

Howard came in to buy an E String, carrying a cup of orange juice, laced with vodka in his hand. He was also troubled and asked me to go next door to Walgreen's for a cup of coffee to talk. I learned then that this person never lacked for conversation. I found out that Howard had just returned from a long tour up the West Coast with Snow. When he got back, his wife had left him and taken everything he owned. All he had was his guitar and amp, stage clothes and those clothes he wore on his back. He had just come from a lawyer, A.T. Levine, and had started divorce proceedings. That was the first thing we had in common as I had just returned home after a divorce in California.

The Nashville I had come back to was not the same. The Arcade and Strobel's was still there, but the old music store was on its last legs. In the first place, sheet music was no longer selling. It wasn't the only music store in town anymore. The Music Mart had opened on Union Street with a Strobel's alumnus heading it, Wayne Snow. There was Sho-Bud on Broad Street and the Hank Snow Music Store had opened on Church Street. Walgreen's was still in its place at the corner of the Arcade and Fifth Avenue, still with a lunch counter. Woolworth's, Kress and McLellands, where Del Wood played and sold sheet music, were still there on Fifth Avenue, but they were soon to go, replaced by a Dollar Store, art galleries and a condo.

Howard was a stranger to me but, then so was everyone else in my home town. It was good to talk to someone and share our troubles. And, Howard was an inspired talker, if not always a good listener. Amazing how an E-string can bring you together!

It was strange that Howard came to Strobel's that day. All the steel players went to Sho-Bud. There used to be a time when all the hillbillies, pop and concert musicians, teachers, band and choir leaders all rubbed shoulders there. I told Howard I remembered Hank "Sugarfoot" Garland, barely sixteen years old, Billy Byrd and Harold (Hal) Bradley all "jammed" there on the new Gibson guitars upstairs with then salesman, Wayne Snow. Once Sam Hollingsworth, the greatest bass player, was walking through the Arcade and stopped in just to tell me I had played quarter-note triplets wrong. Sam was a symphony player, but he also worked at the Opry sometimes. He could play breakdowns on his stand-up bass. Fred Shoemake came in frequently and played "Sweet Loraine" on the piano. Fred was one of the few that still came around. I remembered when we had autographing parties, and George Morgan autographed "Candy Kisses" and Francis Craig autographed "Near You." Howard knew them all, of course.

Howard and I remembered when Nashville first had growing pains and renamed "Hillbilly" as "Country Music." Nashvillians had a hard time accepting that *Barn Dance Music* would become palatable and the "Athens Of the South" would become "Music City, USA."

This is how Howard described our budding friendship: "We fast became good friends, something I had neglected to do with my other wife. Ruth understood the musicians' life and we began to see a lot of each other, mostly in company with my buddies." We had a lot in common. Howard's background was in country music, and mine was in pop. I had played in dance bands. So, we learned a lot about each other's music and style.

Then Howard found out through Claude Sharpe at WSM who was a member of the Opry's Old Hickory Singers, that there was a job opening at the WSM Radio Music Library. Claude arranged a job interview for me with Bob Cooper and I got the job. Ott Devine, program director, became my boss.

Howard's and my life began to parallel. Not only did he introduce me to the "finer things" of country music, but he introduced me to Tootsie and Mom Upchurch. (Mom liked me, good thing!)

When Howard was between tours with Hank Snow, he did other things. He went with Benny Williams to Muscle Shoals, Alabama, to record there. Benny was talented, played five instruments and did imitations. They recorded two sides. When Howard got back to Nashville, he placed it on Todd Records, with Paul Cohen, who had been A&R for Decca. At the time, it had been too much for him to run between New York and Nashville, so he turned the Nashville operation over to Owen Bradley. One side of the record was Benny's imitations. The other side was an instrumental that Benny had written.

They called it "90 Miles From Nashville" as Muscle Shoals was ninety miles from Nashville. Benny said Howard could have publishing on the song. He opened a BMI company he called Locomotive Music Company and then Howard told me, "I want you to learn all you can about publishing." Wow! Where do you start!" Howard had cleared the name and obtained Locomotive with Frances (Williams) Preston, whom he had known since he sold *Grand Ole Opry* tickets at WSM. Then he took me to see Don Warden, steel player with Porter Wagoner, who also owned Warden Music with Porter. (They published "The Battle Of New Orleans.")

Don gave me the basics about contracting and copyrighting, even filling out an EP form, which he titled "Who Shot Nellie." From then on, in those early days, I talked to Dean May at Acuff-Rose, who educated me formally into more of the details, like licensing. She became my mentor. Then I studied everything I could find, which wasn't a lot in those days. So, I contracted, cleared, copyrighted, did my own lead sheet and the song "Ninety Miles From Nashville" started us into publishing.

I had a daughter, Kathleen, who Howard was crazy about. When he was in town, he took her everywhere with him, even to Tootsie's, where the guys gave her nickels and hid her under the table when the police came around. Kathleen loved Krystal hamburgers and Howard said, "She nearly killed me eating Krystals every day." When both Howard and I were working, Grandma Bland took care of her. One day, as she and Howard drove down Woodland Street, she surprised Howard by reading a sign, "Beer On Tap." This was the first we knew that she could read. She had not started Kindergarten yet, but Grandma, an old schoolteacher, had been teaching her. We thought it funny that "Run Spot run" had translated to "Beer On Tap."

In June of 1965 Howard and I decided to get married. We went to Gainesville, Florida, where Howard's brother lived and went to a Justice of the Peace. Kathleen was with us. He looked at us and asked us why we wanted to get married. Howard immediately said, "To give this baby a daddy." Howard called her "The Baby" and "The Baby" she was always to him. Dave Kirby and Glenn Martin at Pamper Music, even wrote a song called "Ruth And The Baby."

About this time the "powers that be" at WSM decided to clear out much of the Library to make room for Dave Overton and his secretary. It was a sad affair to see all the records they destroyed. Not only records, but band arrangements dating back to when *The Waking Crew* began. Marvin Hughes, the director then, would come into the Library every morning and pick three arrangements for the band to play the next day. I set these arrangements up for each instrument for the next day's show. When the purging of the Library began, Marvin and I worked every Saturday, going through arrangements to be thrown away. One day I came back from lunch to find that a locked safe had been opened and Ott Devine had instructed the porter to take the 78-rpm records there out to the dumpster and break them! So there went all the records of the early pioneers like Uncle Dave Macon. Grant Turner trucked out all the hillbilly 78's. They took up a whole wall section. Sheet music was tossed, as file cabinets had to be moved out. Trudy Stamper took a lot of it. That left us with only the LPs and 45s. All that history lost for Dave Overton, who in years past had been removed from his TV dance show, because of shady activities.

It was obvious that things were changing at the station. When Acuff-Rose offered me a position in the Hickory Records Department, I took the job. I didn't really like the record business and when I was offered a job in an attorney's office, I accepted that. It proved to be a good move. They specialized in property and that was good training for the publishing companies to come that I would work for. Years afterward, when I was teaching publishing to the new kids on the block, I would compare copyright ownership to Property Deed ownership. They could understand that.

Then Howard quit his job with Hank Snow: "I had always landed on my own two feet with another job and it never occurred to me that time could change everything. I was twenty-six years old when I came to Nashville and fifteen years had passed. It seemed the road now belonged to the young and I was no longer young. I was forty-one!"

At first, the old Rainbow Ranch Boys tried to work as a unit, playing package shows for acts that had no band. Smokey Smith from Des Moines used them, too, but basically there just wasn't enough work. Then Howard tried to have a band of his own, hiring youthful players: Greg Galbraith, guitar; Jimmy Halfacre, drums' and Ray Crisp, fiddle. But they acted so young! They set off firecrackers in the van, stole oranges in California, and just had a good time. But, as Howard said, "It wasn't that they were so bad, they were just so young. This old man couldn't take it!" Then Ernie Ashworth asked Howard to go on the road with him. Later on, Howard admitted he hated that job more than any he had ever had.

After the pros that Howard had worked for, he regarded Ernest as a rank amateur. Ashworth was just off his first and only number one hit, "Talk Back Trembling Lips." He showed up for their first tour in a white station wagon with great big red lips painted all over it. Howard said, "Oh, no!" Ernest insisted, "This is what I've always wanted." Howard just knew they would be robbed blind. He said, "I had to drive that car from Florida to California." They had four days in Florida and a day in California. They were booked at the Civic Auditorium in Long Beach and when they got there, they parked in front and went in to check things out. Just as Howard thought, when they got back to the car, someone had stolen "Ol' Ern's" new Gibson guitar. Howard said, "I guess they left my steel and amp because they were too heavy to run with."

Howard then went to Canada with Ernest and played sixteen dates there. One date they did was at an ice rink. The stage was extremely high. Right in the middle of "Trembling Lips," Ernest decided to jump down to get with the audience. Then he couldn't get back up on the stage, as there were no steps. So, he ran down the aisle to the back door, ran around the building to the stage door which was locked. He pounded on it until at last a guard heard him and opened the door. Then he ran back out on stage to finish the song. Howard was starting the turn-around when Ernest jumped off the stage, and was still playing when Ernest got back out there. Howard mused, "That was the longest turn-around I ever took in my life."

All in all, Howard worked thirty-six show dates with Ernest. When they came home, Howard, as usual, went down to the Opry on Saturday night to play with Ernest. Once there, he found out that Ernest had flown to a date, taking Little Roy Wiggins along with him. Ernest had made a deal with Howard when they started. He couldn't afford to pay scale then, so he paid Howard in part and after the tours were over, he would pay the balance of what he owed him. I kept an absolute record of what Ernest had paid and what he owed for every date.

There were eighty-five dates, from the West Coast to the East Coast and Canada. Ernest had paid Howard eight hundred and ninety dollars. He still owed him one hundred and eighty-five dollars. When Howard found out Ernest had flown himself and Roy onto his next date, after Howard had driven Ernest all those miles, he went to Ernest's house to collect what was owed. Money was hard to come by in those days, and Howard got nowhere in talking to Ernest. Then for the first time in his career, Howard went to the Union. He figured he needed that money worse than Ernest. George Cooper was President then and he usually took care of things in a short time. He called Ernest into his office and then called Wesley Rose, Ashworth's manager. They got Wesley on the phone and he only asked Ashworth, "Do you owe the boy the money?" Ernest said, "Yes." Wesley told him, "Then pay him!" So Ernest paid Howard right there and they each went their separate ways.

Howard's next job was backing package shows with a band for John Bodin, a promoter. Bill Carlisle was the star attraction. Marshall Barnes, Bill's bass player, and Bill rode together. Then Marshall tried to get Howard fired and take over the band. That was when Howard found out that the business was changing. If you didn't watch out every minute, somebody might try to pull the rug out from under you.

Country musicians could swap jobs whenever needed. They tried to make the band sound as much like the band on the star's records as possible. Maybe they couldn't all interchange with Bluegrass bands, but some few could. Chubby Wise played Bluegrass with Bill Monroe and went directly to playing country for Hank Snow. When Charlie Walker asked Howard to go to Las Vegas with him, Charlie knew Howard could do the job. They didn't even hold practice sessions. Howard was delighted to go with Charlie and he quit the job with Bodin.

Charlie Walker had been at San Antonio, and was rated as one of America's Top Ten Country Music Disc Jockeys by *Billboard* for ten consecutive years. Then, in 1958, he had a hit written by Harlan Howard, "Pick Me Up On Your Way Down." He joined the Opry in 1967, after having the hits "Wild As a Wildcat" and "Please Don't Squeeze My Sharmon." Charlie invited Howard to work a week with him at the Golden Nugget in Las Vegas. The singer flew out there and left Howard in charge of his new Ford Station Wagon. He picked up the bandsmen and girl singer Linda Flanagan in front of Tootsie's at midnight to begin the trip West. Linda was a former winner of the Pet Milk Show Contest on WSM.

Not long out of Tennessee, they began experiencing car trouble. The car would just stop. After sitting awhile, it would start up and later it would quit running again. Finally they got to Henderson, Nevada, stopping for gas. They were tired, dirty, hot and with all their equipment looked like a questionable bunch of individuals. Linda and the drummer got out and started chasing each other around the car. A policeman pulled in, saw them and immediately had suspicions. Here Howard was, in a car with Texas license plates, registered to Charlie Walker. Howard's license was from Tennessee. The policeman asked Howard if they had any firearms. Howard knew that Charlie's gun was in the glove compartment, so he said yes. The policeman said, "Open it slowly and hand the gun to me." He was going to take them to the station, but Howard talked him into calling the Golden Nugget and talk to Mr. Green, who was their talent coordinator. It just so happened that Charlie was in Mr. Green's office and verified what Howard said. Luckily, they weren't arrested, for they didn't have time to spend in a Nevada jail!

After leaving Vegas, they had a couple of days in Texas. Then the little Ford gremlins came back to haunt them, as the car started its old stopping tricks again. Charlie put the car in the shop in that little Texas town, where they spent twenty-four hours in a wooden hotel with no air conditioning as temperatures hovered around one hundred and twenty degrees. After the mechanics couldn't find the source of the problem, they started home, arriving in Nashville a few days late.

Charlie stayed overnight at our house, as the next day he had to fly out again. Howard and I drove him to the airport in the by now infamous car. Sure enough, on the way to the airport, the car stopped dead in the middle of Lebanon Road. We just sat there and eventually it started. Howard took that car and left it outside the building of Charlie's booker, Hubert Long, on 16th Avenue South. He never wanted to see it again! Charlie told him later the Ford dealer finally found a simple problem. There was a little bit of hose from the gas line to the tank that would sometimes close up while it got hot. Howard worked another job with Charlie in Vegas later, but by then Charlie had another station wagon.

The last time Howard worked for Charlie Walker was in 1993, when Charlie was running for State Senator on the Republican ticket. They put out signs on all the roads from Greenbrier to White House in Robertson and Sumner Counties. Howard wrote a slogan for Charlie, which Walker had made up on business cards: "If you want a doer and not a talker, Cast your vote for Charlie Walker!" Incidentally, Charlie almost won, finishing second in a long slate of candidates.

While in Las Vegas, during an off-duty time, the band went to the Nashville Club to hear their band. It just so happened, the steel player announced that he was going to play an instrumental that he wrote. As Howard listened, he was astounded to realize that the instrumentalist was playing a song that Howard had written to record on Hickory Records, published by Acuff-Rose, called "Border Serenade." At the break he cornered the guy and said, "You didn't write that song, I did, back in 1953." The steel player was so shocked, he didn't say a word in reply. What would the odds be that a steel-playing songwriter from Nashville would show up in Las Vegas at a show where another guitarist played a song he claimed to have written, but it was really penned by a guy coming to his show. The odds were in favor of Howard that night at the Nashville Club, if not at the dice table in the Golden Nugget.

Charlie was married to quite a few girls. One of the last was a girl named Diana Sprayberry. She thought Charlie had money and laughingly Charlie thought she had money. Needless to say, that marriage didn't last. Chet Atkins said to Howard one day on the golf course, "I don't know what Charlie does to all those girls, but he must do something."

Other dates, not to be taken seriously, were with Jack Boles. Jack was never a superstar, but he was an excellent showman and always had engagements somewhere. A Nashville native, Jack started entertaining early with the Eagle Rangers, a regional country band. In 1966, Jack had some dates at an Air Force base in Glasgow, Montana, and asked Howard to go along. Jack and another band member, Rudy Lyle, picked Howard up in a pretty well-worn 1953 Cadillac with a trailer hitched on behind. When they started out, Howard immediately went to sleep so he could take his turn driving. It was a long way to Montana and they would be driving straight through. At Louisville, Kentucky, he woke up and discovered they were headed back towards Nashville. Jack said, "Doc, this car ain't gonna make it!" It was making unhealthy noises, but Howard said, "Yes, it will. Turn around and put some oil in it." From then on they kept enough oil with them to feed the old Cadillac. They got into prairie land and the trailer came loose and went out across a field. They re-attached it and finally limped into Glasgow and played the dates. Jack told the Sergeant at the Air Force Service Club what had happened and he loaned Jack enough money to get another car to get them back home. (Howard doubted that Jack ever paid him back.)

Another time, Jack booked himself some dates in Michigan. He couldn't find a bass player or a drummer in Nashville to go, but a friend, Hal Willis, told Jack he knew a drummer and bass player who lived in Seymour, Indiana, who would go with them. Jack made the agreement with them by phone, sight unseen. Jack and Howard pulled into the motel, where they were staying. The drummer who weighed three-hundred-and-fifty pounds, was sitting up in bed, eating a big stick of bologna and crackers. The bass player weighed about a hundred and ten pounds, soaking wet. Howard immediately dubbed them "Laurel and Hardy." The big buy took up the whole backseat and the little guy had to sit on the edge of the seat to be able to fit in the car. As they drove along, the car didn't seem to be driving right. Jack stopped at a station to see what was wrong. The mechanic asked, "Have you been hauling something heavy?"

Howard grinned, "Jack and I laughed all the way to Michigan and back again." All their lives Howard and Jack remembered Laurel and Hardy. Jack wrote Howard a letter which said, "I would always say when a job came up, 'Well, if I can just talk Howard White into going, we will have a good trip!' You would go and we would experience something that would be worth remembering. Now I know why, that of all the steel guitar players that were available, I chose you."

In this manner Howard went *from pillar to post*, and I tried to remain supportive. He even sold ads for what we called "telephone shows" for his friend Ken Marvin. A telephone show was so-called because phones were installed in a room called a "Boiler Room" and you sold ads for a show program book via telephone. The show he worked on was for the fire department for a "Miss Fire Prevention Beauty Pageant."

"I began to hate the idea of loading that guitar and amp one more time. I hated worse the long trips and time away from Ruth and the Baby," said Howard. The life of a country musician was not as fascinating as he once thought, even with the fun they all had together. Country fans tend to think everything is a bed of roses for musicians on the road. How little they know! Like in everyone's life, whether you are a doctor, lawyer or candlestick maker, there's a lot of bitter mixed with the sweet.

Howard once remarked that the really good thing about his life was that he did exactly what he wanted to do, or thought he wanted to do. A prominent lawyer, Jack Norman, Sr., once told him, "I'd give up anything, if I could play like you." At that time Mr. Norman was fascinated with show business and was attending a show in the company of pianist Del Wood, famed for her instrumental version of "Down Yonder" on Tennessee Records. Howard said, "I guess he didn't mean that literally, but it shows there must have been moments when he dreamed of being something besides a lawyer. Me? I never entertained the notion of becoming a lawyer. I just wanted to play music."

About this time, Howard heard about an opening at Acuff-Rose Talent Agency headed up by Jim McConnell. Howard had an interview with Jim, who hired him to start to work the following Monday. On Saturday night, Howard made a big mistake. He was at the Opry and talked to Roy Acuff, fifty per cent owner of Acuff-Rose. Howard told him he had just been hired by McConnell, and how proud he was to be working for that company. On Monday morning when Howard went to work, Jim told him that Roy had just called him and wanted him to put his fiddle player, Howdy Forrester, in that job. Roy wouldn't have known about that job if Howard hadn't told him. Even though Roy was part owner of Acuff-Rose, he didn't keep up with the business. Howard said, "That was a slap in the face. The 'King Of Country Music' and my friend knocked me out of the job."

One day as we rode along I said, "What do you want to do with the rest of your life?" Howard said, "I've a been asking myself that same question." Then I said, "You know, right now the only thing you have to look forward to is being the oldest steel player on the Opry." Howard asked me, "What else can I do?" "Well," I said, "Since you know everybody in town, why don't you go and visit your friends on the business side of music."

So, one day Howard discarded his jeans for a suit and tie and made his way to Music Row. He first went to see Jim Denny at Cedarwood, but he was out to lunch. Then he walked across to see Hubert Long who had a talent agency and a publishing company. Hubert said, "Yes, you're hired. I need a song-plugger for my Moss Rose Publishing."

Howard said, "My guitar stayed in its case and I didn't look back. When I hung up the guitar, I really hung it up. I never went back to it again professionally. I left the picking to the younger guys, just thankful I had once been a part of the whole Opry scene, when it was fun. I realized it was never going to be same for me, as it was before I was twenty-five." The dust gathered on those shiny steel strings that used to vibrate with life.

"There is a time for leaving, although
Some stay to weave the threads
Of the loom and gather the
Harvest in the field."

Charlie Walker

100

15 SO! YOU WANT TO BE IN MUSIC PUBLISHING!

"Music is about making
Something out of nothing
And selling it."

- Frank Zappa

The music publishing scene, to the insiders, hasn't changed all that much. They still live by the motto: "I don't care if it is number one on the charts, it's still a lousy song, besides I didn't write it or publish it."

Song publishing is an extremely rough and political business and gets more so every day. Music publishing in Nashville initially began in 1824, by Western Harmony. They published a book of hymns and instruction in singing, called "The Western Harmony," printed by Carey Harris on *The Nashville Republican* newspaper's presses on College Street (now Third Avenue). On July 20, 1982, Nashville dedicated a historical marker, given by the National Music Publishers Association (NMPA), at the original site of Nashville's first music publishing firm.

When Acuff-Rose Publications opened on Eighth Avenue, it really launched modern day music publishing in Nashville. Others followed and Nashville's fledgling music publishing industry was underway. They were then mostly centered around the WSM studios, then located in the old National Life Building at Seventh and Union Streets (razed in 1981, forever removing those historic studios). Tree Publishing Company, founded in 1951 by Jack Stapp, was housed at 319 Seventh Avenue North in the Cumberland Lodge Building. Cedarwood Music, started in 1953 by Jim Denny and Webb Pierce, located their offices at 146 Seventh Avenue North, in the Albert Building. Both Denny and Stapp were employees of WSM at that time. Some of the music business "executives" had their "offices" at the Clarkston Hotel in the coffee shop, which was between the National Life Building and the Cumberland Lodge Building. Business was not clearly defined in those days and "board meetings" were held daily among them all – publishers, bookers, promoters, engineers, musicians – at the hotel coffee shop to see "what was happening." Deals were made right there! Denny's and Stapp's empire grew without WSM really becoming aware of the truth of the matter.

On March 3, 1956, Denny was named "Country and Western Man Of the Year" by *Billboard* the trade weekly. Six months later, he was fired by Jack DeWitt, WSM president, because Denny refused to divest himself of his publishing interests. Denny didn't suffer financially, for besides Cedarwood, he formed Jim Denny Artists Service Bureau, taking Webb and other acts who had been booked by WSM's Artists Service Bureau with him. (It became the Denny-Moeller Agency, when Lucky Moeller came aboard.) Jack Stapp resigned from WSM in 1958, to devote full time to Tree Publishing. Joyce Bush, his secretary, and musician Buddy Killen went with him. When Tree published the multi-million selling Elvis Presley smash "Heartbreak Hotel," they no longer needed WSM and their salaries to get by.

"Song-plugging" was a term coined in New York City's *Tin Pan Alley* in the days before 1900. Early publishers believed that if a good song, with a catchy melody, could be heard by enough people, it had a chance to become a commercial success. So they invented something brand new - song promotion - and they went everywhere to get their "plug song" heard, and so the terms "song-plugging" and "plugger" were coined. (Songwriter Norro Wilson called it "street fighting.") In those days, "Vaudeville" was the big medium for songs. The big publishing houses plugged or promoted their tunes to the vaudeville stage crowd. Later, they hired people strictly for this function. The business evolved from vaudeville to Big Bands and dance music, on to radio, motion pictures, stage, TV and concert hall. The industry moved to include Hollywood along with New York's Great White Way.

In the 1940's, Fred Rose brought music publishing to Nashville, a natural thing, thanks to the rise of country music. A publishing company's chief asset is its standards, or as commonly called, its "evergreens." Their continued promotion potential means they can be recorded and re-recorded, used in movies, radio and television, etc., over and over. Today, song-plugging is not at the heart of the publishing business, as it used to be. Record labels want artist-writers, who record their own songs or splits writing and/or publishing with others. Splitting of writing and publishing credits is the norm now, leaving an independent writer with fewer sources, unless he or she is in with the right people. You may ask, "How many songwriters does it take to produce a hit?" One song might have three-to-ten writers on it, in other words, one could call it "written by a committee." One veteran songwriter said, "It feels more like building a song, rather than crafting one, as we used to do."

Inspiration used to be the norm. Jumpin' Bill Carlisle wrote a song called "No Help Wanted," and was inspired to do so after WSM called him at WNOX-Knoxville to come to Nashville and join the Opry. When he got here, management said they didn't need him, leaving Bill without a job, and so he wrote "No Help Wanted." After performing with KWKH's *Louisiana Hayride* for a short while, the Opry called him again. Thanks to his new hit "No Help Wanted," he joined in 1953, and remained there until he passed away on St. Patrick's Day in 2003, at age ninety-four.

A typical song-publishing swap story occurred in 1949, when Red Foley recorded "Chattanoogie Shoe Shine Boy." The song was actually written by Fred Rose, who titled it "Boogie Woogie Shoe Shine Boy." As it happened, Fred was also newcomer Hank Williams' producer, and as such he wanted Hank on the Opry. In order to accomplish this, Rose offered his writer's credit to then Opry hierarchy Harry Stone and Jack Stapp.

Neither Stapp nor Stone had ever written a song before, but agreed to the proposition, much to their ever-lasting satisfaction, for the Foley single became a million-selling, number one country and pop crossover disc in 1950. The title was changed to "Chattanoogie Shoe Shine Boy," as produced by Owen Bradley for Decca Records, and it became Red's biggest seller. According to Owen's guitarist brother Harold, the night before their session, Owen called drummer Farris Coursey and told Farris to come up with a new sound by session time. Billy Robinson, the session's steel player, said Farris tried everything the next day to produce a shoe-shine rag beat sound. He slapped chairs, tables, anything available, finally hitting on the sound Owen wanted, by simply slapping his legs with his hands. Songwriter Fred Rose relinquished the right to a fortune, but he kept the publishing rights to "Chattanoogie Shoe Shine Boy" with Acuff-Rose Publications. Of course, Hank Williams sang for the first time on the Opry, June 11, 1949, and not so coincidentally debuted on Red Foley's *Prince Albert* portion, receiving a record six encores from the crowd, and then he became an Opry member.

Hubert Long was an empire man. He saw trends long before anyone else did. He kept his Stable of Stars (actually the title of his talent agency) together by encouraging them to form their own publishing companies and he assessed as much as fifty percent to administer them. He not only had his own, Moss Rose, but he also administered the companies of such notables as Bill Anderson, Ferlin Husky, Marijohn Wilkin and Charlie Walker. When Hubert hired Howard, he was already on a first-name basis with the A&R men at the record companies. Chet Atkins, at RCA, used to split a half-pint with Howard on Saturdays nights at the Opry. Kelso Herston, also a musician, was at Capitol Records, while Owen Bradley was at Decca, and Billy Sherrill and Frank Jones were both at Columbia. All friends!

A song plugger's job was more than just song-plugging. Howard reviewed new music, maintained a liaison with writers, produced demo sessions and, in between, pitched songs. Kelso, at Capitol, called Howard almost immediately and said, "I want to be the first one to record a song for you," and he did. Howard got a personal note from Chet at RCA thanking him for taking him a great song.

Another plus was that the writers liked working with Howard. Once when Howard wrote a song with Chuck Rogers, "The Cold Gray Light Of Gone," in retrospect he remembered, "It was strange how we wrote that song. I had been toying around with a melody on a guitar. Chuck, hearing me play, came in and told me he had lyrics that fit that melody. Sure enough, they fit like a glove. "Howard produced the finished product on Don Jarrell at Bradley's Barn, his first attempt at producing a master session. Millie Kirkham sang the high vocal sounds on the recording. She said afterwards, "You'll get this one placed, Howard." Sure enough Howard got it placed on Stop Records, a label owned by Pete Drake. It was later recorded again, that time by Phil Brown, a Canadian artist on Panorama Records. That was in 1967.

In 1994, it surprised Howard and I to read in a book by Robert Oermann that Bill Anderson took an idea of a song called "The Cold Gray Light Of Gone" to Vince Gill. They wrote it and Vince Gill cut it. Well, you can't copyright a title or an idea, even if you are aware that the writer was "in house" at Moss Rose when the original song was written. At that time, Bill's company was being administered by Hubert Long and Bill was around the whole time, just listening.

About a year had gone by and in that time Howard learned a lot. Hubert held meetings every Monday morning. Howard recalled, "Hubert predicted that one day in Nashville, nearly all the record companies would have independent producers. In-house producers would become a thing of the past." This was a far seeing prediction that indeed came to pass.

Howard recorded a number with George "Goober" Lindsey for Columbia. It was Howard's first talking record, which saw him playing "straight man" to Goober, for "The World's Biggest Whopper." Goober was a hot item then, a star of *Hee Haw*, the long-running TV variety series, co-hosted by Roy Clark and Buck Owens. Howard had one problem, the lyrics talked about Lake Lanier. Howard mistakenly kept saying "Lake Nanier." (Try it, it's hard to say Lake Lanier.) Hubert paid Howard's way into the first Music City Pro Celebrity Golf Tournament, which led the way into many golf tournaments. He also met Charley Pride there. Howard learned a lot that year, notably what a good song was and what song to pitch to whom. Moss Rose proved a good training ground for Howard: "Folks, it ain't as easy as it seems."

Howard garnered a lot of attention, with his position at Moss Rose. Long had an assistant, Audie Ashworth, and without Howard being aware, Audie became jealous of him. When Howard got Chuck Rogers' song, "Louisville" cut by Leroy Van Dyke, Audie and the secretary, Shirley Welch, who were in cahoots with each other, saw to it that Hubert fired Howard. Meanwhile, Chuck called and asked, "Howard, what have they done to us?"

In 1968, Howard was hired by Hal Smith at Pamper Music, to be their production coordinator. Pamper was originally owned by Ray Price and Claude Caviness from California. Then Hal Smith bought the Caviness share in 1959. In the early 1960's, Ray Price sold his fifty-percent share to Hank Cochran. When Willie Nelson became entrenched at Pamper, he bought half of Hank's share, so when Howard was hired at Pamper, Hal, Hank and Willie were owners. It became a great company, located out of Music Row, in the suburb of Goodlettsville on Two-Mile Pike. They had a small frame house with a smaller house behind converted into a studio. Pamper music got hot real fast, Howard said it was due to Hank Cochran. Not only did he write great songs, he was the greatest song-plugger ever. He went to artists' homes and wined and dined them. He could walk into any producer's office and he attracted great writers like Willie Nelson, Dave Kirby, Glenn Martin, Chuck Howard, Don Rollins, Ray Pennington and Carl Knight. When Howard went to Pamper, he took a new, young writer, Neal Davenport, with him. Hal Smith also owned the Hal Smith

Artist Agency, which booked such stars as Ernest Tubb, Jack Greene, and Cal Smith. He also formed a record label, Boone Records, which signed Kenny Price, Linda Flanagan and a few others.

Hal had quite a little empire under his wing. Writers always pitched their own songs, which was a problem. Everybody's songs needed pitching. Ray Pennington had the job before Howard, but they need non-writers in that position, so no favorites were picked. Willie told Howard one day that Howard had got more songs cut for him than anybody. Howard said, "Willie gave me more credit that I deserved. How could you miss with a Willie Nelson song!" A&R men would call and ask Howard, "What do you have new by Hank or Willie?" Artists called also. For instance, Don Gibson called Howard wanting "Half A Man" by Willie.

Howard loved working with the writers. One day, Dave Kirby and Glenn Martin brought him a song they were writing called "Is anybody Going To San Antone." They had written it this way, *"Is anybody going to San Antone or Fargo, North Dakota/ Any place is all right as long as I forget I ever knowed her."* Howard said, "Boys, you can't say *'ever knowed her.'* You need to think of another city besides Fargo, North Dakota, to rhyme with, because 'knowed her' is such bad English." So they went back to the drawing board and came up with: *"Is anybody going to San Antone or Phoenix, Arizona/Any place is all right as long as I forget I've ever known her . . . "* The rest is history It was a big hit for Charley Pride. Howard had pitched it to Walter Haynes, then at Kapp records, for a football player with the New York Jets, who wanted to be a country singer. When Charley covered his record, Walter never did forgive Howard, even though it was Dave Kirby who pitched the song to Charley, not Howard.

Another time a young writer, Arnold Rogers, thought he had a good song for Eddy Arnold. Howard looked at it and noted the title, something like "I'm Glad You Didn't Happen To Me," but suggested a change, as Eddy didn't like negative numbers. They reworked it into the more positive "I'm Glad She Happened To Me" and sure enough, Eddy recorded it.

One thing you learn real quick, however, is that you cannot out-guess an artist. Connie Francis came to town to record, so Howard got his tapes together and went to her hotel room to play songs for her. Buzz Cason and Bobby Russell met him at the door, saying, "Come in and put your head on the chopping block." Hank Cochran was there, relaxing on the bed. Connie didn't like what Howard played for her, but she saw a song in the tape box, "The Welfare Check." She said, "I want to hear that one." Howard said, "Connie, it isn't for you." She insisted on hearing it, and she recorded it and MGM released it as her A side single. It didn't hit, but we sure had a lot of fun with it. When the DJ Convention time came around, Howard had checks printed up that read "The Welfare Check" on them. MGM had a luncheon and Connie's father, George Franconero, and Howard stood outside the Municipal Auditorium, handing out "Welfare Checks" to the DJs and tourists. They attracted a long line of people and got in the newspapers.

That night Howard and I, Connie and her father, all went out to dinner and gave out more checks to the patrons.

Song plugging was fun for Howard and he had great songs, great writers and great producers who would listen. He could just walk in unannounced to see producers like Chet Atkins, Billy Sherrill and Frank Jones or Bob Ferguson. Still, it was always a challenge, for you never knew what they would like. One time he went to see Ron Chancey at ABC, taking in a new demo session by Willie Nelson, and Ron said, "Howard, that's just too pop." Howard said, "Just a minute," went to the car and brought him in another tape. After Ron listened, he said, "Howard, that's just too country." Howard was never discouraged, and later, Ron cut a song from our Locomotive Music Company, on Billy "Crash" Craddock, "Sounds of Music," written by Neal Davenport.

The thinking is that you never get a good song in off the streets, but Howard listened to everything. One time a laborer with a broken leg, had just gotten off his job, and went to Pamper with a song. The girls out in front were scared of him, so they took him back to see Howard. He told Howard his name was Don Stock and said, "I have a hit, if you've got time to listen." Howard always took time to listen and after playing Stock's tape, knew it was a hit idea, but the song wasn't finished just right. Dave Kirby was in the office that day, and Howard got Dave and Stock together, polishing off a humorous take on a wife who abandons her hubby, taking everything, and leaving him homeless. They worked on the song and the finished product was "Her And the Car And the Mobile Home." Howard took it to Porter Wagoner, and he and Dolly Parton cut it and the novelty number appears on their RCA 1972 duet album "The Right Combination: Burning the Midnight Oil."

You can listen to some very bad songs from songwriters, who think they can write. One day a guy walked into Pamper with a song called "Cordell Hull." Hull had been a big politician from Tennessee, who served as FDR's secretary of state. Howard listened and it started off, *"Cor-dell, Cordell Hull, king of Tennessee . . ."* Howard knew immediately it was the same tune as *"Da-vy, Davy Crockett, King of the Wild Frontier."* He said, "You can't do this, it's the same tune as 'Davy Crockett.'" The guy was hurt. "But, but, but this song's about Cordell Hull." How does one explain! You can't steal a tune.

They all worked together at Pamper and got a lot done. Hank Cochran was a gifted writer and a fantastic song-plugger. He would actually live with an artist coming up to record, until they agreed to cut his song. If anyone else came in to pitch a song, while Hank was there, he began talking right in the middle of the song to get attention away from it. It may have been an underhanded trick, but it worked in Hank's favor. He was also good at spotting other potential writers. When he found Willie Nelson, he went to Hal Smith and asked him to take Willie on. Hal said, "I'm paying you an advance of a hundred dollars a month. (Hal also gave him a beat-up old car.) I was going to give you an extra fifty dollars, so I can't afford another advance." Hank said, "OK, give that fifty to Willie instead of to me." And that's how Willie Nelson came to Pamper!

Howard did not have a hint that Hal was about to sell Pamper, until one afternoon on Music Row, he ran into Red O'Donnell, a newspaper reporter. Red said, "What do you think of them selling your company, Howard?" In this manner, he found out that Pamper's catalog had been sold to Tree International, owned by Jack Stapp and Buddy Killen. Howard quickly drove out to Goodlettsville and found out that what Red had said was true. Hal, however, had negotiated a song-plugger's job for Howard at Tree in the contract.

Buddy Killen explained that their attorney, Lee Eastman, had called Jack Stapp and asked if they would like to buy Pamper. Eastman said that Hal wanted it done quietly and carefully." Buddy said, "Jack passed in the hall and said, 'Hey, what do you think about buying Pamper?' I said, 'Let's do it.'" It's common knowledge that Tree paid some two million dollars for the songs, though they didn't buy the Pamper name. Buying Pamper doubled the size of Tree and they got great writers in the deal. Howard said, "Hal had become interested in Renfro Valley, a resort and show area in Kentucky. Maybe he just wanted to do something different, so he sold Pamper to Tree." Then Hal and Hank bought Renfro.

We were all saddened when Hank Cochran died on July 15, 2010. The man who said, "Make it short, make it sweet, make it rhyme," was inducted into the Country Music Hall Of Fame in 2014. He may have been the greatest writer of his generation.

The Pamper writers were absorbed by Tree as was Howard. Howard only stayed for a short while, but was astonished at Tree's operation. For instance, they had no filing system for tapes. They were merely stacked in piles everywhere. The lyrics were in the same situation. If you needed a lyric, you had to look through stacks of them. The first thing he did was to adapt the Pamper system. It became all too apparent that they had hired him to learn the Pamper catalog, and Tree's song-pluggers did not want Howard there. Buddy Killen held a meeting every Monday morning in which he castigated them all for not getting enough songs cut. Howard confided, "The world was spinning too fast around me, and I felt like it was going to let me off with no place to go."

That was when Howard ran into an old friend, Bill Beazley, who had started a new label, Spar. He asked Howard to open two new publishing companies for him and to produce new writer/singers for Spar. Howard gave Tree his twenty-four hour notice and went to work for Bill. Bill was an old hand in the business, having originally been an owner of Tennessee Records, where Del Wood had her million-seller "Down Yonder." Ted Jarrett, who had been with Bill in those days, was still with him in promotion, so Howard guessed they must know something. I went with Howard to help set up their publishing. Howard signed Carl Knight, who had been a writer at Pamper, and Clayton Ford (alias Paul Gene Martin). They were both singer/writers.

Then Howard signed Neal Davenport as a writer. He also added to Spar the artists Linda Flanagan, who had been on Boone, and Carl Phillips, a new artist. Those were fun days, DJ Convention time arrived and Spar had the best hospitality suite at the convention, beating all the "big boys." There was plenty of free-running booze. Everyone came to the Spar suite that Fall of 1969, including Charley Pride, Billy Thunderkloud & The Chieftones, and the Canadian Sweethearts Bob Regan and Lucille Starr. Bob kept trying to call Japan from the phone and the hotel operator kept saying she couldn't reach Japan. Pride was overheard telling Billy Thunderkloud, "You ain't no Indian, you're a N----- just like me."

Clayton had his first release out, "What Money Can't Buy." He, Howard and Carl Knight wrote it. *Record World* reviewed it, saying, "A tribute to things that are free. Will make much coin." Carl's record, "Used Wife Business" had also been released. Howard produced both records. They spent the night making sure these records played over and over on the jukebox. During his time at Spar, Howard continued to produce independent sessions, which he placed on Spar. His production of Carl Phillips' "Vine Covered House" had some success. Howard also produced "Sugar Creek Bottom" on Joe Pain, written by Carmol Taylor, unknown to Howard at that time. Later, Carmol became a dear friend, a prolific writer for Gallico Music, a great drinking partner and my boss.

We were all enjoying this so much that it didn't occur to us that Beazley's main focus was not building publishing and recording, but was on another of his side lines, "sound alike" tapes and their distribution. With no warning, he cut out our side of the business. All things must pass, but Beazley gave all of the songs Howard had contracted to him that had not been recorded. So all these songs were assigned to our Locomotive Music, which really put us in business.

Well, you never know who you will work for next in this business. Joe Allison, who headed what was then Dot-Paramount Records in Nashville, called to offer Howard a position as Nashville manager of Famous Music. Both companies were owned by Gulf-Western in New York. Howard went there and took Chuck Rogers from Moss Rose. He got a song cut for Chuck almost immediately, "In the Arms Of August" by Jim Ed Brown, on RCA. The New York office sent down songs regularly, but mostly what they called country in New York was far from country. However, they did send "Me And You And A dog Named Boo" that Lobo had a big pop hit on. Howard listened and immediately went to see Frank Jones at CBS. He thought it could be a hit for Stonewall Jackson. Frank listened, immediately called Stonewall in, and they set up a special session. Stone's "Boo" made the country chart in 1971, and in fact became Jackson's last Top Ten to date, but charted three weeks longer than Lobo's pop version. We had just bought a dog and Howard said, "If 'Boo' is a hit, we'll name her 'Boo' and if it doesn't hit, we'll name her 'Boo-Boo'." Thankfully, our dog remained "Boo."

New York also sent Howard "Love Story," the title song from the 1970 movie "Love Story." He got the first cut in Nashville on it by Chet Atkins, recorded as an instrumental on RCA. The music business was always fun and one night Joe Allison gave a party at his house and one of the strangest things happened there I had ever heard of, and Nashville had some weird parties. One of the guests was a girl who worked at Columbia Records, who read cards. Everybody there wanted her to give a reading, so finally she said she would read for one person there. She picked out the Accountant for the company. As she laid out the cards, she told him she had never seen anyone so interested in money, he was surrounded by money, he was not interested in women, only money. She also told him he would be leaving the company. Everybody laughed: he laughed hardest of all. A few weeks went by and this Accountant was fired for embezzling funds. His brother, working in Atlanta with the company, was also fired for embezzling.

Looking back, this seemed to set off bad luck. As usual, DJ convention time came up in October. In those days it was a wild time, and it was useless to try and do any business. It was the only convention I know of where everybody congregated just to imbibe as much liquor as they could. All the record labels put on showcases in the Municipal auditorium for the conventioneers, showing off their talent. They also had breakfasts, lunches, and dinners. Dot- Paramount was no different. All their talent was in town to be on the show. Howard's special friends, Lucille and Bob Regan, were in town, to record for Dot and attend the convention. We all attended the Dot-Paramount Breakfast, and the show afterwards. Joe Allison had written the script for the show and emceed it, for he was good at that type of thing. However, Joe got drunk, and instead of sticking to the script, cussed out all the Dot-Paramount dignitaries down from New York. When they got back to New York, they immediately fired Joe, and sent Jim Foglesong to Nashville to run the label and publishing.

Jim was different from the Music City crowd, cold and haughty, seeming like a typical New Yorker. New York told Howard that Jim was not the talented producer that Joe was, so Howard surmised they needed a good "pencil pusher." Jim's claim to fame was that he had sung with the Fred Waring Singers, which was kind of a joke among his peers. It wasn't long before Jim replaced Howard and the whole office with his own regime. That's the way it works in show business. As time went on, Jim became noted for his goodwill and politeness. Years later, Jim was working for Capitol Records and they fired him. Howard used that moment for retaliation. At Christmas, he sent Jim a Christmas card and wrote on it, "I got mine and now you got yours. Love, Howard White." We used to see Jim at parties after that, and he was most courteous.

Howard learned, too, that the world of business was not unlike that of a musician's, very unstable. That was when we decided to begin publishing, in earnest, on our own. We activated Locomotive Music and brought in Neal Davenport to write. Howard began getting cuts: Neal's "Beaver Creek" and "Ain't Life Easy" were recorded by George Hamilton, IV, best known for the number one "Abilene." Additionally, "Eve's Garden" was cut by Eddy Arnold, and "Wanted Man" by Jerry Wallace, both songs written by Neal. The latter song made Top Forty in 1975.

One day, Howard remembered the song "What Money Can't Buy" by Clayton Ford and Carl Knight, which was still with Spar, as it had been cut by Clayton. Howard thought maybe he could get it back since so much time had elapsed. He made a trip to Jack Johnson's office to pitch the song for Charley Pride who Jack was managing at that time. While there, Howard struck up a conversation with Jack's secretary. He told her that if she could get that song to Pride, he would give her a hundred dollars. Pride was living in Texas at that time. Somehow she got it to him, Charley loved it and Howard paid the secretary the hundred dollars. Then Howard hustled over to Bill Beazley, and asked him if he would assign the song back to him. Bill said he would, provided Tommy Downs, the engineer at Spar, would give his okay. Tommy, who thought he smelled a cut, said he would give it back to Howard if Howard, in turn, would assign fifty per cent back to his Doney Music. Well, what can you say? He held us up, but then as now, the theme song in Music City is, "Fifty per cent of something is better than a hundred per cent of nothing." So, Bill assigned one hundred per cent to Locomotive, and we allowed fifty per cent back to Doney.

Charley cut the song at RCA, but it didn't come off the way producer Jack Clement wanted it, since they were aiming for a single; however, they called two more sessions for that one song, but each time it got worse. It started on a high note and Charley just couldn't reach it. Finally, it was released in a 1971 album. Nonetheless, that album - "Charley Pride Sings Heart Songs" - became album of the year, charting number one sixteen weeks, which didn't hurt sales a bit. Howard got other cuts on the song, including a duet cut by Mel Tillis and Sherry Bryce.

One day, an old friend, steel player turned businessman, Don Davis called Howard and asked him to come by his office. Don was in business with Harlan Howard at Wilderness Music. They wanted Howard's catalog, so they struck a deal. They bought the two hundred songs in Locomotive's catalog, not the name, and in addition gave Howard a job, as Don's assistant. Everybody loved Harlan. Frances Preston, at BMI, wrote Howard a note that read, "Great, Great!" Harlan Howard was a fine writer, who had once written for Pamper Music. Among his hundreds of standards are "Heartaches By the Number" and "Pick Me Up On Your Way Down." Harlan's songs have been recorded over and over.

Howard continued doing "his thing" at Wilderness, but almost unnoticed, the music publishing business was changing, even back in 1972. Some years before, a few people like Billy Sherrill at Epic began to see there was money in publishing. Record sales might amount to nothing, but because of radio play, the BMI or ASCAP monies earned on a song might amount to a lot of income. If you had publishing or writing, or maybe both, on a song cut by a big artist, you could make money, and screw the record sales. If the record sold it was icing on the cake. More and more producers began joining the ranks. And then the artists got in the game. It got harder and harder to get a good song cut. You better have the greatest song in the world, if you wanted to get it recorded. A few songs were being cut from Wilderness, but not nearly enough. Tree, who owned half of Wilderness, put the pencil to it and cut backs began. Everyone knew that Billy Sherrill and Al Gallico were in business together with Algee Music and even artists like Tammy Wynette had a publishing deal with Gallico. Buddy Killen was seen giving checks to Sherrill. Payola in all forms ran rampant.

About this time, Howard went to a Chet Atkins Golf Tournament in Port St. Lucie, Florida. Howard always claimed he got more songs cut playing golf than any other way. While he was on the way back, I got word that his father had died in North Carolina. When he got to Atlanta, he called me and I asked Howard if Bob Jennings was with him. When he said yes, I told him the news regarding his father. I was surprised when Howard said, "Yes, I know, I saw him in the clouds when I was playing golf yesterday." I immediately called Wilderness and told their secretary, Shirley Welch, what had happened and that we would have to go to North Carolina as soon as Howard got back. Shirley said, "Well, they will fire him when he gets back if he goes." Shirley was the same secretary at Moss Rose, who was responsible for getting Howard fired there. We had to go, but when we got back, sure enough Don fired Howard.

Howard had then been in the publishing business ten years. New people were arriving in Nashville every day, hoping to get into the business in some way. He noticed that they were younger than he was, a natural evolution. Howard talked to Hal Smith about opening Pamper again. It had been over five years since Hal had sold to Tree, the required waiting period by contract. But by now new games were being played by the producers, writers, artists and record companies, all of whom wanted a portion of the publishing to cut a song. They even sometimes asked for part of the writing, as they knew they carried all the aces. Neither Hal nor Howard were used to this. Hal still would not give up any portion of a song to such blackmail tactics.

Neal Davenport was still with Howard, and wrote a good song, "Pure Plain Sweet And Simple Love." Howard went to Ronnie Milsap's office to pitch it, and they liked the song. Turned out, however, they wanted seventy-five per cent of the publishing and twenty-five per cent of the writing. Howard and I talked it over. I called Neal and said that the publisher would give up the percentage of the publishing, if he wanted to give up part of his writing. Howard would never give up writing, that was the composer's heart. Neal said, "No, not even for a Milsap cut." So that was that!

Another happening at Milsap's office occurred when Howard stopped by to see Tommy Kerkeles who worked there and was a golf buddy of his. They had a locked outside door and a call button. Howard pressed the button on the intercom and the conversation went like this:

Question: Who is it?

Answer: Howard White

Question: Who are you with?

Answer: I'm by myself.

Question: (after a pause) Whom would you like to see?

Answer: Elizabeth Taylor, but I don't suppose she's there.

They let him in, proving that a sense of humor usually wins entrance. Another time I went up to see Kerkeles about some business for Porter Wagoner. I noticed on the corner of Kerkeles piled up desk was a little brass bowl with some white powder in it. I thought, "Oh, oh, cocaine!" Well, we finished our business, never mentioning the stuff in the little brass bowl. Then Kerkeles said, "Oh, my goodness, the maid left her cleaning powder in here." He didn't have to say anything. I still believe that was the first time I ever saw cocaine anywhere on Music Row.

In about 1976, Hal and Howard agreed to call it quits. Suddenly, Los Angeles and New York had come to town, always quick to get in on wherever money is being made. Nashville was flooded with artists, musicians, writers anything else you could name. Howard said, "I would have been happy to see Pamper catch on again, but it was not to be."

That was when Henry Strzelecki, a fantastic bass player and a golfing buddy emerged. He had somehow put together a record company and four publishing companies. He had a backer who put up a lot of money, and soon both Howard and I would work for him.

After the Strzelecki days, Howard and I worked for Colonel Dave Mathis for eight months. Only one exciting song-plugging story happened while there. Howard had pitched a song to RCA's Bob Ferguson, a producer for Jim Ed Brown and Helen Cornelius. Bob called me at the office and told me to find Howard immediately. Jim Ed and Helen were in the studio right then and they wanted to cut our song; however, they wanted to make some changes. I reached Howard at Mercury Records. Jim Ed and Helen were cutting two sessions that day. Helen wanted to re-write the chorus of the song, and cut it at the 2 p.m. session. That's exactly what happened. Howard got there, called Colonel Dave, and told him Helen wanted to change the chorus and wanted fifty per cent of the writing.

Wasn't that typical? Dave called the writer in Kentucky and said, "How would you like to have Helen Cornelius as a co-writer?" That's exactly how the deal went down. Helen got fifty per cent of the writing and it was released as a B side. Dave's company went broke and they sold all their office furniture to Carmol Taylor and Norro Wilson. Then I went to work for Carmol and Norro.

Much, much later, after Howard retired, a strange thing happened regarding "What Money Can't Buy," the song that Charley Pride cut. A call came in from a lawyer in Chicago. He said that the owners of Doney Music had died and that company was in limbo. He said, "There is only one song in the company that is earning money and it's the song, "What Money Can't Buy," if you want to buy Doney Music, we will sell it to you for one hundred dollars." All this time, we had thought Doney Music belonged to Tommy Downs, but it didn't. It belonged to Helen U. and Henry E. Doney. Tommy Downs was only administering Doney Music in Nashville for the Doneys in Lake Forest, Illinois. Now Tommy was dead and we realized he had deceived us. We jumped at the chance to buy the fifty per cent that the

Doney's owned. Since we originally had owned fifty per cent and had sold it in the transaction with Wilderness Music, we didn't have any part of the song. Now, suddenly, by a twist of fate, we had fifty per cent of that song again. We made the deal with Bryson Burnham, executor of the Doney estate, starting a new publishing company with it: Howard White Music. We were never sorry.

Back when Nashville was still called "The Athens Of the South," before David Cobb at WSM had called Nashville "Music City USA," the music scene was vastly different. Many hit artists, such as Ernest Tubb, Hank Snow and Webb Pierce, were not great singers, but they were stylists. If they only knew three or four chords on their guitars, it was said, "They didn't play enough to hurt their singing." When they counted their money, no doubt, they laughed all the way to the bank. Their secret weapon was that they treated their fans as friends and neighbors.

As country music became less and less country and developed more and more into pop and country rock, Nashville lost that traditional image. As the Opry lost their power as country music trendsetters, the "big boys" waltzed in and took control. What do the older fans say now? "We don't hear country music on the radio anymore." They are right. The stations are not playing traditional country music much anymore. It's hard to tell, when scanning down a radio dial, just what kind of a radio station you've found. The record companies' new blood insist that they offer exciting, youthful talent to a new breed of country listeners. The old style listener is called the "middle age market." Where does that leave the traditional country writer and publisher? If the publisher wants to survive, he has to find writers that are aimed at the new sound.

Maybe, without realizing it, we've brought this on ourselves with all the new technology. In the "old days," music was recorded directly to disc. When tape was developed, it was a decided improvement. Then we went from two-track to eight-track, to sixteen-track, to twenty-four-track and beyond. It meant that we could over-dub, "punch in," or "stack" anything in order to go from one note to a multitude of sounds. The rock people started it first, but Nashville wasn't far behind. Sound became more important than the singer. Then they developed a little machine that could move the singer's voice up or down. It didn't matter if he or she sang flat or sharp, that little machine could "fix it." Mort Thomasson, an early engineer, and one of the greats, said, "The worst thing we ever did was go to eight-track."

Recording was primitive in Nashville's early days. RCA brought their own engineers and equipment down from New York, at first. Then Aaron Shelton, George Reynolds and Carl Jenkins, engineers at WSM, got permission from the station to use a studio, when idle, to operate a recording business. They called it Castle Studios (as WSM's logo was "Air Castle Of the South"). Don Davis described recording there, "Then there was no room for the lathes at WSM, so they installed them on 15th Avenue, WSM's old broadcast house. The signal had to travel through phone lines to the transmitter, before recording it to the belt-driven master cutting lathe that etched a mono track onto an acetate disc. The engineers placed a phone call to 15th Avenue and said, 'We're rolling. Are you ready out there?' Then they would hear, 'Yeah, we're rolling.' The light would come on and we'd record direct-to-disc."

After a time, WSM told the engineers they would have to take Castle somewhere else, so they made a studio out of an old ballroom, at the Tulane Hotel on Church Street, a block down the hill from WSM. Millie Kirkham, who had her high soprano recorded more than any other singer in Nashville, remembered the Castle Studios at the Tulane: "I remember working there a lot with Dottie Dillard, as background singers. They called us the Tulane Sisters. I also remember working for Paul Cohen for Decca. We recorded in a house on 16th Avenue South. They created an echo chamber out of the stairwell."

In 1945, Mort Thomasson installed recording equipment for the Brown Brothers, Bill and Charley, who opened Brown Radio Productions at 4th Avenue South and Union Streets. In 1953, the Browns left town and Mort and Cliff Thomas set up Thomas Productions in a "garage." That building is gone today, lost to Interstate 65. Porter Wagoner made his debut in Nashville there. He said, "When a truck went by outside, you had to stop recording because that sound was heard on the tape."

From these primitive beginnings, the Nashville Sound developed. Of course, now we have the finest state of the art sound studios and equipment. No matter how many great singers, producers or musicians there are, first there must be a great song. Wesley Rose once said, "No matter what, the song's the thing." Chet Atkins noted, "The world is full of singers, but the only ones that are successful are those who have a great supply of great songs to sing."

Regardless of what Rose and Atkins once said, it is now sad, but true, a great song is only as good as the record label it's on and the singer who sings it. The record labels have independent promoters, free-lance record pluggers, who have an uncanny knack for getting radio stations to play certain records. These promoters work for any company who can afford to hire them. Some are so good that a record company sometimes keeps them on retainer.

In the 1950's and '60's, country music was easy to promote. It became very hot, selling millions of records. Then, there was always a place to get your record played. Now it's almost impossible. The texts on promotion have all been rewritten. The whole truth boils down to it takes big money these days to promote a record. Radio listeners don't make the hits. The labels that "spend their money in the right places" do. Record promotion is no different than advertising any other product. After all, it would be ridiculous for the record company to play a record on a street corner in hopes a passerby might go out and buy the record.

Sometimes it even seems that somebody out there is trying to prevent a hit record, rather than making it a hit. Once when I was working for

Sound Factory Records, owned by Phil Baugh, we had a good country record by Sammi Smith going up the *Billboard* chart. Sammi previously had the mega-hit, "Help Me Make It Through the Night." Tom McBee was in charge of promotion and her record was in the number twelve spot and *Billboard* had scheduled the record to go into the Top Ten the next week. But when *Billboard* came out that week, Sammi was not in the Top Ten, she wasn't even in the Top Hundred. She had been completely dropped out of the charts, meaning no radio play. Somebody, somewhere had killed that record. It's one thing to take a record that's doing well and just take it off the air. Despite the fact that *Billboard* had it high in the charts and radio was playing it, it was actually pulled off the air and out of the charts.

Was there – and is there – payola in the music business? Payola is a contraction of "pay" and "Victrola." It supposedly went away in 1958, when Alan Freed went down for taking bribes to play records on his *The Moondog Show* when on WINS in New York. But, payola did not go away. A promo man in Nashville laughed and said, "It all began with country hams and whiskey, progressed to motel rooms and women, and then topped out with lots of money and dope."

By the 1980's, it was said that the record industry may have been paying out forty million dollars to indie promo men to pay the DJs to play music. After 1960, Congress passed a statute making payola a misdemeanor offense, punishable by a maximum fine of ten thousand dollars and one year in prison. No one has ever served a day on payola charges. In the 1950's, the DJs had been easy to bribe, but then the promoters turned to the Program Directors. This meant they needed to pay off only one person rather than all the DJs at a station.

In the old days, the stations were owned independently. That made it easier to get radio play. In today's market we have "institutional payola," that is, the stations are owned by conglomerates, notably Clear Channel Communications, Cumulus Media and Citadel Broadcasting. This makes it easier for the promo people. All they have to do is call a conglomerate, which then calls their stations to tell the DJs what to play. Clear Channel owns one thousand and five radio stations as of this writing. These stations are being paid to play the same fifteen songs over and over, sometimes not even identifying the artist.

Ahmet Ertegün, head of Atlantic Records for forty-seven years, said, "To get a hit record, it takes hard work, an understanding of music and songs, how the song will work with public tastes – and then there's LUCK."

Of course, luck is involved, but hits don't just happen. Joe South wrote a song he simply called "Rose Garden" and recorded it on Introspect Records. Then Lynn Anderson recorded it and Columbia released it as "(I Never Promised You A) Rose Garden" in 1970. At that time, Lynn was singing on *The Lawrence Welk Show*. Paul Gallis, an independent promoter from Chicago, then promoting for Columbia, heard her record. He told a DJ, Jack Lee, about it. Lee worked for WTMJ, a powerhouse station in Milwaukee. Lee knew nothing about the record and had not been serviced by Columbia.

Gallis called Columbia telling them the stations he was promoting had not been serviced. Columbia said they would take care of it, but didn't. Gallis said, "Columbia blew it, even though I knew it was a hit the moment I heard it." So he called Al Gallico, one of the biggest music publishers in the business, whom he also worked with. Gallis told Gallico, "Columbia Records has a hit in Anderson's 'Rose Garden' and they don't even know it." Gallico, in his wisdom, said, "Call Bill Lowery of Lowery Music in Atlanta. Lowery owns the publishing. Tell him I told you to call him." When Gallis called Bill, he said, "If you can help me, you're hired."

Paul Gallis took the record and ran with it, looking for pop play. When he took it to WLS-Chicago, they played it continuously. Columbia had a roster of major artists, but when WLS broke the record, nothing could stop it. It not only became a great country record, it became the biggest pop record at that time. Without a great promo man, Columbia would not have had the great success that "Rose Garden" became. It sold a million or more discs, made number one country, number three pop, and earned a Grammy Award, as well. Sometimes, as Lowery Music and Gallico Music did, the publishers also spend money on promotion in order to get their song heard. It's all a round robin, from singer and writer, to publishing company, to record company, to promo men to radio.

Gallico's Carmol Taylor co-wrote "Red Wine And Blue Memories," with Billy and Mark Sherrill, and Joe Stampley recorded it, peaking *Billboard* at number six in 1978. Then one day Boudleaux Bryant, then a writer with Acuff-Rose, called Linda at Gallico and asked if she would send him a copy of "Red Wine . . ." She said she would, but asked him why he wanted it? He said, "We think it got a little too close to our song 'We Could.'" The melodies were similar. When Linda told Carmol, he said, "My, God, we were trying to stay off 'Green, Green Grass Of Home' . . ." Gallico was sued and he went to court with a musicologist, who proved that all three songs had their melodies taken from a Public Domain (P.D.) song. Al Gallico bewailed, "I never made any money out of that song after paying the court, the lawyer and the musicologist."

Lawsuits happen sometimes, particularly if the song is a hit. Once Howard asked Hank Cochran if he had a hit lately? Hank replied, "I don't know. I haven't been sued lately." Paul Simon once said on *The Tonight Show*, "If you borrow from one source, they call you a plagiarist, but if you borrow from three sources, they call you prolific." Neither Carmol nor Sherrill would consciously steal from another writer, but there are only eight notes in a scale, and most country songs back then had only three chords and a seventh, so melodies sometimes crossed over.

Another publishing story that I became involved in was the time I went to work for Reed Music, Inc. Ben and Reba Reed were in the glass business and a bus leasing business in Florida. They wanted to start a recording, publishing and booking business and had a girl singer to record, Melissa Kay. We put out a record on her, which Norro Wilson produced, but eventually Bob Bean, the booker, could not seem to get her booked.

We decided she was too old, not pretty and couldn't sing. According to the Reeds, God spoke to them and told them to help her. The Reeds also wanted to begin publishing. I told them we couldn't start a company with writers off the street. The best way to get started was to buy a promising company with credits. They agreed.

Then one day, a small company in Kentucky, Muhlenburg Music, called me saying they wanted to sell their company. They came down to see me. I asked them what they had in their company. Among others, they had four songs in their company that a newcomer, Garth Brooks, had cut and were "in the can." (Recorded, but not released.) It so happened I had just been showed a preview of the Brooks' new video, "If Tomorrow Never Comes," by the video company, and it had knocked me out. They said they wanted one hundred and twenty-five thousand dollars for their company. I called the Reeds in Florida and said "You need to buy this company, if you don't have the money, borrow it, Garth Brooks will be the next artist to hit." Reba Reed said, very sarcastically, "You really think so?" She called back and her Florida CPA said it wasn't feasible. One of the songs that was released on Garth Brooks from that little publishing company was "Two Of A Kind Workin' On A Full House," which hit number one. The Kentucky people decided to hold on, when we didn't buy it and the first year they made more than double the one hundred and twenty-five thousand dollars they had asked.

Right after that, Zoe Tapscott brought us an Alan Jackson tape for our record label. Zoe was then Alan's manager and literally Alan was unknown. I presented the tape to the Reeds and they also turned that down. They said they didn't hear anything they liked. Lucky Alan Jackson that the Reeds turned him down! He went on to Arista Records and became an instant superstar.

Success stories have been told, I imagine, since Pop Stoneman first sang his "event song" recorded in January 1925, "The Sinking Of The Titanic" on OKeh Records. Hank Snow dominated the charts in 1950, with his hit "I'm Movin' On." As the years have gone by, stories about how instant "overnight" successes were attained have made interesting conversation. We tell about how "Lucille" recorded by Kenny Rogers hit, only after reportedly being turned down by every other artist in town. There was even a story about how Hal Bynum, the writer, jumped on the desk of a producer's secretary and threatened to remove his clothes if she didn't let him in to see the producer. "For the Good Times," written by Kris Kristofferson and recorded by Ray Price, sat in Buckhorn Music's catalog for five years before it was "discovered." Success stories never stop. It's the hope a writer pins his hopes on.

The latest success story I know about (2014) concerns a Johnny Cash album that was recorded for Columbia Records between 1981 and 1984. Cash had been dead a decade, but his son, John Carter Cash, resurrected the Master. When Columbia dropped Cash from the label, they never released all the songs he recorded. Gary Gentry wrote a song for an album,

"I Drove Her Out Of My Mind," and Billy Sherrill produced it. Gary, who had hits like "The Ride" by David Allen Coe, "The Corvette Song" by George Jones, and "1959" by John Anderson, had despaired of ever having the release by Cash. Gary remembers the day his song was cut, April 12, 1984. He was there in the studio and Sherrill asked him to change the last line of the song, which he did. Now, thirty years later, the album, "Out Among the Stars" has just been released, with Gary's song in it, and he's praying for a single. It seems impossible but it looks like we haven't heard the last form Johnny Cash – or Gary Gentry.

By the time all this happened, I was sixty-two years old and ready to retire. I was tired of the innocents in charge, who didn't know right from left. I retired from Music Row and kept right on doing administration for a lot of independent companies. In 1990, I wrote my first book, "Every Highway Out Of Nashville."

A good song stirs the heart. A great song is characterized by the millions of just plain folks, who associate with that particular song, in one way or another. Songs mean different things to different people. In his song "Little Things," Willie Nelson sang about his ex-wife, their son Billy, Sam and Peg who lived next door, and the Freeway that had taken over his part of town. We identify these little things with our own individual walk through life. A lot of people have exes and Billy becomes our child, Sam and Peg could be any neighbor we loved and we all know of roads that have displaced people. We associate! That's why a simple song like Willie's becomes a hit. Those are the songs that make us think of happy or sad times.

Norro Wilson, former producer at Warner Brothers and RCA, told me that the days of "street fighting" (song-plugging) were over. Getting a song cut today is mostly playing the right politics, and writing with the "right" person. It's this monster we've created, right here in Music City, that we have handed over to the younger writers and publishing business as their inheritance. Howard said, "I liked the publishing business as it was. It isn't fun anymore." Things were vastly different when Fred Rose and Roy Acuff started the publishing boom in Nashville. But that was then and this is now. Time marches on and waits for no one. They said it then and they still say: *"Well, my boy, it's not a bad little song, I can change a word or two here and there, Which will make me a co-writer, Put it into my publishing company, And I'll cut it."*

FROM RUTH WHITE'S SCRAPBOOK . . .

White brothers
(from left) in 1937:
Howard, Billy
and Jimmy.

Piano prodigy Ruth Bland (White), age six.

Howard's idol Jerry Byrd

Sailor man Howard in 1944

Howard's first professional band (from left) Speck Morris,
Herman Porter, Howard, Hoyle Henley and Dan Gibson.

Howard, the man of steel.

Pioneer 'Daddy' John Love.

Howard's first record, with The Golden Valley Boys, (from left) Harvey Rayborn,
E.C. Beatty, Shannon Grayson, Howard and Millard Pressley in 1948.

121

In 1951 Knoxville, The Don Gibson Band featuring (from left) Sed Addis, Blackie Lunsford, Don, Billy Kirby and Howard.

Legendary songwriter Arthur Q. Smith, Red Kirk and Howard at WNOX-Knoxville in 1951.

Mom Upchurch (standing), Junie Dunn (left) and unknown friend, '53.

Howard at Mom's with Joel Price, in the early 1950s.

Howard and Strollin' Tom Pritchard.

Louise (Mom) and John Hackler, bar owners

Howard with Mother Maybelle and daughters Helen, Anita and June Carter in 1951.

Howard (left) with 1953 Cowboy Copas troupe in Indianapolis, featuring Merle (Red) Taylor, Cowboy, Ray Edenton, Kathy Copas and (hidden) Hardy Day on bass fiddle, in the Lyric Theatre.

Howard (left) with Clinch Mountain Clan in 1960, including Jimmy Elrod, Stoney Cooper, George McCormick, Wilma Lee and Joe (Flapjack) Phillips performing on the Grand Ole Opry.

Howard plays first Sho-Bud guitar.

The Davis Sisters, Georgie and Skeeter,
with White in mid-1950s.

Moon Mullican

Grandpa Jones

Howard (from left) with music
buddies Ken 'Loosh' Marvin,
Buddy Spicher and James
'Goober' Buchanan, during their
'historic' 1958 Hank, Jr. tour
with 'Miss Audrey.'

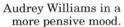

Audrey Williams in a
more pensive mood.

Buddy Emmons (right)
with his buddy Howard.

The Light brothers, Larry and Ronny, in their Knoxville days.

The boys in the band backing Wilma Lee & Stoney Cooper,
having their own 'Big Midnight Special.'

Don Slayman, a Morgan music
man, also known as 'Suds.'

George Morgan in his chart-topping
'Candy Kisses' heyday (1949).

Pamper Music, house of hits, located on Two-Mile Pike in Goodlettsville, boasted
writers Harlan Howard, Hank Cochran, Ray Price, Willie Nelson.

Morgan in the era
Howard toured
with George's
colorful crew.

When Howard
White plays,
Luke Brandon
listens!

The 1957 Opry ball team at Sulpher Dell Park, Nashville, line up: (front) Cowboy Copas, Bill Williams, Jesse Saunders, George McCormick, Howard, Jackie Phelps, Teddy & Doyle Wilburn; (rear from left) Bob Moore, Hawkshaw Hawkins, Ferlin Husky, Jerry Byrd, Harold Bradley, Judd Collins, Ott Devine and Roy Acuff, manager.

All-star cast performing at Portland OR Memorial Coliseum in 1964, included (front row) Howard, a KRDR staffer, KRDR's Tom Cauthers, Ferlin Husky, KRDR manager Clair Murser, Steve Melnichvek and Ray Montee; (back row) Chubby Wise, Ralph Jernigan, unknown, Pearl Butler, George Jones, Hank Snow, Ed Hyde, Carl Smith, Webb Pierce, Carl Butler, Dave Dudley, Ernie Cutshall and Johnny Finman.

Canadian icon Wilf Carter (Montana Slim) with daughters Sheila and Carol on tour.

Hank Snow and Shawnee, smartest steed at Rainbow Ranch.

Hank's Rainbow
Ranch Boys (from left)
Howard, Chubby Wise
(front), Ed Hyde and
Ralph Jernigan.

The Jean Shepard-Hawkshaw Hawkins Show in late 1950s.

More than 30 years after their first tour, Jean presented
Howard with an autographed picture.

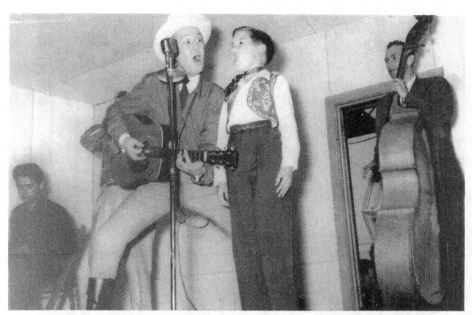

Red Foley sings with Larry Butler - who would grow up to produce the likes of Kenny Rogers - at a Florida show, backed by Howard and Tommy Warren.

The Opry's Lonzo & Oscar duo: Lloyd George a.k.a. 'Loosh' Marvin as Lonzo to Rollin Sullivan's Oscar.

Hollywood actor Leo Gorcey gets a music lesson from Howard in 1965,
on the set of their film 'Second Fiddle To a Steel Guitar.'

TV band (from left) Walter Haynes, Jerry Byrd, Ernie Newton, host Joe Allison,
Harold Bradley and Bobby Sykes in 1960s.

Howard on the Nashville movie set of 'Second Fiddle . . .' with Minnie Pearl and camera crew members in 1965.

Dolly Parton and Porter Wagoner sign RCA pact in 1967, as witnessed by label's Chet Atkins and Bob Ferguson.

Howard tackles Moss Rose Publishing paperwork in 1967.

George Franconero, Connie Francis' dad-manager (left), and Howard hand DJ Conventioneers fake 'Welfare Check' and single, during 1968 DJ Festival in Music City.

DJ Hall of Famer T. Tommy Cutrer chats with Johnny Cash.

October Records executive White signs Carl Knight to a
contract on the indie label in 1976.

King of Country Music Roy Acuff welcomes Kathleen White
backstage during December 1984 Opry show.

Hall of Famer Fred Rose's home studio on Rainbow Trail, where the legendary music man produced Howard in 1953, for his Hickory Records label.

Perky Donna Stoneman takes the mic during a late 1960s' Stoneman concert, featuring brother Van and their Hall of Famer dad Ernest (Pop) Stoneman, while brother Jimmy's hidden behind sis.

- Photo courtesy Joe Lee

Ruth and Howard greet Gabe Tucker at Nashville Union Hall.

Carmol Taylor during 1975 BMI awards gala with (from left) Al
Gallico, Norro Wilson, BMI chief Ed Cramer and Lillian Evans.

Ruth with Norro (standing) and
Carmol on Music Row.

Howard visits with Murray Nash at
1989 WNOX reunion.

Little Buddy (Jennison) chats it up with hero Willie Nelson.

George Jones shares some time with songwriter John Riggs.

Watch out when Buzz Cason, Howard and Joe Funderburk team up.

Henry Strzelecki and Howard
sport their latest cowboy duds.

Singer Hank Locklin, a
longtime Opry attraction.

BUDDY HARMAN

HENRY STRZELECKI

WILLIE RAINSFORD

TERRY McMILLAN

PHIL BAUGH

BUDDY EMMONS

BOB BEAN TALENT AGENCY

NASHVILLE SUPERPICKERS
38 MUSIC SQUARE EAST
SUITE 217
NASHVILLE, TENNESSEE 37203
(615) 242-0541

SPRINGFIELD PIKE, NEAR BAKERS

Overview of Springfield Pike near 1973 Akeman murder site.

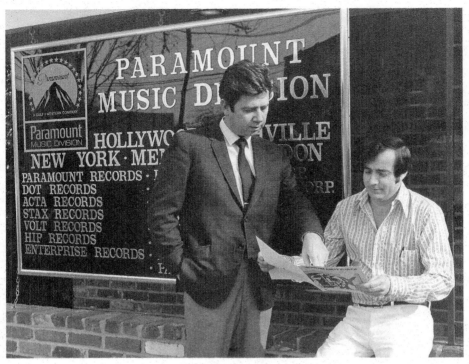

Howard and Paramount Music Division's Chuck Rogers check out
the latest dirt covering the Nashville music scene.

Competing in the tournament were (from left) J. L. Sullivan, plus an unknown
smiling face, and Howard, Smiley Wilson and Joe Allison.

Following a game of golf, we find (from left) Doug Hall, Eddy Arnold, Dianne and Henry Strzelecki with Howard White, relaxing.

There's time for a photo following a friendly get-together of music pals Ray Edenton (front), Don Slayman, Howard (behind him), and standing DeWitt Scott, Jerry Byrd, Lloyd Green and Joe Allison. – *Photo courtesy Billy Robinson*.

Howard, with Ruth, received 50-year Life Member pin from Nashville Union President Harold Bradley and Business Agent Buddy Harman.

Kathy Hughes and her friend Howard.

Howard played a role in a Charley Pride hit 'Is Anybody Goin' to San Antone.'

Ruth with Carl Knight and Joe Lee.
- *Photo courtesy Mike Streissguth*

16 THE STRZELECKI

"I'm a long tall Texan
And I ride a big white horse..."

- Henry Strzelecki

There are a lot of great musicians in Nashville, but the one that stands out in my mind is the bass player, Henry Strzelecki. Howard met him, not as a musician, but on the golf course. Then they drove together to Florida to play in the annual Chet Atkins Golf Tournament. When Howard returned he told me that Henry had received financing from the Pepsi Cola Corporation of South Carolina to open a record company and publishing. Henry wanted both of us to work for him, Howard as a song-plugger and myself as a publishing administrator (and/or general flunky).

After an organizational period of a few months, we opened an office in the United Artists (UA) Towers, on the fifth floor, right in the heart of Music Row. It was 1976. Henry took all involved to dinner at Mario's, and it was there I got my first look at a very energetic person. He was a small-ish man with red hair and freckles, which I thought might indicate a short temper. I found out I was right, but most of the time, he was a teddy bear. Howard called Henry "his little buddy." So we were destined to work for this very funny Irishman (really?) with a Polish name. That began a friendship that has lasted all through the years.

Henry came to Nashville from Birmingham, Alabama, with his big bass fiddle in 1960, at sixteen years old. He "cut his teeth" in Nashville, playing jazz with people like Hank Garland, Beegie Adair and Doug Kirkham. It was Hank Garland, a famous guitar player, who got Henry into session work with Owen Bradley at Decca. He was producing an unknown singer, Baker Knight. (Knight was a songwriter who wrote Ricky Nelson's "Lonesome Town" and Elvis Presley's "The Wonder of You.") Besides Garland on guitar, and Henry on bass, that first session also included Farris Coursey, drums; Marvin Hughes, piano; and The Anita Kerr Singers. After that, Chet Atkins hired Henry to play on sessions with Eddy Arnold, Skeeter Davis, George Hamilton, IV, and Jim Reeves. Shortly thereafter, Billy Sherrill began using Henry on all his sessions with the likes of George Jones, Tammy Wynette, Johnny Paycheck, David Allen Coe and Charlie Rich. Besides country acts, Henry backed pop icons, notably Fats Domino, Perry Como, Gordon Lightfoot, Simon & Garfunkel and Roy Orbison. Henry could switch from upright to electric bass with ease, whatever the producer wanted. He could even bow that bass when needed. Henry was a natural-born showman and you could see his great big smile as he played that great big bass on *Hee Haw* for thirteen years. Henry was a humble man, who said, "I would say I have a whole lot to be thankful for. Mainly, it was a matter of being in the right place at the right time with the right tools."

147

Actually, I heard first about Henry from Karen Kelly, a gal I worked with at attorney John Cobb's office. Henry and Karen were writing songs together. At the time, I wasn't interested in wannabe songwriters. After all, everybody in Nashville was a songwriter. That was in the 1960's. I didn't give Strzelecki another thought until 1976, when I went to work for him.

When we opened the offices of October Records, Copper Music (ASCAP) and Strzelecki Music (BMI), Henry was working three and four sessions a day. The first thing I had to do was to learn how to spell S-t-r-z-e-l-e-c-k-i. To this day, I am about the only one in Nashville that can spell it right. Henry brought me his publishing companies in disarray. He was a great record producer, the greatest bass player, a fine songwriter and golfer, but not a good organizer. My first priority was to get those publishing companies in order, so that Howard could find a lyric in order to pitch them. Howard also brought with him two fine writers, Carl Knight and Neal Davenport.

I also had to deal with personalities with egos, who only wanted to see Henry, not Howard or me, just Henry. George Richey came in one day and asked to see "Mr. Strzelecki" about a song. I told him Henry was in a session and could Howard or I help him. Richey said, "I'll wait." I said, "Fine, but Henry has two other sessions after this one." Richey stomped out.

The financing company's aim was for Henry to produce and manufacture ten albums in three months. Henry spent day and night in the studio. I spent day and night keeping up with Henry, booking sessions, writing checks, typing union contracts, copywriting and licensing songs. We raced from studio to mastering, to pressing, to album cover manufacturers. Howard worked full speed getting new writers and songs and plugging songs. Our aim was to sign artist/writers. Our artists recorded as many of our songs as they could and their own self-written songs, which they contracted with us.

Of course, we had a lot of fun, even though there were a lot of problems in the U.A. Towers. We went through two floods and a fire. One day, I heard the fire alarm go off and walked into the hall to see Merle Kilgore, also a fifth-floor resident, kicking the elevator door. When I asked him what he was doing, he said, "There's a fire. We've got to get out of here." I said, "Take the stairs, dummy." I went back in Howard's office and told him he had to exit the building because of fire. He had a songwriter there, Jean Crouch. Then I went into Henry's domain and told him we had to leave. He was playing the music so loud, he couldn't hear the alarm. When I went back to get my purse I saw that Howard and Jean had deserted us, so Henry and I went down five floors of steps together. As we went down, we passed the firemen with hoses and axes going up. There was no answer when we asked them where the fire was. Howard was waiting for us outside and we all recessed to the St. Charles, across the street from us in the Four Star Building. We had a few drinks until 5 p.m. and by that time it was all clear. The fire had been in singer Tommy Overstreet's office, and had been quickly extinguished.

The next day Merle Kilgore was mad as a wet hen. Thinking he had to get his tapes out of the office or they might have been lost in the fire, he had grabbed them all and put them in two waste-baskets and carried them out. When we all got back to our offices, Merle just set them down as they were and went home. During the night, the cleaning people emptied the waste-baskets into the Dempsey Dumpster outside. The next scene was Merle inside the Dumpster hunting for his tapes. Merle was a funny guy. He told me he could make the telephone rise off my desk if he wanted to, but he had been "de-programmed," as the spirits were banging on his house so loud at night that he couldn't sleep.

Our first "glitch" was a controversy over the first name we had chosen, Omni Records. Our logo, already printed, was O.R.I. Then we found out we couldn't use Omni because the Omni Entertainment Center in Atlanta, Georgia, already had exclusive rights to the name. We discussed everything beginning with an O from Octopus to Octagon, finally arriving at October. So we began a union-affiliated label with October Records, Inc.

One day, the musicians union in Los Angeles contacted me, informing me that a L.A. musician had not been paid by October. We had not used any musician from L.A. Delving into the matter, I found out there was a non-union label in California called October that had not paid their musicians. I left this unhappy situation to the West Coast people to figure out.

We released a single from the Lloyd Green album and promoted it into the *Billboard* charts. Lloyd had the last steel-guitar instrumental ever charted. Henry hired Ted Jarrett, who Howard had known from Spar, for promotion and Ted did a great job getting our records to the distributors. (Many years later I wrote a book about Ted, "You Can Make It If You Try," published by the Country Music Foundation.)

Music business jobs seem to not only begin, but they come to an end. The day came when Pepsi Cola had what they wanted, ten master album sessions sitting in the vault at CBS Studios, a nice fat tax shelter. They closed our doors.

Henry kept his publishing companies and Henry and I kept our publishing association, as I did his publishing administration on the side. Henry was the sole writer of the song "Long Tall Texan." It is now in his own firm, Copper Music. It has been recorded over and over by people like the Beach Boys and Lyle Lovett. It was even used in a TV series, *Heroes.* Henry has always earned money on this, his signature song, and his recording career never skipped a beat.

A few years later, Henry formed a band called The Nashville Superpickers. He next formed a new company called Sounds Like Nashville, with an attorney, Joe Binkley, Sr. I went back to work for Henry and Joe. The Superpickers were recording on Paid Records, and they were booking out in California and England. The band originally was Henry, bass; Phil Baugh, guitar; Buddy Emmons, steel; Buddy Harman, drums; Buddy Spicher, fiddle; and Pig Robbins, piano. Later on, Bill Pursell and Willie Rainsford also played piano and Terry McMillan joined on harmonica. Johnny Gimble also played fiddle for a short while.

Musicians always think they have problems. They had been booked at Knott's Berry Farm in California, and I had made their plane reservations. When they got back, Buddy Harman came to the office and said, "Ruth, why did you book my ticket as Murrey Harman instead of Buddy?" I said, "Because your name is Murrey." He said, "But everybody calls me Buddy." I said, "My problem was I had three Buddy's: Buddy Harman, Buddy Spicher and Buddy Emmons. The airline wanted names. Since Emmon's name is 'Buddy', you and Spicher lost." "Oh," was all he said.

Then Phil Baugh came in and complained because they only had forty-five minutes between planes in Dallas. Never mind, that if they had waited for the next connection, they would have waited three hours in the Dallas airport. But that was the least of the problems. The booker at Buddy Lee's Agency had booked them at Governor's Park, thirty miles south of Chicago. I had a limo booked at O'Hare Airport to take them down to the venue and a hotel booked near the venue. On the night before they left, a friend living in that area, whom I had called and told to go see them, called and said, "Ruth, Governor's Park never heard of The Superpickers." I quickly called the booker at home. A mistake had been made on the contract. They had really been booked thirty miles north of Chicago. I had to call and change the limo service, cancel the old hotel rooms and book a new hotel. Booking mistakes caught by a stray friend!

They were then booked at the Portsmouth Festival in England. It rained and the show sponsors didn't make their "nut," so they didn't pay The Superpickers. Johnny Cash, also on the show, paid them out of his own pocket. That taught me a lesson. Never book outdoor festivals, especially in England, where it always rains.

There was never a better group than these, all session players, but session work got in their way. Some wanted to stay home and make the money in the studio rather than on the road. Eventually, it was just all over. Sounds of Nashville had a girl singer, Trilly Cole, whom Henry produced. She had a great record, "Keep On Believing," but she just never hit. She was just another girl singer from the Alley, performing at the Captain's Table.

Once Henry, Joe and I went to the Captain's Table to hear Trilly sing. The Captain's Table was on the corner of the "Alley" and Church Street. There were no parking places, so Joe said, "Just park here on Church Street, part on the sidewalk. I know Mickey Creitner, owner of the club and he won't mind." Can you imagine! The busiest street in downtown Nashville! A few hours later, when we came out, both cars were gone. They had been towed away by the police. At midnight, all three of us took a taxi to the tow-in lot to bail out Joe's Jaguar and Henry's Mercedes. I was convulsed in laughter, as Joe paid the fine in his three-piece suit and bowler hat. Howard and I laughed at this story for years. I don't think Joe or Henry thought it very funny. Mickey Creitner didn't care where we parked, but the Nashville Police Department sure did.

Henry always wanted to be more than just a musician but somehow his business ventures didn't last. Eventually, when The Superpickers went back to playing sessions, and when Trilly Cole's record didn't hit, Sounds Like Nashville closed their doors for good. Joe Binkley went back to practicing law, full time, and Henry to playing sessions.

Henry Strzelecki, now retired, is a golf addict and still plays golf every day if it isn't raining or too cold. Besides being a great bass player, or maybe because he is so great, Henry has always been popular with the ladies. I asked one of his followers once why she liked Henry so much. She said, "Ooh, he's so cute!" I guess that sums it up in four words. Friends are like the notes of a song: One melody, One harmony, Together they make music.

Guitar virtuoso Hank Garland with bassist pal Henry Strzelecki.

17 CARMOL TAYLOR

"I can see us now riding in a brand new wagon
Happy as a king upon a throne
Papa wearing overalls and Mama with her bonnet,
Riding in a brand new wagon going home."

- Carmol Taylor

Was there ever anybody like Carmol Taylor? Probably not! Carmol was one of the good ol' Alabama boys, though one of a kind, a diamond in the rough, an under-educated, but brilliant man.

When Howard and I first met Carmol, we were both working for Henry Strzelecki in the UA Tower. Carmol was writing songs for Gallico/Algee Music next door. Many artists had scored with his songs. A few were George Jones ("The Grand Tour"), Tammy Wynette ("My Man"), Joe Stampley ("Red Wine and Blue Memories") and George & Tammy ("We Loved It Away"). Billy Sherrill, at Epic Records, brought Carmol to Al Gallico and there he met Norro Wilson and George Richey. They teamed up to write great songs together. With Al Gallico and his boy Billy Sherrill on your side, how could you miss.

Norro said, "He just kind of showed up at Gallico's and we wrote some great songs together." As a songwriter, Carmol's ideas became a valuable commodity. Carmol was also a performer and recording artist. He was recording for Elektra Records when we met. He had one hit under his belt, "I Really Had A Ball Last Night," a Top Twenty he cut in '76. He was riding high, and followed that up with "That Little Difference," a catchy number, singing *"There's a little bit of difference / Between a man and a woman / Thank God, for that little bit of difference."*

Carmol came from a farm in Brilliant, Alabama, and even though he had only the first month of a fifth grade education, it didn't hinder his music ability. He was a big guy, built like one who had walked behind a mule in the fields. By the time he was fifteen, Carmol was playing professionally in the Alabama-Mississippi area for shows, square dances and radio. His ability to write songs showed itself early, before he came to Nashville. He penned "Sugar Creek Bottom" and "Flat Rock River Land," both recorded by artists on independent labels.

In 1976, he began a fledgling publishing company, Taylor Made Music. He lost no time in signing a newcomer, Gary Gentry, of Athens, Tennessee, and a fellow Alabamian, Laney Smallwood, to a contract. He couldn't ask Linda Kimball, secretary at Gallico, to type his contracts, as that would be a conflict of interests, so he would walk next door to my office, and ask if I would mind typing a contract. Of course, I didn't mind; we all loved Carmol. Gary was to become a fine songwriter himself. He immediately gave Carmol,

"Drinkin' and Drivin'," which Carmol got cut by Johnny Paycheck (a Top Twenty tune). Laney wasn't only a songwriter, she was also a talented vocalist. Carmol got her a record deal with Fred Foster at Monument Records, where she recorded a Taylor Made song, "I'm Sure To Cry." Then Ron Muir gave Carmol a song, "Slow and Easy" (credited to Barbara Muir and Fred Kelly), which Randy Barlow recorded for Republic Records. It went to Top Ten in 1978 on *Billboard*, so Carmol's little company was doing just fine.

Carmol and Norro Wilson called me at home one night from a BMI party, saying they had decided to open a publishing company together. I could tell they were really high, at least on this idea. They wanted me to work for them and their "Canary Music." Of course I agreed. Colonel Dave Mathis had just shut down his office and I needed a job. It turned out that they couldn't clear Canary with BMI, so they settled on Taylor and Wilson Music; not very original, but logical. We leased an office in the Screen Gems Building and, of course, needed office furniture. I knew that Mathis was selling out, so I called him and he agreed to sell everything to them for eight hundred and fifty dollars. That included two desks, typewriter, adding machine, chairs, shelves, ice box, and most important, a cold drink cooler to put their beer in.

Howard and I met Carmol and his friend, Monroe Fields, at Dave's office with a truck to help move out the equipment. What a disaster it turned out to be! It was hot that day and when we got there, the door was locked. Carmol and Monroe were not there yet and we waited and waited. When they finally arrived, Carmol told an unbelievable story. He had gone to his bank, Third National on Music Row, to get the money, but the bank had just been robbed and they were closed for business! Carmol was in a panic, but called Norro, who took him to his bank to get Carmol his money. When Carmol and Monroe arrived, we learned that the building manager had locked the doors to Dave's office, allegedly for unpaid rent. We had a heck of a time explaining to the building manager that we owned the furniture, not Dave Mathis. The manager wanted the furniture for the unpaid rent. Howard found the custodian, who quietly unlocked the door for us. During the delay, Monroe disappeared to a local bar, so Howard, Carmol and I moved everything out, keeping as low a profile as we could manage. After we had loaded everything, Howard asked Carmol, "What if the building manager had come out and stopped us?" Carmol said, "Then I would have physically hit him!" That's how we started up Taylor and Wilson Music, Inc.

We finally opened the office, and so began the most fun either Howard or I ever had in the music business. On the first day, Carmol called me into his office and quietly said, "I want you to understand that I never sleep with my secretaries." Of course, I knew that Carmol had never had a secretary before. I played it just as serious as he did, "I understand completely, Carmol."

Carmol stayed in Nashville all week and on the week-ends, he worked shows or went home to Alabama. During the week, when Carmol was in town, every day was a fun day. Ever the entertainer, Carmol held court about 4 p.m. every day, the cocktail hour. Howard caught on real quick and under Carmol's orders, brought in a quart of Windsor Canadian, a package of Vantage cigarettes for Carmol, and a bag of ice every day. If the Windsor Canadian ran out, he would pass the hat to buy another bottle. Carmol said, "The advantage of having Ruth work for me is that I got Howard in the bargain." Music Row literally descended upon us, including writers, musicians, bookers, secretaries, and nobodies, they all dropped by. At any time after 4, you might find Norro, John Riggs, Phil Baugh, Henry Strzelecki, Ronnie Robbins, Linda Kimball, Mark Sherrill, Wayne Carson, Bill Bleckley, Joe Taylor, Bob Bean, Paulette Carlson, Hurshel Wigginton or Monroe Fields. And if they got there early, well, it was 4 o'clock somewhere.

One night, Joe Taylor, Carmol's booker, locked himself in the bathroom. He had too much to drink and he just fell asleep. The guys banged and banged on the door, and finally decided to break it down. When they got to Joe, he had really passed out. It was raining outside, so they carried Joe out, sat him under a tree and left him there. Then they all came back in and the party continued. Once, Phil Baugh told me, "I don't come for business, just to see who is there and have a laugh."

We started off with a couple of lucky breaks. Epic Records had released "Drinkin' and Drivin'" by Johnny Paycheck. Carmol moved Gary Gentry, who wrote it, from Taylor Made to Taylor and Wilson. Right on the heels of that, Norro recorded John Anderson on another Gentry song, "1959." That Warner Bros. release peaked at number seven in 1980, so we felt pretty good about ourselves.

Carmol was notoriously bad on directions. One night, Howard, myself and Carmol were part of a crowd that went to the Stockyards, a night club owned by Buddy Killen, situated on the historic spot of the real Nashville Stockyards. We listened to the band for a while, then left. Carmol said, "Howard, you're going to have to lead me home or I'll never find it." Howard said, "Carmol, we live North and you live South. It's very simple. You just go right down this street to I-65 and go South. You can't miss it!" Now any good hillbilly knows you don't say, "You can't miss it!" Well, we each headed our separate ways. The next day when I got to work, Carmol said, "You know where I ended up? Bowling Green, Kentucky! That's about sixty-six miles north of Nashville. Carmol went at least two hours out of the way. Guess he really didn't know North from South.

Writer-singer John Riggs probably spent more on-the-road time with Carmol than anyone. He went along with Carmol to help drive and to sing some on his shows. One day after a show, as they rode along quietly toward home, Carmol broke the silence, saying, "Why do we do it! Why do we do it!" John said, "What, Carmol?" "Sit up all night and drink all the whiskey," Carmol said sadly.

In Tupelo, Mississippi, there was a place Carmol played with some regularity, called Bill's Lounge. One time he drove over to Bill's and looked up at the big flashing sign outside. It read: "Tonight - cat fish - all you can eat - $5" Carmol was furious: "Can you imagine, advertising cat-fish instead of Carmol Taylor playing here tonight!"

Carmol had an immense U.S. map which covered the whole wall behind his desk. One day I noticed him leaning back and studying that map for a long time. Finally, he said, "Well, I'll be darned. I didn't know you had to go through Mexico to get to Hawaii." I said, "No you don't, Carmol." He replied, "Yes you do, come look at this map." I explained to him that the mapmakers put Hawaii as an inset down by Mexico, because it wouldn't fit on the map otherwise. Carmol listened, but didn't completely believe me. His parting shot was, "Are you sure?"

Carmol, Norro and George Richey wrote a song and used the tune to the old public domain song, "Beautiful Dreamer." Carmol played it for Danny Darst at Gallico, who said, "It's beautiful. Who wrote this?" Carmol honestly replied, "Me, Norro, George and Stephen." (Stephen Foster, of course, penned the original "Beautiful Dreamer.") At another time, as John Riggs and Carmol rode along, Carmol, the good ol' Alabama boy, said to John, "Well, tomorrow is the 4th of July and you know how it'll be; the blacks will be celebratin' with watermelon parties." John asked, "What do you mean, Carmol?" Carmol said, "Well, you know, the 4th of July, that's the day Lincoln gave the blacks their freedom." John said, "No, Carmol, that's the birthday of the United States of America. That's the day our country got its freedom." Carmol paid attention, but at the end of John's explanation he remained doubtful. "Are you sure?" he asked.

Carmol's strong points may not have been geography or history, but if you asked him how much money it would cost to build a nine-by-nine shed, he would mull it over in his mind, counting how many boards, plywood, etc. it would take, and come up with an almost exact figure.

One evening, after a club date in Indiana, Carmol became friendly with a lovely girl who agreed to go back to his room with him. John was with him, so all the way back to the motel, Carmol spent a lot of time whispering to John that he needed to go get coffee after he dropped Carmol and the girl at the motel. John just ignored Carmol and followed them to the room. As Carmol put his key in the door, he whispered again, "John don't you want to go and get some coffee." John said he really didn't need any. Carmol mouthed, so the girl wouldn't hear him, "Yes you do! Get some anyway!" Carmol and the girl went in and shut the door, leaving John standing there. John waited until he was sure Carmol would be undressed; then he knocked at the door. Carmol appeared in his boxer shorts. When he saw it was John, he angrily said, "What do you want now!" John said, "The place was closed." Carmol mused, "Then go sit by the pool." John, deciding he had kidded Carmol enough, went down by the pool and waited, laughing so hard he could hardly walk. The next day, Carmol fumed all the way back home because John had spoiled his night with the girl he'd never see again.

Carmol got quite a surprise in Columbia, South Carolina. He was playing "The Skyline Club," for Jim Davis, and it was near the air base. The club was noted for a huge open parachute hanging on the ceiling. In the club's dressing room, Carmol opened a locker to hang up his clothes, and found all lined up were a bunch of KKK robes. It seems the club was not only noted for its parachute, it was also the headquarters for the local Ku Klux Klan.

One day while John was "riding shotgun" with Carmol on Kentucky's Bluegrass Parkway, a toll road, they had just paid their first toll and driving along saw a house that had been burned, leaving its chimney standing. After a couple of miles more, they decided to get off the exit and get some coffee. When they got back on the Parkway, however, they didn't realize they entered heading the wrong way. A little further on, Carmol said, "Look a'there, John, there's another house burned, with just a chimney standing." Then they came to a toll gate. Carmol remarked, "This parkway sure has a lot of toll gates." Then it hit them. They were going back through the same toll-gate they entered. Carmol said, "Same damn house, shit! The sun's behind us, same damn toll-gate, shit! We're going the wrong way!" They got off at the next exit, retraced their route, paid at the toll booth again and Carmol said, "I can hear that girl back there at the toll booth saying, "Look at that old man and the bald-headed wonder. They must be crazy. Now don't you tell anybody about this, John." Well, that's not where the story ends. When they got back to Nashville, they pulled into the back parking lot of Country International Records, home of Sherman and Joy Ford. John rushed in as Carmol parked the car. John immediately told all the people sitting there about their escapade. When Carmol walked in, Sherman said, "Well, look who we have here, Wrong Way Taylor." Carmol said, "John, you bastard, you told!"

Carmol's friends from Alabama and Mississippi descended on the office constantly. I called these rebels "The Tupelo Mafia." To name a few, there was Gene Simmons, who once had a hit, "Haunted House." There was Andy Wood, who had a Tupelo recording studio called "Slaughterhouse," Dave Hall, a D.J. from Laurel, Mississippi, Bill Lancaster, a writer and owner of the Paradise Motel at Montgomery, Alabama, and writers Don Hobson and Terry Morgan. We also entertained a big guy from Louisiana, Big John Mihalec, who worked on the oil rigs and was managing an artist, "Little Cajun Margie." The times spent in that office on 16th Avenue South, will never come again. But we can and do retell Carmol Taylor stories.

Billy Sherrill, Norro and Carmol went to Nyack, New York, to pick up a car Billy had ordered. They had taken a chauffeur-driven limousine from the airport. Billy and Norro were in the back seat, Carmol rode up front with the driver. The driver was pointing out the sights to them and as they rode along, the driver said, "There's Grant's Tomb." Then he turned to Carmol and asked facetiously, "Do you know who's buried in Grant's Tomb?" Carmol thought a minute and then said, "No, who is buried there?" Norro said he and Billy, in the back seat, laughed so hard they had to get down on the floor of the limo to laugh.

Carmol drank a lot every day and as evening approached in the office, and it became difficult for him to get up and make his own drinks, you could hear him yell, "Ruth! Fix me a drink!" I fixed his drinks like he liked them, a lot of ice, with whiskey, and no mix.

Once Carmol planted strawberries on his farm in Alabama, but he knew nothing about growing strawberries. When he came back to Nashville, he asked John how strawberries multiplied. John explained that when you plant them, each plant puts out about ten runners, so you judge how many plants you need to plant by that. Carmol said, "Ye Gods! I planted three hundred plants! I'll have enough strawberries for the whole state of Alabama!"

Howard and I made a trip to Nashville, Michigan, with Carmol. On the way back, as we were passing through Louisville, Carmol said, "Howard, you've got to stop. I've got to get to the restroom." Now this was at a time when they were widening I-65 and there was nothing but concrete barriers on either side of the lanes. There was nowhere to exit or stop. Howard had to keep going and Carmol was sitting on the edge of the seat with his hands on the dash, saying, "I've got to go," every few seconds. Finally, we got to a place to exit. Howard took it, but there was no sign at the exit as to which way there was a gas station. We took a right and saw nothing, turned back, finally finding a gas station. Carmol got out of the car before it stopped and ran to the rest room. Guess what! The door was locked. Carmol's luck! Howard quickly got a key and Carmol finally got into a restroom.

I was at my desk one day and the phone rang. George Richey, at the other end of the line said, "This is an emergency. Tammy (Wynette) has been kidnapped! Let me speak to Carmol." I put Carmol right on the line and when he hung up, he came running through my office with his gun, (a "hog leg") stuck in his belt. He always kept that gun in his desk. I asked him, "Where ya going, Carmol?" He said, "I've got to go rescue Tammy." As he ran out the door, I yelled, "Let me know what happens." I didn't hear anymore until I called his girl friend, Shirley, that night. She said, "Oh, Tammy's all right. She's home now after being treated for some bruises." Well, it might have been a hoax, or a publicity stunt. No one ever knew, but none of us at the office believed she had really been kidnapped. But it made all the nightly news and all the newspapers.

One day a cute gal, little and blonde, "bopped" into the office all smiles. She said her name was Paulette Carlson and she was a singer. I asked her where she was from and she said, "Minn-e-sota?" She had that cute Minnesota accent, putting the emphasis on " . . . sota." I introduced her to Carmol. Everybody in the office that day was completely charmed. She had written a song, "The Bed You Made For Me," which we all instantly knew was a hit song. Carmol said, "I can get that cut by Tammy Wynette." Paulette said, "Oh, no, I want to cut it myself." (She said "meself.")

Well, Paulette became our friend and she bewitched everybody, Carmol, Gary Gentry, John Riggs, and whoever met her. Nonetheless, her song laid in our catalog. Carmol took her to Norro, at Warner's, but there wasn't room for her on that label. He couldn't pitch "The Bed" because she wanted to cut it herself. He couldn't record her himself, because he was too tied up in producing Laney Smallwood at Monument. Time moved on and Paulette went on the road for a while, singing with Gail Davies. Then Norro moved from Warner's to RCA. He decided to record Paulette. They did four songs, including "The Bed." Paulette asked us to release the publishing and we did, hoping for the best for her. Then RCA made a mistake. They didn't release "The Bed" and Paulette didn't hit. RCA let her go, but gave the publishing on "The Bed" back to her.

Finally, Paulette joined a group from California, Highway 101. They recorded their first record on Warner Brothers. It was "The Bed You Made For Me." Paulette gave Warner's fifty per-cent of the song, so she ended up with all the writing and fifty per-cent of the publishing. The record hit like gangbusters. Later on, as most groups sometimes do, they split up. Paulette married, had a little girl and moved to Montana. I saw her in Reno, Nevada, at the Golden Nugget, playing a rare get-together with Highway 101, and then again in Nashville, recently. She talked about coming back to Nashville. Paulette has a rare, great voice. I always called her a "country Stevie Nicks." Today's market is different, but I hope she makes it again.

It was a long time ago, but I remember well the afternoon of November 30, 1978, when I was working at my desk in Carmol's office. Suddenly a girl from Waylon Jennings' office, located just around the corner on 17th Avenue South, came bursting into my office in hysterics. It seemed that Barry Sadler had come into her office, yelling that he was going to kill Lee Emerson. Sadler was co-writer with Robin Moore, who had penned the 1966 hit, "The Ballad Of the Green Berets." Emerson was the writer of "I Thought I Heard You Calling My Name" (Porter Wagoner). After she had calmed down a little, she left. I assumed she had gone back to work, but I learned later that she had left town and never returned.

I knew that both men were volatile. Lee Emerson had been in prison in Memphis. He had come back to Nashville to resume his writing career, but got caught up in Nashville's "wild side." Then he and Sadler got into a wrangle over Emerson's ex-girlfriend, Darlene Sharpe. It was rumored that Emerson had become a mental case. Sadler was equal to or meaner than Emerson. He hung out in bars, mostly at the Hall Of Fame Motor Inn. He liked to talk about his escapades and told friends of mine - Phil Baugh and Sherman Ford - about his adventures as a Green Beret Medic in Vietnam.

When I met Barry Sadler, he was with Phil Baugh. I never met anyone with as little empathy as Sadler. He looked mean to the core. So I was not surprised to learn that on December 1, the day after his rant in Waylon's office, Sadler had shot and killed Lee Emerson. He shot him with a .32 caliber pistol, while Emerson was sitting in his van outside Darlene's apartment. The police said later that Sadler had then placed a .38 pistol on the floor by Emerson's feet, called the police and reported that he had shot Emerson in self defense.

Sadler retained my friend, Joe Binkley, Sr., as his attorney. Joe had previously saved the Brown cousins from the electric chair in the Stringbean murder case. I figured Joe was going to lose this case big time. At first the D.A.'s office charged Sadler with second-degree murder, but later, he pleaded guilty to voluntary manslaughter and received a four-to-five year prison term. I then thought Joe had provided a great job of defense, but it got better. Four months later, a judge gave Sadler four months in the workhouse and two years probation. Joe had wrought a miracle.

Then I told Joe about the threats Sadler had made the day before he shot Emerson. Joe looked at me seriously and said, "I'm glad you didn't tell me that before we went to trial." I sure wouldn't have! If you're smart, you didn't cross Barry Sadler. Sadler left Nashville and went to Guatemala in the mid 1980's. He was there in 1988, and while he was riding in a taxi, he was shot in the head. News reports said he was "shot under less than explained circumstances." *Soldiers of Fortune* magazine said he was transported to the Alvin C. York VA Hospital in Murfreesboro, Tennessee, where he died November 5, 1989, at forty-nine years old. The rumor mill in Nashville said he had been a secret service agent for the U.S. government. I suppose no one will ever really know.

After a year-and-a-half, things didn't go too well at Taylor and Wilson. We contracted a lot of songs and did a lot of demos. Carmol was so busy enjoying himself, however, he couldn't find time to pitch songs. He would go to Norro at Warner's, or Billy Sherrill at Epic, but he never went anywhere else. Once Carmol asked Howard if he knew Jim Vienneau at MGM. Howard said, "Sure, I'll set you up an appointment." Howard reached Vienneau at home and Jim agreed to see Carmol the next day at noon. Carmol came running into the office at 11:55 the next day, He had not gotten together any of our songs, so he grabbed an out-dated song he had written, "Papa's Wagon," and ran over to Vienneau's office. When he got back, I asked him if Vienneau liked his song. His only answer was a shake of the head.

Finally, Norro decided to sell his half of the company and sold it to Kenneth Watts. Taylor and Wilson then became Taylor and Watts. Both Norro and Carmol, being writers for Gallico, had signed papers at the beginning, agreeing they would not write for their own company, but Gallico did not like it that his writers had started their own company. His thinking was that they would help their writers. Then Norro and Billy both began telling Carmol they didn't like our songs. I began hearing rumors that Gallico had told Norro and Billy to cut us off, and not cut any of our songs. I told Carmol, but he wouldn't believe me. We had received one hundred and twenty five thousand dollars in advance from BMI, to open the business. A publishing company generally does not get royalties in for a year after a record release. For that reason the advance was necessary.

I heard directly from sources that Gallico had told Frances Preston at BMI to cut us off. Believe me, Al Gallico had that power. In a Nashville music magazine, Gallico was quoted as saying, "I put 'my boy,' Billy Sherrill, in at Epic and I put 'my boy,' Norro Wilson, in at Warner's." That way he could get his own songs cut. We had two major cuts, "1959" by John Anderson and "Drinkin' And Drivin'" by Johnny Paycheck, but we had not received the royalties from these releases. There was no doubt we were struggling. The office finally had to shut down.

Our main writer, Gary Gentry, asked me what he should do. I advised him to go up to Gallico Music. Billy Sherrill liked his writing and I bet they would sign him. That's what he did and they did sign him to their Algee Music immediately. As time moved along, Gary got a lot of songs cut by Billy Sherrill. I got Carmol a new deal, sharing an office with Sy Rosenberg. I was to work for both of them with a twenty-five dollars a week raise. In the meantime, Henry Strzelecki called me and said he had a new deal with Joe Binkley and wanted me to work for him for the amount I was supposed to get from Sy and Carmol. I put Henry off. On the day Carmol was moving into the new building, he took me to lunch. On the way back he said, "You know, Ruth, jobs are hard to get now." I agreed. When we got back, Sy sheepishly informed me that they couldn't afford to give me that raise (split between the two of them). I called Henry and said I would be at work on Monday, and gave my one-day notice to Carmol and Sy. Carmol hired a few girls, but none of them worked out, so I continued doing his work at night when he had something that needed doing. But the days of wine and roses were over.

I was working for Porter Wagoner when Carmol discovered he had lung cancer. All of us were heart broken as everybody loved Carmol. He kept saying he had the flu, but finally he went to a doctor at Vanderbilt Medical Center, where he was X-rayed and found to have cancer. Carmol wouldn't believe it and went to Dr. Perry Harris, who agreed to do a biopsy in his office. Carmol was deathly afraid of hospitals. That doctor missed it and told Carmol he didn't have cancer. But Carmol got sicker with those "flu" symptoms. Finally, facing the fact that he was very sick, Carmol went into a Birmingham hospital, since he didn't trust Nashville. They also diagnosed him with lung cancer, not giving him long to live. He came back to Nashville and Norro and I, and a lawyer, drew up his will, naming me as co-executor. John Riggs met Carmol on the street and Carmol told John he needed three hundred dollars, his well-pump had gone bad and his lawn mower had quit. John freely gave him the money.

He went home and then came back to Nashville one last time. He came into my office at Porter's and told me he was desperate for one hundred and twenty five thousand dollars. When his mother died, she left her property divided between Carmol and his siblings. He had borrowed that much money from the bank in Brilliant to buy the land from his siblings. Now, when he died, his wife, Louise, would have no money to pay the bank. I told Carmol I would try to help him. I called Sherman Ford, who had previously bought Kenneth Watts' half of Taylor and Watts Music. I told him of Carmol's plight. He told me to tell Carmol to go to his office. Sherman paid Carmol the one hundred and twenty five thousand dollars he needed immediately and then owned the other half of Carmol's company. Carmol went home, paid off the bank and never came back to Nashville again. The last thing he ever said to me was, "Please take care of Louise. They will eat her alive." I didn't know who "they" were, but I promised.

In December 1986, Howard and I went to his funeral at a little Baptist Church in Brilliant. The church was filled to overflowing. Bill Bleckley, a booker, was standing on the steps and said, "There's no way you can get in." I said, "Watch me!" As Howard and I walked down the aisle, someone came up to me and said, "Are you Ruth from Nashville?" When I said yes, he said, "We're saving a seat for you." Carmol was laid to rest on a hill in the little graveyard next to the church. I stayed until the last clod of dirt was in place.

Carmol was always "gonna get to something." He was "gonna" put a new tin roof on his mother's house, he was "gonna" sell Elizabeth, his mule, he was "gonna" get his own line of horses and he was "gonna" get the carburetor fixed on his 1979 big black Lincoln, with four hundred thousand miles on it. He never did any of the "gonnas." The pump was always going bad on his well, his lawn mower still needed fixing, the "power bill" was always due, and the Lincoln sat in the yard waiting for a carburetor, but, we all loved him, all his friends from here, Alabama and Mississippi. John gave him the three hundred dollars when he needed it, Sherman bought his publishing, so he could pay for his land and Norro and I saw to it his legal problems were taken care of. He told me once, "Ruth, you're the only one I can trust." In truth, I was always just honest with him.

Carmol might have been a certified character, but God gave him talent. The preacher said at his funeral that Carmol accepted his Savior, near his beloved horses, in the stable. There were so many people attending his funeral, they had to stand in the yard. He's really on the "Grand Tour" now: *"Step right up, come on in / If you'd like to take the Grand Tour . . . "* (Carmol Taylor-George Richey-Norro Wilson, 1970.)

18 "LOOSH"

"If a man does not keep pace
With his buddies,
Maybe it's because he hears a
Different drummer."

- Henry David Thoreau

A history of country music would be remiss if they left out the biggest character of them all, Lloyd George, a.k.a. Lonzo, a.k.a. Ken Marvin, and a.k.a. "Loosh." Officially, he was born Lloyd Leslie George in Haleyville, Alabama, June 27, 1924.

When he recorded his biggest hit, "I'm My Own Grandpa" in 1947, with duet partner Rollin (Oscar) Sullivan, as Lonzo & Oscar, he was still Lloyd George. Three years later, he became Ken Marvin, so some called him Ken, but he called himself "the luscious one." Friends in the music business shortened that to "Loosh." He was always "Loosh" to us, because it fit.

Loosh was the original Lonzo of the famed comic duo Lonzo and Oscar. He played that role for two years. "I'm My Own Grandpa" hit the Top Five in 1948, on the RCA Victor label. Lonzo named their back-up band, The Winston County Pea Pickers. It was in 1950, that Loosh changed his stage name to Ken Marvin, bought himself a big white hat, and tried his luck as a solo country singer. However, it seemed that Ken Marvin could not become the big star he thought he was destined to be.

It appears Loosh was his own worst enemy, as he really did not respect people in charge. For instance, he needed money and the Opry only paid a small amount for an appearance. At that time, Jack Stapp and Jim Denny had equal powers toward assigning these Opry spots. Loosh went into Stapp's office, without knocking, and said, "Jack, Loosh needs a spot on the Opry Saturday night. Miss Clydie (his wife, Clyda) needs some new shoes!" Jack looked at his schedule and said, "I'm sorry, but all the spots are filled." Loosh went directly to Jim Denny's office and said, "Mr. Denny, my fans are demanding that I appear on the Opry Saturday night. How 'bout it!" Denny looked at his schedule and said, "Yes, we can use you for a guest spot at 9:45 and 10:15." Ken said, "Thank you," turned and went back to Stapp's office, barged in, saluted and said, "Screw you, Jack, Loosh doesn't need you anymore."

Joe Allison, then an announcer at WMAK, bought a fine cowboy suit, second-hand from Tex Ritter. He sold it to Loosh for fifty dollars. Loosh didn't have the fifty, but promised to pay Joe in a week. Three weeks went by and he still had not paid Joe. Joe found out that Ken was going to be on the Opry on Saturday night, so Joe made sure he was there too. Loosh wore Joe's suit that night and Joe situated himself in the wings where Loosh would have to walk right into him, when he came off stage. When Loosh finished his song, he skipped right past Joe, waved his hand and said, "If I knew you was gonna be here, I wouldn't have wore it."

George Morgan loved Loosh, but he also loved the laughs that Loosh gave him. He heard that Loosh was not doing well, so he offered him a spot on his show. He was a fine showman and he really wowed the audience. After the show, some of his fans went backstage, but Loosh locked his dressing room door. One of the fans asked George, "Why won't Ken come out of his dressing room? We wanted his autograph." George, very seriously said, "Failure has gone to his head."

Once Loosh was on the road with Bun Wilson, a comic. Bun had just taped an *Ozark Jubilee* show and wanted them all to see it. Bun entered a room at a motel, and alerted them so they could all watch him on TV. Then the show, supposedly with Bun on it, was replaced by Snooky Lanson's show. Loosh laughed and laughed, and from then on called Bun, "Snooks."

When Bud Wendell came to the Opry as manager, after Ott Devine retired, George Morgan took Loosh down to the Opry with him. Now, Loosh had been through quite a lot of Opry managers, Denny, Stapp, D. Kilpatrick and Ott. Loosh, having been at the Opry since 1947, and didn't let another new Opry chief phase him one bit. George introduced Loosh to Bud Wendell. Loosh, who liked to shock everybody, said, "Hello Bud, how'd you like to go screw yourself?" George kept a straight face and said, "Loosh, I don't think you know who this is. This is the new Opry manager, Bud Wendell." Loosh looked at Bud and very calmly said, "Yes, I know who this is. He's the new Opry manager. Now, how'd you like to go screw yourself?" George, of course, doubled over with laughter. This was the kind of gag George loved. He could depend on Loosh to deliver.

One night, while playing cards, Loosh, George and Danny Dill wrote a song about an uncouth fowl which gave off a terrible odor, had a buzzard-like head and sharp, beady eyes. This "Butris Bird" was responsible for all the dastardly acts in the world: *"He flies through the skies, forever in search / Of those with a fear and a dread / Then he hounds the unfortunate wretch to his death / And shits on his grave when he's dead . . ."* The credits were given to Howard by Loosh in this manner: "Loosh, idea; George Morgan, story; Danny Dill, poem." It's hard to believe that the man who wrote the sentimental classic "Candy Kisses," George Morgan, would write a song like the "Butris Bird," but George, as he grew older, liked to make fun of songwriting.

This account happened while Suds Slayman and Loosh were both working for Morgan. Suds was known for being tight, and even he always said, "I'm not stingy, just tight." Suds never loaned money or bought a beer for anyone. They were driving along with five musicians in the car. Suds and Loosh were in the back seat, with Suds sound asleep. Loosh slipped Suds' billfold out of his pocket, taking out twenty dollars. Then he put the billfold back just like it was. When Suds woke up, Loosh said, "Boys, stop at the first market we pass. I haven't bought y'all a beer for a

163

long time and ol' Loosh wants to treat y'all." Boy, was Suds happy! Free beer! Later, when Suds looked in his billfold, he discovered he was missing twenty dollars. They all laughed and laughed. The boys told Suds what Loosh had done, so Suds realized he had been had. He was as mad as anyone had ever seen him. Suds never did get over the fact that all the guys were drinking on his money.

Loosh called a half-pint of whiskey an E-flat. And you can bet he always had one in his pocket. One night, Howard and I were spending a quiet evening at home. About midnight there was a knock at the door and there stood Loosh and Clyda with a quart of vodka. They were already smashed and had obviously been arguing. Loosh's routine that night was, *"I hear the stage a'comin,' clippity clop, clippity clop."* He meant that the stage was coming to take Clyda away. Every time Clyda would open her mouth, Loosh would go through his routine again, *"I hear the stage a'comin,' clippity clop, clippity clop."* It was not a fun time. Fortunately, they left when the vodka ran out.

Don Davis, steel player with George Morgan, used to room with Loosh when they were on the road. He said that Loosh used to stand in front of the mirror, without his shirt on, flex his muscles and say, "I look just like Richard Widmark," a real misnomer. A fiddle player, Johnny Tona, sometimes played with them and Loosh would always comment, "Tona has a stance like Rubinoff and he sounds like Harkreader." (Rubinoff was a violinist and Harkreader was an old-time fiddler.)

Loosh used to tell Howard that when he retired, he was going to get himself a big beach umbrella and sit out by the highway, pour himself a big drink and wave at all the hillbillies driving by on their way to show dates. Yet, he never retired in the normal sense. When he died, he couldn't have picked a worse time, because it was the same time frame that Grant Turner passed. Grant was the much-loved Dean of WSM Opry announcers, who was also a member of the Country Music Hall of Fame. So everybody in Nashville, who was in the music business, went to Grant's funeral.

Ol' Loosh was truly a colorful person, a good showman and a certified character. He died in Cookeville, Tennessee, at age sixty-seven, on October 16, 1991, and hereabouts all his friends said, "You know, Loosh died the other day." He really deserved more than that, lamented Howard White, "Not one tear was shed at his grave, and though I didn't cry, I do wish somebody had."

19 THE HAPPY BOOKER

"Exercise caution in your business affairs;
For the world is full of trickery.
But let this not blind you to what virtue there is;
many persons strive for high ideals;
and everywhere life is full of heroism."

- Max Ehrmann, attorney/essayist.

Interview with Smiley Wilson (1990): Of all the unsung heroes in the music business, the booker or promoter is at the top of the list. These pros book and promote dates for artists for a percentage, but no glory. Notice that when a big artist accepts an award, they always thank everybody, God, the kids, their wives or significant other, the producer, their record company, musicians, but never, no never, their long suffering booker or promoter. Maybe the artist fees like the percentage the bookers receive is all the thanks they need. They have been called "flesh peddlers." However, the booker is the one that keeps the artist working, so he can pay for his home, boats and Cadillacs.

In spite of this, all the bookers and promoters seem happy. Howard was never a booker, although that was his objective when he went to work on Music Row. Chance took him to Hubert Long where he began a life in the publishing business. In the years when he was a musician, Howard knew the bookers and promoters well. His favorite booker was a friend and golfing buddy, H.K. "Smiley" Wilson.

Smiley and his wife Kitty were entertainers in the beginning, so they knew intimately the life of the artists and musicians. They traveled the road with Ferlin Husky, were on *Country Junction*, a TV show for years and they were duet partners on the Opry with Cousin Jody. Smiley also played guitar and Kitty slapped a mean stand-up bass. "Miss Kitty" was renowned for saying exactly what she thought and Smiley was equally as famous for his straight line, "Now, Kitty... " Smiley lived up to his name, Smiley, he was always smiling. After Smiley and Kitty retired, Smiley became a booker. He was known for being honest. He knew the business and all the other bookers and promoters. He could read their pedigrees.

Smiley and Kitty both passed on, but before that, Howard and I met with them on a sunny day in nearby Ridgetop, Tennessee. We reminisced about the old show business personalities from days gone by. I doubt if there is anybody out there today as colorful as these early "carnival people."

Smiley said, "I remember Larry Sunbrock. He was a promoting rascal. He would do anything to promote a show. One time in Washington, D. C., Larry had a rodeo and a show coming in. He couldn't get newspaper advertising, so he hired me to go to the stockyards and let the cattle out. Bulls and cows were running all over Washington. It made the front page with cops herding the cattle and brought attention to his rodeo. On his circuit there were signs in all the dressing rooms, which said, 'Have you ever been Sunbrocked?'"

Howard asked, "Do you remember Cracker Jim?" Jim was an early booker from Miami, Florida, booking shows into the Dade County Auditorium. Smiley laughed, slapped his leg, and said, "I sure do! Jim insisted on introducing the acts on his shows, although he was the worst announcer ever. His lead on, regardless of the star was, 'Now here's . . . ' He never changed his intros a bit."

Connie B. Gay was a promoter based in Washington D. C. Once he was promoting a big show and the union told him he would have to hire thirty local standby musicians. He went out and bought thirty push brooms and told the union to have their musicians be there at 2 p.m. When they arrived, with their instruments at 2, Gay told them to grab the brooms and sweep the floor. They said they were musicians, but they swept the floors anyway, after Gay told them they wouldn't get paid if they didn't sweep.

Smokey Smith arrived at the Civic Opera House in Chicago with his show. As usual, they had their books and records to sell at intermission. Then the concession people at the auditorium told them they couldn't sell, but they would, and take thirty-five per cent for doing so. Smokey said, "Okay, but we will play straight through and won't stop for an intermission." The concessioners said no to that. Smokey told them that his contract didn't mention an intermission and they wouldn't stop for one. They could just smell the popcorn and hot dogs. Then the concession people backed down. Smokey's crew did the selling and paid only ten per cent for the privilege of selling.

Fact is, Smokey was always ready to help a friend. Lazy Jim Day was playing in Des Moines and once after he drank a little too much, he told the hotel's parking attendant that he wanted to go to Tuscola, Illinois, to see his kids. So, the parking attendant told him that he knew a guy that had a car there and would be gone three or four days and Lazy Jim could borrow that car. He gave Lazy the keys and Lazy took off, but about an hour out of Des Moines, the road made a sharp left turn, but Lazy didn't, and wound up in a cornfield. The police found him and took him to jail, charging him with D.U.I. and car theft. Smokey found out and bailed him out. Lazy was put on probation and could not leave Des Moines for a year. He took a job at Reliable Rugs. One day, Smokey came home to find a paper plate tacked up on their door saying, "I'm leaving town. Thanks. Tell Slim Hayes at the radio station and Joe at Reliable Rugs goodbye. Thanks to you. Goodbye."

Smiley's eyes got misty when he remembered Joe L. Frank, the very first big-time country promoter. He is remembered in country music circles as the father-in-law of Pee Wee King. Smiley said, "J. L. booked a lot of Opry acts. He was probably the first booker to 'package' a show. We always got paid on his shows. Some unscrupulous bookers took the money and ran. J. L.'s main objective was to fill the auditorium. If he saw there wasn't going to be a full house, he sent little boys out on the street with tickets to give away. He used to hold contests. He would use Curly Fox and Natchee the Indian for a fiddling contest or hold a yodeling contest with Texas Ruby and Tex Waterbury. Chester Studdard was front man for Ernest Tubb, and J. L.'s advance promo man. J. L. took the country acts out of schoolhouses and the like, and put us in theaters and auditoriums."

In the old days, the artists would stop at radio stations and promote their records on the way to their next show date. Howard said he remembered one time when Copas parked his car in front of a radio station in Gadsden, Alabama. When he came out all four tires were flat. Copas raised Cain, because he didn't make enough money to buy all four tires at one time.

In the early days, as Howard and Smiley remembered, WSM booked their Opry stars through their own Artists Service Bureau for fifteen percent off the top. Jim Denny managed that bureau for a time. Then Denny left WSM to form his own Artists Bureau and publishing company, and the Opry gradually phased out their artist business.

When Howard and Smiley were playing the Opry, the Opry was a focal point part of the country music business. The old National Life Building at Seventh and Union Streets, home of WSM, became a hangout for musicians, singers, bookers and promoters. A number of hustlers clustered like vultures in the lobby, using the free phones inside to create the impression they had offices there. Oscar Davis and Colonel Tom Parker hung out constantly, using the free phones to their advantage. This became a concern for the owners of National Life until, finally Bill Williams, in charge of Opry public relations, got the task of having the phones disconnected. Then Parker tried to weasel his way into empty studios to use the phones there.

Next, Howard and Smiley thought of A. V. Bamford, who was one of the first to line up good, profitable tours from Texas to Minnesota. He owned a big country music radio station in Texas, and would line up eight or ten dates, not worrying about the distance between them. It was the Bamford bookings that prompted the old canard about throwing darts at the map to see where the next booking date would be. Incidentally, Xavier or "X" Cosse worked with Bamford initially and later wed and managed gospel artist Martha Carson, famed for her hit, "Satisfied."

Both Howard and Smiley agreed that Hubert Long was the smartest of the Nashville bookers. Hubert perfected the art of keeping his artists by selling them on the idea of letting them keep their own publishing, as long as Hubert could keep fifty per cent to administer their publishing, known as split publishing.

Smiley's kindest thoughts were for Harry "Hap" Peebles from Wichita, Kansas, probably the second man to package country music shows. Smiley said, "He was honest, always paid his acts, even if he lost money himself. He never owed anyone a dime. He was the first to bring country music into big State Fairs. He knew the secret of advertising and used it to his advantage. His circuits were cities like St. Joseph, Kansas City, Wichita, Salina, Topeka, Omaha and Des Moines."

Then there were the so-called "Phone Shows." They were a natural for country music shows. These "Boiler Room" operations or "phone shows" are so-called because promotion was done by phone solicitation from one room. The promoters sell ads for the show program by phone, then the programs are sold at the show. If done honestly, they're great. In this manner the show is paid for before the show is held, and the sponsor doesn't have to depend on straight ticket sales for income. Some of the people in charge of these operations, however, are dishonest, which gives the honest phone promoters a bad name.

Smiley said, "There used to be a man called "Pop Watts," an ex-serviceman, who booked shows at Army camps. He hitchhiked from one post to another and booked Army base shows. The Army respected him. He also would be the comic on their shows."

Howard and Smiley thought fondly of Dick Blake, a pilot who flew P-51s in World War II. Before he came to Nashville, he was a promoter in the Indianapolis area. He also had a nice Country Music Park and, in addition, booked acts into the Lyric Theater. At one time, Blake booked acts for "The Shower of Stars" in St. Louis, as well. He owned a tavern on Washington Street in Indianapolis, naturally enough called Blake's Tavern. When Howard first met him, he was working Indianapolis on a Sunday, and Blake opened his bar, so that Howard could have a beer. Blake was an understanding promoter, who finally came to Nashville to open a booking agency. Howard told Smiley, "He belonged here," and Smiley agreed.

Howard remembered T. D. Kemp from the 1950's, when Howard was working for Copas. Kemp was booking country acts in the Southeast. Kemp would book his singer-brother Hal Kemp in swank places in New York, but as Howard recalled, "The country acts were booked in places less than swank." Smiley laughed and added, "Yes, the joke was, 'Have you ever worked the Kemp Circuit?'"

This was the last conversation Howard had with the happiest booker we ever knew. Smiley was tough as whang leather (not unlike granddad's tough old razor strop). He only left show business once to become a U. S. Marine during World War II. Only a strong guy like Smiley could have lasted on a kidney machine for nine years. This time, he left show business for good. Before he died, he told his friends gathered around him, a story of a rainbow in the sky between the clouds on a sunny day. He believed that was God's sign to him. Smiley had a lot of faith in his wife, Kitty, his daughter, Rita Fay, his friends, country music and above all his God.

Howard said, "I miss a lot of friends who were 'happy bookers' in this business we call music. There's Dick Blake, Hubert Long, Oscar Davis, Shorty Lavender and as they say in show business, many others. But Smiley Wilson, my old friend, I miss him most of all." As Cowboy Jack Clement once said, "We're in the fun business. If we're not having fun, we're not doing our job."

20 AFTER THE GLITTER FADES

"How many times have you heard someone say
If I had his money, I could do things my way
But little they know that it's so hard to find
One rich man in ten with a Satisfied Mind."

- Jack Rhodes and Red Hayes.

There was a cult of country music artists who glittered brighter than the stars in the Heavens. They appeared in the most striking costumes they could have tailored. Porter Wagoner, Webb Pierce, Faron Young, Hank Snow, Ernest Tubb and Little Jimmy Dickens, just to name a few, were all attired for their fans in sequin-adorned Western attire.

No one knows why this Western cut seemed to set the style for Opry performers. The first bands were hill folks, who played and dressed traditionally. Later, a lot of artists hailed from Texas and Oklahoma or points west when the sequin image emerged. Maybe it's because their tailor of choice, "Nudie," hailed from California. Whatever, these stars gave their fans a show, not only in music, but in eye appeal. When they walked on stage, all of them sparkling, their fans got their money's worth. The bands looked like a band; their clothes all matched. Whether it was The Rainbow Ranch Boys, The Texas Troubadours or The Wagonmasters, their fans knew who they were. For these performers were, above all, showmen. When Howard was a Rainbow Ranch Boy, he put on his Western cut pants, a white dress shirt with silver collar tips, boots, string tie, he looked every inch the performer on stage.

Members of Porter Wagoner's Wagonmasters band all had suits like Porter's, maybe not quite as glittery, but still impressive. There came a time when Porter was almost the sole survivor of these sequin-clad artists. As time went by, his suits became more tailored, but still artistically sequined by Nudie. Porter claimed to have a couple hundred of these sequined suits that he confided cost about eight thousand dollars apiece. While this figure may be slightly exaggerated, he did have a lot of them and they were expensive.

Nudie Cohen, the tailor, was born in Kiev, Ukraine, and immigrated to America about 1911. He became the most famous tailor for Country and Western stars from California to the East Coast. Nudie has left us, but his stylish work's being carried on by his former son-in-law, Manuel Cuevas, who actually relocated to *Music City USA*.

Porter Wagoner was born in 1927, in Howell County, Missouri, outside of West Plains, the youngest son of a sharecropper. He grew up "knowing the rear end of a mule." His father and elder brother were ill, the others left the farm and this left the youngest brother, Porter, to do most of the farm work. He grew up fascinated by a couple of black boys who played fiddle and guitar on the streets of West Plains. His brother and sister could play a little guitar, so they showed Porter a few chords. Back then, country people just naturally played string instruments. I know that Howard learned to play by watching the neighbors, and I assume Porter did the same. It mattered not if you were from a farm in North Carolina or Missouri, music was a bigger and better thing than what you were doing, and it filled you with a dream you didn't dare speak about, for fear of being laughed at. Your only recreation on the farm, was the radio, which brought you the music.

Howard dreamed of a Jerry Byrd steel guitar sound. But Porter dreamed bigger, of someday being like the heroes he heard on WSM's *Grand Ole Opry*: Roy Acuff, Ernest Tubb or Bill Monroe. Porter had to quit school in the eighth grade and go to work full-time on the farm. Still, it didn't stop him from dreaming more and more of a country music career. Like most beginning singers, he started singing in his hometown. When he moved to West Plains to work at the local supermarket at age fifteen, his boss heard him sing, and put him on his sponsored local show. Porter became an instant success in West Plains.

From there, he moved up to KWTO-Springfield, thanks to a bus driver who brought him to the attention of the station's program director. The year was 1951, and Porter formed his first band. He drove to Springfield in a 1940 Chevrolet with slick tires. Soon, Si Siman, a KWTO executive, personally contacted Steve Sholes at RCA in New York City. Impressed, Sholes flew to Springfield to audition Porter and on the spot signed him to a contract.

Porter made his first recording session at KWTO studios, September 19, 1952. Actually, he did two sessions that day, cutting eight songs. His first release, "Settin' the Woods On Fire" and the others to follow, did nothing really. In 1953, he came over to Nashville to record, but nothing came out of that either, although two of the musicians were Chet Atkins on guitar and Papa John Gordy on piano. Then in 1954, Don Warden, a steel guitarist, Speedy Haworth, playing electric rhythm guitar, and Porter on open string guitar, recorded "A Satisfied Mind" at KWTO. The Porter Wagoner sound was born. They were the only three musicians on that session, which only cost RCA forty dollars to record. Then they recorded the pure sound of a hillbilly trio vocal, and overdubbed the bass fiddle. That Wagoner *Billboard* charting, which hit number one for four weeks starting July 9, 1955, was so striking, covers followed by Jean Shepard and Red Foley, each hitting Top Five.

During this period, Porter was actually working with Foley on *The Ozark Jubilee* telecast from Springfield. Foley, in fact, schooled Porter in the art of recitations. Meantime, Porter became the number two man on the *Jubilee*, after Foley. Along with his hit records and regular appearances on network TV the *Jubilee* gave him, Porter became nationally important in country circles. It must have been hard to leave this security blanket, but in 1957, Wagoner came to Nashville to sign with the *Grand Ole Opry*. From that point on, his career skyrocketed.

Howard, who preceded Porter at the Opry by a few years, said, "I saw right away that the Opry's newest artist had the ability to sell himself on stage." His fans believed in him. Whenever Porter did "Trouble In the Amen Corner," a recitation at the Opry, while I was working for him, we were flooded on Monday at the office with requests for lyrics and tapes.

At one time, Porter boasted the longest-running, most-watched syndicated show on television. His show's sponsor was Black Draught Syrup, and when Porter told viewers it was "good from the inside out," his fans rushed to partake of this "marvelous laxative." It had to be that sincere country boy look that sold them on it.

Meanwhile, hits followed hits and Porter was riding high. Although Porter had brought his wife, Ruth, from Springfield to Nashville, rumors began flying about so-called escapades with his show's female singers. He was initially paired with "Pretty Miss" Norma Jean, later with Dolly Parton, and a few that weren't so famous.

Porter's greatest success story was Dolly Parton. Dolly joined *The Porter Wagoner Show* at the right time, when Norma Jean departed. Fred Foster, at Monument Records, had released some unexciting records on her, but she was showing great promise. Howard remembered Dolly doing demos for Moss Rose when he was working there. Porter found their voices blended well together, and he took Dolly to Chet Atkins, asking that she be signed; however, RCA did not want Dolly. Then Porter pulled a strictly "Porter-type thing," telling Chet he would give up his royalties to pay Dolly's sessions. Needless to say, Dolly was an instant success, mainly thanks to Porter's sponsorship. Her first RCA releases were hits, but they were also duets with Porter, who incidentally never had to give up any royalties.

Their first duet in 1967, "The Last Thing On My Mind," made them an instant Top Ten duo, quickly followed by "Holdin' On To Nothin'," another Top Ten, and "We'll Get Ahead Someday," a Top Five record, both in 1968. They began winning duet awards each year, and finally, in 1970, she garnered her first Top Ten solo single, "Mule Skinner Blues," a revival of an old Jimmie Rodgers blue yodel song of that title.

It seemed as if Porter's plans were working out. He and Dolly wrote songs together and published them. He had management on Dolly, but in the end Dolly had bigger plans. Little arguments between them became big disagreements. Arguments cropped up at the TV show, sometimes about make-up and then about his productions of her records. Finally, Dolly wanted a new producer to record her with more of a pop sound. Chet and RCA encouraged her. Suddenly the situation was reversed, his only hits then were the duets with Dolly. Eventually, she left Porter, and the lawsuits began. Gossip backstage at the Opry was that Porter was finished. A song was written about a falling star that used to travel in a great big bus, but now traveled in a little van. It sure sounded like Porter.

Porter quit RCA and stopped going on the road. He gave his band to Dolly, including Don Warden, his mainstay. As if in a dream, Porter watched Dolly get bigger with a 1980 movie, "Nine To Five," while his career and money seemed to be fading away. Then the IRS came down on Porter for back taxes, so he had to go back on the road, and hired new Wagonmasters.

All of that happened before I went to work for him. He was still in his building on 18th Avenue South in 1984, when he hired me as office manager. Then he let The Wagonmasters go, hiring an all-girl band: Wanda Vick, fiddle; Lisa Spears, steel; Patti Clements, keyboard; Becky Hinson, bass; Nancy Given, drums; and Glenda Knipfer, guitar. We even held a contest to name the all-girl band and the winners were Nellie and Ruth Poe, of Mountain View, Arkansas. Their winning name was The Right Combination. They were fitting winners, who once had performed as The Poe Sisters, the first females to work for Ernest Tubb. This new band sparked Porter's career for a while. It was a natural booking arrangement for a man with his reputation as a womanizer, and it stirred up plenty of publicity. Our CPA asked, "Now, which one is he going to pick out of the herd?" He picked Glenda, the pretty guitarist from Alabama.

Porter was easy to work for, and we never had a cross-word. In five years, we only had two bookings that went amiss. One was in Canada, for fifteen days in Ontario. In the middle, a festival was booked. I was always afraid of outdoor events, as they could be rained out so easily. In this case, Bill Anderson, booked on the same festival, called me from his Nashville office and said he had been stopped at the border, because the festival was canceled. Porter, already in Canada for other dates, called me the next day, saying the promoter had run off with the money, and they weren't paid. I knew he was upset, so I said, "Porter, you were already up there with other dates and half of the money is in the bank." Porter murmured, "I guess you're right." We always had half the money in the bank, before Porter even left town.

Then there was another gig at "The Little Opry" in Indiana and they didn't have the money to pay after the show. They promised to pay, but never did. But of course, half of the money was in the bank, just as usual.

One time I sent him to Mobile, Alabama. Before he left he said, "Ruth, that's care package country." When he got back, I asked him how the show went. He said, "Well, when I looked out the window of the hotel on Main Street at noon, and there was not a car in sight, I knew nobody would be at the show." He did get paid.

Porter always hated it when he didn't draw a crowd. Once in his hometown of West Plains, he didn't fill the auditorium, so he got angry and refused to get off the bus to sign autographs. The town was so angry, they threatened to take his name off the street they had named for him, Porter Wagoner Boulevard, which crossed Jan Howard Avenue. (Yes, the Opry's Jan Howard, who was also a native or favorite daughter, as the saying goes.)

One winter I booked Porter in Watertown, New York. The weather there was terrible. The bus with Porter and the girls left here in the afternoon. I was in bed, when the buyer started calling me at home. "He'll never make it here," he said, "We've got seventeen inches of snow and it's still falling." Knowing Porter had to almost be there, I said, "He will get there, call me when he does." This went on for several hours, back and forth. Finally the buyer said, "I'm sending out the state police to guide him in." "Great," I said, and added again, "Call me when he arrives." The calls stopped. No one called me. The next day I called Porter at the hotel. He said, "Oh sure, no problems at all. We had a full house." The next weekend he was booked in Baltimore. Did he go? No! He heard there were predictions of sleet.

Another night he and the girls were waiting for the bus at the office to go to Pennsylvania. Porter called me at home, "Ruth, Porter Wagoner can't ride this bus: it's dirty." (When talking about himself, he always said "Porter Wagoner.") Okay, so I called the bus company and they sent another bus. Porter called again. "Ruth, Porter Wagoner can't ride on this bus. A hub cap is off." Okay, I called the bus company again. They sent another bus. This time it broke down before it got to Porter. Then I called the booker, Don Fowler, a long-suffering man. Luckily, Bill Anderson was in the area and not working on that day. He replaced Porter, but I still had to call Porter's doctor, Dr. Perry Harris, and get a letter from him for the buyer saying Porter was sick. Dr. Harris was always available when needed for such things.

I suppose there was no way to avoid leaving things behind sometimes. Most things were left because of always loading in the dark. Most country bands left out of Nashville somewhere around midnight. One day, Porter and his band arrived at their date somewhere in Pennsylvania and discovered all their cords were missing. Now this could be disastrous, when all the band members play electrical instruments. Meanwhile, back at the office, I came to work and found their cords all in one duffle bag, sitting right where they left them, in the driveway, where they had loaded the bus the night before. At the end of the day, Glenda called, wanting to know if I found their cords. Thanks to Federal Express, the cords were drop-shipped to the band at a Fed- EX office nearest them for their next date.

I just never knew what would happen next in that office. Like the time Porter was booked in Enterprise, Alabama. I called the buyer, as I always did before a show date, to ask if everything was okay and if he needed anything. I talked to a very nice man who proceeded to tell me the history of the town. He said, "We are the only town in the United States to have a statue to the boll weevil." I said, "Oh y'all grow a lot of cotton." He said, "No, ma'am, we used to, until the boll weevil came through."

Then I got a call from some guy in Ohio, who said we had to stop using the name "Right Combination" for our band. His band had been using that name for ten years. I took a second to think, then I told him, "Well, I think YOU had better stop using that name. Porter and Dolly had a record out, 'The Right Combination,' fifteen years ago." He said, "Oh-h-h-h!" I never heard another word from him.

Another time a lady called the office from Chattanooga and gave me hell because she had gone to a Gatlin Brothers show and it was so dirty she had to leave. I asked her why she was calling Porter Wagoner's office. She said, "Because y'all were the only ones with a number in the phone book." That was possible as Nashville was known for having the most unlisted phone numbers.

There was also the case of the missing wagon wheel from Porter's office yard. It was really a big buggy wheel that proclaimed that this was the office of Porter Wagoner Enterprises. It stayed gone for a year and we guessed it was gone forever. Then one day a new intern booker at Buddy Lee's Talent Agency, Pat Logan, called and said he had found Porter's wheel. Pat was a recent graduate of Vanderbilt University and said he had spotted it at one of the college's fraternity houses. Pat returned it. I never did ask him the question foremost in my mind, "Did you know the theft of our wagon wheel first-hand?" Anyhow, we did not place the wheel in the yard again, causing the fraternity brothers to steal on new grounds.

Things were going along pretty well, until Wanda Vick, fiddle player, called me at home one Sunday morning. I said, "What are you doing home, Wanda? You're supposed to be in Pennsylvania." She said, "Porter fired me, and sent me home on a plane." It seemed that none of the girls liked their bus driver. Wanda, as spokesman for the group, went to Porter and asked for him to be replaced. Porter refused. Words were exchanged and Wanda called him Hitler. Porter, of German descent, resented that, so he sent Wanda home. Wanda was replaced by a musician named Kathy Ann Kuhn, but went on to form an all-girl group Wild Rose ("Breaking New Ground").

From that point on, Porter seemed to be on a roll. Somewhere in Indiana, on their day off, he caught Becky and Nancy having pizza and a beer at the hotel bar. He fired them, too! (Porter did not drink anything.) Ed Chambliss, the old drummer from The Wagonmasters, succeeded Nancy (who joined Wanda in Wild Rose). Lisa was the next to go and Hank Corwin, also a former Wagonmaster, replaced her. Hank was a great steel player, originally from New York. When he came aboard, he helped me in routing their trips, for he knew all the short cuts. It became evident to me that Porter was going to get all his boys back. That's what happened. The girls were replaced with the boys. Except Glenda! After all, Glenda was his personal manager.

About this time, Porter decided he wanted a divorce from wife Ruth, whom he had been married to since his West Plains days. I recommended attorney Joe Binkley, Sr. But Nancy Hurt, the office bookkeeper, and I delayed proceedings as long as we could. Porter thought he would get an easy divorce, because he hadn't lived with Ruth for some twenty years. He had given her a monthly payment, a home, a Cadillac and paid her utilities all those years, but life isn't always fair. Muriel Robinson was the judge in their case and she was tough on philandering husbands. I had to testify about Porter's show dates. One thing Nancy and I had to be careful of, was to not hurt Porter's ego. I couldn't tell the whole truth, that he was older and with no hit records, his price was falling.

The end result was that Porter lost. Judge Robinson awarded Ruth a lump sum of one hundred and seventy-five thousand dollars, and a one hundred and fifty thousand dollar life insurance policy on Porter. The Judge also gave her thirteen hundred dollars a month alimony. Porter was allowed to keep his office building, his home on Pennington Bend Road and his boat. Judge Robinson granted Ruth the divorce on the grounds of cruel and inhumane treatment. Porter admitted in court that he had a number of affairs and was now living with a girl in her twenties (which sounded like bragging to me).

The end result at the office was that we had to sell the building on 18th Avenue South in order to pay Ruth the lump sum awarded her. Someone testified in court that Porter's net worth was from seven hundred thousand to nine hundred thousand dollars. I was never sure how they came up with that figure, unless they added property into the mix. We sold right away and rented another building closer to Opryland, which is what Porter wanted. I struggled to get Porter moved. Things were never the same after that.

Another job landed in my lap, paying one hundred dollars more a week. We were leasing buses from Ben and Reba Reed of Florida and they wanted to open a publishing, record and booking company. Howard and I talked it over and both of us decided it was time to move on. I moved Porter to the new office building and then moved on to work for the Reeds at Spence Manor. I hired Bob Bean to do the booking and we opened up Reed Music, Inc.

On October 28, 2007, Porter Wagoner died of cancer at age eighty. He was still an institution at the Opry. There seemed to be an understanding between him and an audience, that he and his music was real country. His jokes were corny though, for instance, "Put a picture of me in your corn crib and there won't be a rat left." Or, when he pulled up his pant legs to reveal his knobby knees, the audience still laughed big. But when he sat on a stool and told them about Brother Irey in the Amen Corner, there wasn't a dry eye in the house. He was always an entertainer, a shade above the new acts, who could only say, "And here's my next record . . . " They say that Dolly was with him and sang "I'll Always Love You," for him, just before he died. That was the song she said she wrote for Porter, when they went their separate ways.

Porter told me a lot of things I can remember, like, "You meet the same people going down, as you met going up." Once when I asked him if he was attending a music business gathering, he said, "No, they'll shake your hand, while they're looking over your shoulder to see who's there more important than you." I think he was right.

I believe that Porter always remained true to his roots. He spent more time at the Opry in his later years by choice, preferring to be there, rather than out on the road. He seemed to have more to tell people than what he recorded last and, of course, his recording career had been over for some time. His glitter had been fading, but he still wore sequins that sparkled in the stage lights, maybe not quite as bright. Porter always believed the audience came first.

I'm sure "The Thin Man From West Plains" died with a satisfied mind, believing that the country music fans would always love him, as he had loved them. The 28th of October was the day the glitter faded for good: *"When life has ended and my time has run out / My friends and my loved ones, I'll leave there's no doubt / But there's one thing for certain when it comes my time / I'll leave this old world with a satisfied mind."*

Porter Wagoner entering backstage dressing room.

21 FORE

"Oh say can you see
That flag from the tee
It's so hard to make a five
With a bear staring you in your eye
I'd proudly tell you my score
But please don't make me lie anymore
Oh say does that sand trap
Cause you to cuss and act mean
Can you blame it on your clubs
Or is it just one of those things."

- Howard White.

On a Wednesday night, with the help of the "Wednesday Night Choir" and a little wine, Bob Jennings dreamed up a real, honest-to-goodness golf tournament for the duffers in the music business to participate in, at prices they could afford. It was to be a tournament that they all could play in: artists, musicians, songwriters, publishers, bookers, etc., without fear of embarrassment, if your ball stayed in the rough. Thus was born the First Annual Four Star Golf Tournament International in the year of our Lord, 1969. The "Four Star" was planned as a two-day affair on a Monday and Tuesday, but from the start, Bob planned Saturday and Sunday (Mother's Day) as practice days, so it really was a four-day event. It was held about forty miles from Nashville at the Henry Horton State Park.

They all stayed at the Inn there and, from the onset, the fun they had topped the golf game they played. Everyone loved Bob's tournament because the emphasis was on fun, rather than golfing skills. Darrell Royal from the University of Texas; George McIntyre, Vanderbilt Coach; and Frank Lary, former Detroit Tiger pitcher were invited guests and played every year. There were some good golfers from the music industry, like Chet Atkins, Henry Strzelecki, Pee Wee King and Bob Beckham, but most were like Howard, an 18 handicapper, and, as he said, "That ain't good!" Then there were some good golfers who raised their handicaps extremely high. Howard said, "Not saying they cheated, but they won constantly. However, nobody cared." As Howard said, "Don't try to play sober, you won't play any better."

Everyone thought Howard was naturally funny, so Bob decided that Howard should entertain at the banquet providing Howard would "Keep it short." After all, Howard came free. The first year he did his act impromptu, the old imitation of Roy Acuff he had done for years. Bob and the crowd absolutely fell out. Afterwards, Bob sent Howard a picture and on the back he wrote, "Since one picture is worth a thousand words, this makes us about even."

The next year Howard approached Bob and said, "You are putting me on the show, aren't you." Bob said, "Keep it short!" Howard then wrote a new routine. He started with a little Roy Acuff, but then sang new words with apologies to Webb Pierce, who was there: *"Wondering, wondering how to play golf / Wondering, wondering how to knock some strokes off / Every hour of the day I'm in the wrong fairway / I keep wondering, wondering if I'll ever learn to play."* ("Wondering" was Webb Pierce's first number one hit.) Then he kidded Eddy Arnold who was also there, noting:*"Make the bogies go away / Give me a par or two today / Keep the big trees out of my way / And make out of bounds in play."* That, of course, was a take off on Eddy's mega-hit "Make the World Go Away." Howard closed his act with the above *"Oh, say can you see . . . "*

That year, Howard was presented with the Perseverance Award. He also made the news. A *Music Row* publication read, "Howard White was a winner for something, and did a little of his Roy Acuff act, which is so real you think you are at Dunbar Cave." The next year, Howard said, "Bob, I'm going to be on the show right?" Bob said, "Keep it short!" Howard really planned a routine that year, because he heard that Glenn Snoddy of Woodland Studios was going to be there, and record him on a mobile unit. His routine went something like this: "A lot of stories have been told about how and why Columbus discovered America. Well, I think I finally found out the truth. I was over in Spain last year, and this old Spaniard told me that he had heard that Columbus used to hang out at the El Toro Tavern, with an hombre named Fernando Cortez Smith and a midget they all called El Low Boy. They drank beer and wine and listened to the original Little David play on his harp.

"There really wasn't much going on, except bullfights and bull-washes by the Spanish Boy Scouts, to raise money for the Uno Baptist Church. Columbus said, 'Boys there ain't nothing going on here. Let's look for greener pastures.' Queen Isabella was Columbus' 'special' friend. That day she was having a party at El Holiday Inn, so Columbus stopped off and asked her if she would sponsor a trip to the New World, and she said she would, if he would bring back four tickets to the *Grand Ole Opry*. Pretty soon he got three ships and he and his friends were on their way. They stopped off at Cuba to get a couple of six packs and they found some Indians who said, 'Who go there?' Columbus said 'Christopher Columbus, Fernando Smith and El Low Boy and could you tell us what you are smoking?' The Indian said, 'That weed we grow. You are welcome to try it, but don't give any to El Low Boy, it might make him high. Why you come here?' 'We got tired of bullfights and harp music and we got plans for this new country. You need some baseball, football, tennis, and track, not to mention Bingo and horse races, back to back. And we're gonna name a baseball team up in Cleveland for you, and you're going to have plenty of room for your teepees, but you're gonna have to let us pick out your lots.'"

Well, Glenn taped it and we have a copy, but that was the end of that. However, Bob sent Howard another picture. This time it said, "Well, at least I'm clean, cute and original." Billy Edd Wheeler, (one of the Wednesday

178

night choir) wrote Bob and said, "Tell Howard I've got a job for him, just perfect for his brand of humor, writing for a TV show that was cancelled before it got started."

Everyone in the business wanted to play in the Four Star. Bob Jennings was really gifted. He came to Nashville from Auburntown, Tennessee, and joined WLAC-Nashville. He fronted his own band, then had his own early morning show. In 1952, he was named DJ of the year. He recorded on Challenge Records and emceed *The Stonemans'* show. He also became manager of Four Star Music in 1961.

So much fun was had at that golf tournament. A bunch congregated in Kitty and Smiley Wilson's room because they brought enough food and drink for two golf tournaments. They all moved from room to room, just to see what might happen next. Knowing the music crowd, anything could happen. For instance, Webb Pierce and Faron Young were playing together and they were overheard arguing, when Faron failed to make a putt and his ball landed between Webb's ball and the cup. Webb said, "Faron, pick up your ball." Faron said, "Hell no, putt around it." Rusty Adams (Coco the Clown) set the all-time record for the most strokes, one hundred and thirty five! Howard was the only golfer to get a real birdie. A robin flew right into his drive and was killed instantly. That foursome gave it "last rites" before they played on.

As business goes, Joe Johnson, owner of Four Star, decided to build a monstrous office building. He mortgaged his successful publishing company to do it and lost everything. Four Star closed and eventually Acuff-Rose bought the Four Star catalog. Bob went to Acuff-Rose Publications and the golf tournament went right on with a change of name to the Acuff-Rose Golf Tournament.

In the first year of the Acuff-Rose tournament, Bob put Howard on the show again, after saying, "Keep it short." Howard wrote a parody of Acuff-Rose's biggest hit, "Tennessee Waltz." Golfers like Webb Pierce expected Howard to roast them, so Howard wrote and sang (and believe me, Howard could not sing): *"I was trying to play golf/At the Acuff-Rose golf tournament/When two old friends, I happened to see . . . It was Webb Pierce and Max Powell, And they were standing in the fairway/Some two hundred yards from me/I saw Webb as he drew back his powerful swing/And the ball rolled right on the green/It's too bad they were playing number 7 at the time/Cause the ball rolled on number 13 . . . Webb, don't feel too bad, 'cause I've done things like that/Winning's not everything in life/Sometimes it's hell when you don't play too well/And you've got a 250 pound wife . . ."*

Every year Howard did his bit at the banquet shows and Bob always said, "Keep it short!" Lots of golf tournaments followed, the Chet Atkins International, The Floyd Cramer Celebrity Golf Tournament, The Jerry Chesnut Open-Closed, The Jack Greene Tournament and The Chuck and Georgia Chellman Tournament. Howard was invited to them all. He was not a great golfer, but he kept 'em laughing.

The golfers played on, but time changes everything. Suddenly, the game was taken seriously. Too many bankers, lawyers and CPA's, etc., were playing. The fun began to diminish. Howard said, "I believe Bob's tournaments were, for more than a decade, the high point for all. I never won, but in 1975, I won a trophy for 'Appearing To Have The Most Fun.' I can still hear The Reverend Ralph Hart shout 'Heavenly days' the day he made a hole-in-one. He always blessed my ball to keep it from going out of bounds. I can still see Billy Edd Wheeler doing an Indian Dance when he hit a good drive. Once Bob and I bet Smiley Wilson we could beat him going home. Smiley passed us so fast his golf cart never touched the ground. On Sunday nights, Bob always took us out to eat at Stan's."

Bob Jennings died in 1984. Howard played golf with Bob's son, Don, and Smiley Wilson, but golf was never the same for Howard again. Howard remembered, "Bob wasn't there to see me win the 'Johnny (Peanuts) Wilson Sportsmanship Award.' And he wasn't there with his infectious laugh to spur me on at the shows. I performed at no more golf tournaments. After all, who would be there to say 'keep it short.'"

Bob wrote a very prophetic letter to Howard that he treasured. It said: "In future years, after you have forgotten if you won or lost, you no longer remember any of your bad shots and the groans about the sandbaggers have faded, maybe this picture will bring back a few fond memories of the good weather and friendship we all enjoyed at this occasion." And Howard said with tears, "Oh yes, Bob, I will not forget."

M.C Bob Jennings during 1981 Acuff-Rose tournament warns crowd Howard's about to deliver his Henry Horton address.

22 THE DJ'S GOLDEN AGE OF RADIO

"When the last moonshiner buys his radio . . .
Something will pass that that was American,
And all the movies will not bring it back."

- Stephen Vincent Benet

At first, country music was heard mostly on phonograph records (78-rpm), but, as the depression wore on, and the price of records became too expensive, radio became the king of the day. People either owned a radio or they knew someone who did. Radio, in the long run, was less expensive than buying records. In 1927, for instance, it is said that one hundred and four million records were sold, but by 1932, the figure had slumped to six million.

As radio began to enjoy its dominance, radio personalities were born. This was the Golden Era of radio, the time when we all turned on our radios to hear our favorite artists, announcers or the news. When broadcasting began, live programming was all we had. DJs were a thing of the future. For talent, stations depended on the music available in their own locales, few of whom were professional. The newsmen reported local disasters, floods, droughts, blizzards, storms, fires, etc. This was the time when even commercials were as popular as hit songs, such as the one Roy Acuff wrote for the *Opry's Prince Albert Show*. Do you remember? *"Howdy all you friends and neighbors / Join us in our Prince Albert show / Tune up your five-string banjo / Lay down your fiddle and your bow / Throw back the rug on the floor / Light up your old corn pipe / Everyone will have some fun / At The Grand Ole Opry tonight . . . "*

The following are stories about some of the most colorful radio personalities of our times. In 1940, Judd Collins was an announcer at WSGN-Birmingham and was reporting the South Eastern Track Meet at Legion Field there. Jack Harris, WSM sports announcer, was supposed to join him there to report for Nashville; however, at the last minute, Harry Stone called WSGN's manager to ask him if WSM could take their "feed." Harris was ill and couldn't make it. So it was agreed on and Judd wasn't aware that WSM was taking their feed. On Monday morning, Harry Stone called Judd in Birmingham and said, "Are you the young man that reported that track meet the other day?" Judd said, "Yessir." Stone asked him, "How'd ya like a job at WSM?" Judd was astounded, but managed to say, "Goodness gracious! How much does it pay, Mr. Stone?" Stone told him it paid thirty five dollars a week, Judd told me, "That was fifteen dollars more than I was making, so I went to Nashville and went to work the following Monday. Seems I auditioned and didn't know it."

Collins was assigned to work the *Grand Ole Opry* on Saturday nights, because, as he said, "Nobody else wanted to work on Saturday nights." The Opry was being held at the War Memorial Auditorium, across the street from the station then. Judge Hay, Ford Rush, Louie Buck and David Cobb were there. When Judd went on, his basic job was reading commercials. He went there the same month as Minnie Pearl and Owen Bradley. Judd said, Minnie loved the Opry so much that she stood around absolutely intrigued. She was a real trouper."

When World War II came along, Judd joined the military, becoming a pilot and flying twin-engine planes. He lost touch with WSM then, but on Saturday nights, he'd turn his radio on to WSM despite his co-pilot and navigator's objections. "Turn off that damn hillbilly music," they'd say.

After his time in the service ended in 1945, Judd went back to WSM. By then, the Opry had moved to the Ryman Auditorium. It was a great time for the Opry and so many servicemen came to the show. Tennessee was an ideal spot for Army maneuvers. That, together with all the bases around Nashville, created a whole new audience from service members who loved country music, and those just looking for something to do on Saturday nights.

Judd said, "It became a very big-time show. To me, the big attraction was the people. There was a family reunion every Saturday night. Everybody in the world came through those doors. I treasured that association. I remember Dick Norris, a free-lance policeman, who was the guard backstage. He seemed to know just who to let in."

WSM started paying additional monies to announcers for making promotional spots. Things were good. Then Judd decided he wanted to go back to college, so he took his entrance exam at Vanderbilt University and passed. Soon afterwards, he and Louie Buck were sitting back stage at the Opry and Judd said, "Louie, I'm going back to college." Louie said, "Why Judd, you're a damn fool! You and I are making money on these 'hillbillies,' you have a house and two children. You need to work." Taking Louie's advice, Judd kept on working, giving himself a year to make a decision, and of course never quit.

Naturally, Collins came into contact with all the artists. One night he and Loretta Lynn were sitting side-by-side putting on make-up, when Loretta's agent came to the door. "Loretta, next week we'll be in Houston, Texas. Just wanted to tell you that we've sold a lot of tickets for next Saturday night." Loretta said, "That's fine, but I'll be canning beans. I won't be there next Saturday." The agent almost dropped his hat, "What do you mean you won't be there!" Loretta said, "I mean I'm canning beans next Saturday and I ain't goin' to Houston." She didn't go either. Judd said he had to admire her for sticking to what she believed.

Among Judd Collins' favorite memories concerned Louie Buck and occurred one Saturday night after Judd finished *The Purina Show* at 8 p.m. He was going to get a beer on Broad Street, when he spotted Louie sitting in his car in front of a pawnshop there on Lower Broad. Judd tapped on the car window and Louie opened the door and told Judd to sit down. Louie was listening to the NBC Symphony. "What are you doing listening to the symphony when you're fixing to do the *RC Cola Show*?" Louie answered, "This is my kind of music." Judd said, "I thought that was a strange twist to his personality. Then I came upon him one day in Studio C playing the piano. He told me that he taught himself to play." Louie said, "How do you think the man who invented the piano learned to play? He taught himself!" Judd mused, "And yet, he really was one of the hillbillies."

In 1945, Collins was working day and night. His Saturday's began at 5:45 a.m. on *The Martha White Show* with the Carter Family, Mother Maybelle, daughters Helen, June and Anita, with Chet Atkins on guitar. Judd remembered that Chet always wanted to sing and they wouldn't let him. Judd's day ended Saturday night after the Opry concluded at midnight.

One afternoon at WSM on the fifth floor, the switchboard operator rang him and said there was somebody waiting to see him. He told her he would make the station break and be right out. As he walked out, a tall skinny man said, "Are you Judd Collins?" When he said yes, the man said, "My name is Hank Williams and I'm from Montgomery. Charlie Holt sent me to see you. He said you'd get me on the Opry." (Holt was an old friend of Judd's, then running a radio station.) Judd replied, "Hank, I'm glad to meet you and I'm glad to hear from Charlie, but I can't get you on the Opry. I don't have anything to do with that. Jack Stapp is back there right now rehearsing *The Prince Albert Show*. I'll take you to see him. He's the man who makes the decisions." Judd could tell that Hank thought he was fluffing him off, but Judd took him to Stapp and introduced him.

As time went on, Fred Rose actually got Hank signed to the Opry. A few years later, Judd and Louie Buck were sitting backstage when Hank came in, all dressed up. He sat down beside Collins and said, "Judd, what kind of car are you drivin'?" The announcer replied, "I'm driving a 1948 Plymouth and it's a Jim Dandy! Why?" Hank got up to leave and said, "I just thought I'd ask. I just bought Audrey a new Cadillac today, same color as mine. I just wondered what you was a'drivin'."

Television came to WSM in 1950. Judd said, "We spent long hours talking about TV." What do you think television is going to be like, was a favorite discussion. None of us knew. I'd never seen television. In reality, we thought television would complement radio, thought they'd just roll a camera in the studio, take a station break and there it would be, WSM-Television. We just thought that when you did *The Martha White Show*, there the camera would be and you'd be on television. It wasn't like that, of course. It was a separate business. I thought it would be part of the radio station. It certainly was not! We didn't know anything about TV."

After TV began, the radio shifts Judd was working were no longer possible for him. He did some Martha White commercials and National Life syndicated series for a while. Some of them were done at the Ryman and some at the WSM Studios. One of the artists that appeared was a very young Willie Nelson, all dressed up like a business man with short hair.

Judd was really impressed by him, because his appearance was so clean cut. Years later, the next time he saw Willie, he appeared in long hair, a beard, ragged clothes and a head-band. During the late 1950's, Judd was phased out of the *Grand Ole Opry*.

Collins was still doing the Opry when he saw Jack Stapp with Elia Kazan. Jack told Judd that Kazan was doing a movie and maybe Judd might like to talk to him. Judd told Kazan that he didn't know anything about movies, but he'd like to have a part in his film. Then Judd forgot about it, until one day he got a call from an agent in New York, saying they wanted to talk to him about being an announcer in a movie "A Face In The Crowd." They wanted Judd to go to New York, saying it would take about a week. Andy Griffith and Tony Franciosa were in this movie, along with Lee Remick, Patricia Neal, and Walter Matthau. Others such as Burl Ives, Mitch Miller and Walter Winchell were doing cameos. There were Opry people in it too, Sammy Pruett, Suds Slayman, Odie and Jodie, Autry Inman and Rod Brasfield. Big Jeff Bess was also included. They filmed at a theater on the lower East Side. Judd said, "It was educational for me. I had such a small part, like one line. When I came home, it opened in Nashville at the Tennessee Theater, the marquee read, 'A Face In the Crowd,' starring Andy Griffith, Rod Brasfield and Judd Collins."

Judd was the Esso Reporter at WSM-TV, when New York called and offered him the job of doing the Esso News in New York. Judd and his wife went to New York. An advertising man took Judd to NBC. While they were there, a real estate agent took Mrs. Collins to look at homes. When Judd got back to the hotel, his wife was crying. She said, "I can't imagine coming up here and rearing my children. You can come, but we're not." Judd's wife had been his childhood sweetheart, so they went home and Judd stayed at WSM. He was really disappointed. He said, "I thought that was my shot at the big time, but she was right in the long run."

"Those were the good years," Collins said. "Our station was the best. National Life insisted on doing everything right." He continued, "I'm sorry the Opry has gotten away from the Judge Hay philosophy. He was very serious, no bugles, no drums. He knew what direction he was into. On the other hand, what they call country music now ain't country, but more popular now than it ever was. It seems to prosper now. I don't understand why somebody doesn't start a thing and say, 'This is where you find real country music.' Branson was in a perfect position . . . but they didn't do it."

Judd then added, "I loved the Opry. One night I was on my way home, listening to the Opry and Minnie Pearl, and Rod Brasfield came on. Rod asked, 'Where were you born, Minnie?' and Minnie said, "Born in a hospital.' Ron said, 'Were you sick?' Minnie answered, 'No, I just wanted to be near my mother.' I had to stop the car and laugh. So many good friendships resulted from all those years, lots of memories." (Here Judd paused and sighed. I did this interview with Judd Collins in 1991. He died in 2008.)

WSM had the most-loved radio personalities on the air. One of the more respected was Grant Turner, who was an announcer there for almost half a century. Grant came to WSM on D-Day, June 6, 1944, at age thirty-two, hired as a staff announcer and one of Hay's assistants at the Artists Service Bureau. Grant loved radio, he loved WSM and the Opry, and its artists.

Turner was the serious type, so serious that the fun-loving country artists liked to pull jokes on him quite often. One evening, Grant was interviewing Bill Carlisle for his show, *Nashville Jamboree*. Bill had clued the engineer in on the gag he was about to pull. Grant thought he was taping for real as he began the interview, like this: "Here on *The Nashville Jamboree*, it's great to have a guest like this, seeing him jump higher and higher, then hardly jump at all. Bill Carlisle's songs just get better all the time." Bill responded, "Thank you, Grant." Grant: "Just having you on the show is a great joy." Bill: "Oh, shit, I know that." Grant: (He never let on he heard what Bill said.) A lot of folks don't know you come from Kentucky. That was your home, wasn't it?" Bill: "Yeah . . . well, wait until I scratch my ass (Bill's laughing)." Grant: (Panicking) Now! What are we going to do! Start over? Start over! I guess." Engineer: "Let's take another tape." Bill: "Sorry, I forgot we were taping Grant (Bill chuckles)." Grant continued the interview, never stopping once to laugh. Of course, he knew that anything could and did happen when Bill Carlisle was around. Grant began his career at KYFO in Abilene, Texas. He was inducted into the DJ Hall of Fame in 1975. God love Grant Turner; he died as he lived, loving every minute of the work he took so seriously.

One of the most outstanding announcers was T. Tommy Cutrer. He was born in Louisiana in Tangipahoa Parish, which is on a river of the same name. Cutrer grew up in Osyke, Mississippi. In reality, he didn't mean to be in radio. He dreamed of life as a professional prize fighter or a football player, but after age thirteen, due to Osteomyelitis, he was unable to play sports. He took art at his school, St. Mary Of The Pines. One day, while listening to Woody Haysack on the radio, he turned to his father and said, "Does that fellow on the radio get paid?" "I suppose so, son," answered Dad, who was a log hauler and didn't know about those things. From that moment on, Tommy's mind was made up. He wanted to be on radio. One day he walked into WSKB at McComb, Mississippi, and met George Bloomingstock. Tommy said, "I want to talk on your radio, if it pays money." George asked him if he wanted an audition. Tommy said, "What's that?" George gave him some news and commercials to read and Tommy passed the test.

He was given a fifteen-minute program called *Music In the Garden*. All he had to do was talk a little about the song being introduced, push a button that started the turntable at the transmitter, then the music started and he turned his mike off at the same time. Tommy said, "That engineer was a genius." Bill Lowery (later of Lowery Publishing) was a DJ then. When Tommy came, Bill left and went to KWKH-Shreveport. Tommy worked three hours a day for thirty cents an hour, riding the Greyhound Bus to get there, which cost him twenty-nine cents a round trip. He stayed there three months, then left and went to WCSU in New Orleans.

185

"Actually," Tommy said, "WCSU was the only job I was ever fired from." He was to have been the morning newsman. He had only been there for two weeks, living only a block from the station, when one morning his alarm didn't go off. Instead of opening the show at 6 a.m. as scheduled, he arrived at 8. They let him go from his new twelve dollar and fifty-cent per week job. He walked across Canal Street to the St. Charles Hotel and the station there hired him for the night shift. "That worked out fine," Tommy said.

Tommy always had the desire to go to Nashville. There were no radio schools in those days. He just listened to other announcers, trying to get rid of his rural, Louisiana accent. He never graduated from college; just had to learn to speak distinctly by himself.

Connie B. Gay asked him to manage his Ashland, Kentucky, station. Tommy agreed to talk to him, but at the same time Chet Atkins produced a session on RCA with Tommy. Tommy said, "It didn't mean anything. Probably, RCA figured I would play their records, if they put out a record on me. It may have been an early method of payola." Tommy sells himself short. I just listened to a release of him on Mercury Records, "The Farmer And the Lord." Backing him were The Chanters, consisting of Buddy Killen and Kitty and Smiley Wilson. It was a fine recording.

Chet Atkins asked Jack Stapp to look into getting Tommy on WSM, so Stapp asked Tommy to come in for an audition. When Stapp told him that the job paid one hundred and twenty-five dollars per week base pay, Tommy told him, "Well, I make one hundred and fifty dollars in Shreveport." Stapp told him that only one man made one hundred and fifty dollars there and that was Judd Collins. Then he paused and said, "Now we have two." That was in 1955.

Tommy turned down the job at Gay's station that paid that plus fifteen per-cent of what he sold. He had made the same in Shreveport, but there he also had a band with which he made additional money. They had been playing at the Skyway Club, booked by Tillman Franks. In that band were future well-known Nashville musicians Floyd Cramer, Tommy Bishop and Jimmy Day. Also in the band was Floyd Ellis, who went on to play with jazz legend Pete Fountain. Tommy had been a drummer, but he had an automobile accident in Shreveport and lost a leg. After that, he hired D. J. Fontana, who later played with Elvis Presley.

WSM put Tommy on at 7:05 p.m. *The Opry Star Spotlight*, until the news came on at 10, except when a baseball game was on, which began at 7:30 p.m. After a few months, Tommy and his wife were not happy. Back then you worked a year before WSM trusted you with a commercial. He and his wife were renting a little house with Gabe Tucker and his wife, Sunshine, on Due West Avenue. Tommy decided to talk to D. Kilpatrick about his problems. After he left Kilpatrick's office, D. called Stapp and told him he was fixing to lose Cutrer. "He's on his way to resign," said D. As Tommy made his way to Stapp's office, Stapp waylaid him in the hall and told him that he wanted him to audition for a thirty-minute show, *The Pet Milk Friday Night Show*. It was beamed on two hundred-plus stations, and Tommy landed the show.

With talent and good luck, things began to fall in place. He got the job with Pet Milk's show, then a salesman with Martha White Flour told them that WSM had a new announcer he thought could sell flour and corn meal for them. So Tommy got the Martha White-sponsored Flatt & Scruggs fifteen-minute early morning show that Grant Turner had been doing, followed by a TV portion that Judd Collins had been doing. Then he got the Saturday night Opry's Flatt & Scruggs Show, as well. At about the same time, Louie Buck bought the RC Cola bottling plant in Beaumont, Texas. Louie resigned from WSM and Tommy even got his commercial spots. All this happened in a couple of months.

Tommy and his wife decided they might stay in Nashville after all, so they bought a home on Brush Hill Road that had belonged to Roy Acuff. Oswald told them how famous that house was. It was to that house that Acuff and his band had brought money home in a "tow sack" on the weekend, after playing schoolhouses, etc., during the week. They would put the money under the bed until the banks opened on Monday morning.

Lester Flatt and Earl Scruggs had an old bus. One night after the Opry, Tommy went with them to Jackson, Tennessee, to do a show. They were coming home about 3 a.m. when Tommy went back to rest in a bed. Tommy took off his wooden leg and fell sound asleep. All of a sudden awakened by Lester, calling out, "Wake up, Tommy. The bus is on fire. Get out as quick as you can, but take your time." Tommy smelled smoke, so he grabbed his leg under his arm and went hopping down the aisle. He got to the door, stepped down, forgot his leg was under his arm, went tumbling down the steps and fell in a ditch. Uncle Josh asked, "Are you hurt?" Tommy said, from where he'd fallen, "Hell no, save your self, lad!"

It was WSM's loss when T. Tommy Cutrer left to buy a radio station of his own in Jackson, Mississippi. Tommy had done everything he dreamed of and some things he hadn't dreamed about. He was in the chicken business in Texas, owning three outlets. He almost retired. He raised quarter horses. In 1969, he and his family moved back to the Nashville area, buying a house in Cottontown. It was cold, raining and sleeting, the day they moved in. Then the announcer, T. Tommy became State Senator, T. Tommy Cutrer.

While a Tennessee Senator, he was chairman of the very powerful Transportation Committee. He was responsible for bringing double trucks onto the Tennessee highways, which helped the Teamsters and the freight industry. Then he decided to retire again, but the Teamsters came to him and asked him to work for them. He was valuable to them, because he knew legislation. He was with the Teamsters for twelve years. Tommy may have been a politician, but he always had music in his soul. He and John Hartford co-wrote a song, "The Cajun Waltz." *"Oh, I'm a gonna go to the Fey-do-do/Down on the banks of the bayou go/Swing my cherie with the dancing feet/Then have some crawfish biscuits to eat/I'm going to go to the Fey-do-do/Do a little dancing to the Cajun Waltz . . ."* Think it might become a hit some day?

I did the interview with friend T. Tommy Cutrer in 1992. Tommy loved his home in Cottontown. He said, "I've made a few trips to Washington, D. C. and I'm not sure I'd like it there. I love it here with my chickens, cows and ponies, all of it," Tommy was seventy-four years old in 1998, when he died.

During the early years WSM featured live music on its broadcasts. *The Grand Ole Opry* built an audience that no one imagined, all done by radio. Programming then was heavy on concert bands, classical musicians and well-known dance bands. Beasley Smith had a show called *Mr. Smith Goes To Town.* The Lion Oil Company sponsored *Sunday Down South.* Francis Craig's show was *Sunday Serenade.* In 1950, Ralph Christian suggested a new show called *Eight O'Clock Time* featuring the staff band. Dave Overton took over Christian's spot in 1952, changing the name to *The Waking Crew.* Due to their comedy efforts, personnel laughingly called it "The Wrecking Crew."

The Waking Crew continued long after other radio stations in their country gave up on live music. It broadcast from Studio C in the old National Life Building. The *Waking Crew Band* did their last broadcast March 25, 1983, after a succession of great band leaders, Beasley Smith, Owen Bradley, Marvin Hughes, Bill McElhiney and Joe Layne. The *Nashville Banner* said, "There's been a death in Nashville's radio family." WSM's decision to drop the historic radio show ended an era in American radio. WSM was the last station to employ an on-air band. The only live broadcasts now are the *Friday Night Opry* (formerly called *Friday Night Frolics*) and the *Grand Ole Opry* on Saturday and in the summer, Tuesday night.

DeFord Bailey was the first black man on the Opry. His harmonica reels and breakdowns were recorded and released as both "race" and "hillbilly" records. He learned to play harmonica as a child, while staying in bed for a year with Polio. It was Bailey's "Pan American Blues" that preceded Hay naming the *Grand Ole Opry*. As a child, Bailey hung out under a Tennessee Central train trestle, learning to duplicate that train sound, as the old Pan American locomotive roared overhead on its route to New Orleans.

As time moved along, Bailey became a main attraction in Opry package shows. They called him "Our Little Mascot." When the Opry decided to change its image for a more "citified" audience, suddenly Bailey became an issue. Judge Hay had the unpleasant task of firing him, because, officially, "he failed to learn new tunes." In firing Bailey, WSM lost a Nashville Sound harp player before there was a *Nashville Sound* and before we had Charlie McCoy and Terry McMillan.

Bailey went to work in his own shoeshine shop and, according to accounts, refused to play in public for decades. By 1947, Bailey's sign on the wall of a 12th Avenue South shoeshine shop read, "Shoe Shining Taught Here." Red O'Donnell interviewed Bailey and he told Red, "I had to quit my radio work. My heart was acting up and I had to take it easy." When Red asked him if he really taught shoe shining, Bailey's answer was: "Yas suh, I teach shoe shining. I do it for nothing. My students are schoolboys. I suggest they take instructions for about a month, but most of them play hooky after two weeks. I've been teaching them off and on for about two years. I guess I've graduated about three hundred, all boys. Shoe shining is an art, but most of the shoeshine boys these days are what we old bootblacks call 'hit and lick guys.' They dab a little polish on, hit the shoes with a rag, make a lotta noise, pass at the shoes with a brush and say, 'thank you, boss.' This may be a fast age, but I can remember when I spent fifteen minutes on a pair of shoes. I used the old soap and water system as a starter. You don't see that anymore."

In the 1970's the Opry attempted to make up and Bailey acknowledged them warily. Bailey died in 1982, but the harmonica wizards of today, cannot claim they were the first to record here. DeFord Bailey was a master of the clickety-clack sound of a train on his harp.

Sometimes it's good to remember the little people that were not hit artists or musicians that helped to keep the cogs turning at WSM and the Opry. From 1930 until 1963, a small, gentle black man we all called just "Clifford" made his way in and out of the WSM fifth floor offices during the week, and on Friday and Saturday night at the Frolics and the Opry. He was hired by National Life as a porter, but to all of us he was the original "shoe shine boy" that some folks called "Lightning." His full name was Joseph Clifford Hampton, born in Elloree, South Carolina, and by profession, a barber. When he began his trade, he had to stand on a chair to reach his customers.

From the time he was hired in 1930 by National Life, Clifford was a favorite of Edwin Craig. One day, when Mr. Craig went to play golf at the Belle Meade Country Club, he spotted Clifford's son, Joe. "Little Clifford, what are doing here?" Mr. Craig asked. When Joe told him he was a caddy at the club, Mr. Craig said, "You tell them to give you my bag." From that time on, Joe started up and stayed at Belle Meade for twenty-two years. Now he is a Pro at Ted Rhodes Golf Course.

Clifford retired after thirty-four years. During that time he kept the whole Opry's boots shining, becoming an important personality in their lives. I remember him coming into my office in the WSM Library and shining Claude Sharp's boots twice a week. Nobody ever knew that Clifford played piano, or that he had six children and sent them all to college. He did his job quietly with a big grin. No one ever knew just how much National Life valued his services. To WSM and the pickers at the Opry, "Clifford was his name and shining was his game." It was said by several people that Harry Stone and Jack Stapp in 1950, got their inspiration for the hit song, "Chattanoogie Shoe Shine Boy," from Clifford. Stone and Stapp are both gone and Clifford died in 1978, so we'll never know for sure. Yet, as noted earlier, Fred Rose really created that classic song, but who knows, maybe ol' Fred knew Clifford, as well, and if the "slap-slap-slap" of his shoe shine rag inspired its writer, then Clifford could've played a part in one of the biggest records ever played by a DJ anywhere. (Howard and I interviewed his son Joe a.k.a. "Little Clifford," to get all the facts in 1992.)

189

Clifford Hampton

DeFord Bailey

Judd Collins

Bill Carlisle and sisters Minnie and
Martha Carson

23 OTHER PIONEERS OF RADIO

"Don't talk unless you can improve the silence."

Olde New England Saying.

Because of the dominance of the *Grand Ole Opry* and WSM Radio in things country, we tend to forget that in Nashville, not all the radio personalities were connected with WSM. There was WLAC, WSIX and WMAK, along with WENO-Ranch in Madison. They created their own place in the hearts of Nashvillians, during the Golden Age of Radio so, let's look back at the other side of radio in Nashville.

WLAC, owned by the Life and Casualty Insurance Company, went on the air in 1926. They were located on the top floor of the old L&C Building, and then moved to West End Avenue. In 1939, they moved to the top of the old Third National Bank Building. WLAC concentrated on programs with small musical groups, like Bobby Tucker, a pianist, who was an early staff pianist there, Mary Elizabeth Hicks, a pianist and organist, Charlie Nagy, a violinist and Luther Heatwole, cello, did a program for Crazy Water Crystals (a health additive). In 1943, WLAC employed a small staff band, under the direction of Charlie Nagy. When he died in 1945, Fred Murff became music director. In his band were Brooks Kirk, bass, Jack Charamella, guitar and Mary Elizabeth Hicks, piano. WLAC also did a remote show from the Andrew Jackson Hotel Grill. Bill "Hoss" Allen awarded cash prizes to members of the audience for identifying mystery tunes.

When the DJ or record shows first came about, WLAC moved quickly to employ disc jockeys. John R. (Richbourg) ran the first R&B show on WLAC. Bill "Hoss" Allen and Gene Noble, between 1946 and 1973 had what they believed to have been the largest audience of any record-spinning program. Gene Noble convinced Randy Wood of Gallatin, Tennessee, to buy advertising spots on his nightly show on WLAC. In only a couple of weeks, *Randy's Record Shop* was receiving arm-loads of mail and by 1950 was selling as many as 500,000 records a year from the advertising on Noble's DJ show. The show popularized such artists as The Hilltoppers, Pat Boone, Chuck Berry, Bo Diddley and Billy Vaughn. Randy Wood became so popular, he began his own record label, Dot Records. Johnny Maddux recorded his first record on Dot, which was an instant hit, "Crazy Bone Rag." Dot Records became an instant success in 1950. In 1967, Dot was sold to Paramount Pictures. The power of the DJ started it all.

One of the most-beloved announcers at the fifty thousand watt WLAC was Bob Jennings, *The Old Farmhand*. In about 1948, Bob fronted a band on WGNS-Murfreesboro, sponsored by Monarch Flour. The band called themselves The Eagle Rangers. In the band were Billy Robinson, steel;

Floyd Robinson, guitar; Jerry Rivers, fiddle; Jack Boles, fiddle; and Bobby Moore, bass. Once a man from Wildwood, New Jersey, came down to Nashville to play his "Saw." He guested on their show and said he could book them in a theater on the pier at Wildwood. They all went to New Jersey in the saw player's '46 station wagon. When they arrived, they found the whole pier had been condemned. Jennings, who had never been away from home before, called his wife, Robbie, long-distance and actually cried. In 1950, Bob joined WLAC, again fronting the Eagle Rangers. Big Jeff Bess was also there at the time. Then Big Jeff departed to do his own show and, one-by-one, the others moved on to other jobs.

Jennings' early ambition, as a kid in Auburntown, Tennessee, was to be a singer like Eddy Arnold. He admired Arnold so much that once, on the way to an Eddy Arnold show, he had a flat tire and drove all the way from Auburntown to a school in another town, on the rim. He was afraid he would miss some of the show, if he stopped to change the tire. As a young boy, Bob started singing over an old-fashioned telephone to members of his party line. No doubt, WLAC seemed like his door to fame when he got there. By 1955, he had his own DJ show in the early mornings on WLAC.

In 1957, Life and Casualty completed a tower at the corner of 4th and Church Streets, which still stands as a downtown landmark. Jennings, with his old cowbell, rang out from WLAC, in the tower, after its completion: "This is Bob Jennings, your old Farmhand, coming to you from WLAC Radio in downtown Nashville." In 1959 Bob was voted DJ of the year. He had received one hundred and twenty thousand pieces of fan mail from twenty-eight states. In 1966, Bob became the announcer for the Nashville-produced syndicated TV show, *The Stonemans*, featuring the legendary 1920's icon Pop Stoneman, and his children Roni, Van, Donna and Jimmy. The Stonemans, after years of hard struggle, became a force in Music City when this half hour 1960's program began going into homes everywhere.

Cowboy Jack Clement and Gene Goforth, a music promoter, from Chattanooga, started the syndicated show for The Stonemans. Goforth booked talent for Lake Winnepesaukah in Rossville, Georgia, near Chattanooga. Lake "Winnie," for many years, was a popular country music and amusement park. Nearly all the country music stars worked there. Suds Slayman recalled working at Lake Winnie with Cowboy Copas in the early 1950's. He didn't remember much about the show, but did remember that they traveled to the date in a 1952 Cadillac and they sat their whiskey, a gallon of moonshine, on the floor of the Cadillac to keep it cool (which is why he probably didn't remember the show). He did recall he and Gene Martin rode on the roller coaster and Gene was so "high" and cut up so much that the man in charge threw them off.

Jennings was also the announcer on TV's local *Carl Tipton Show*. Theirs was really an old-time country show which Carl and Sophie Tipton performed every Sunday morning on WLAC-TV. One thing that made Bob popular about town was his constant drive to do something better all the time. In 1961, he became Southern Division Manager for Four

Star Music, making Four Star one of the leading country music publishers, boasting hits like "Release Me." When Four Star closed, he moved to Acuff-Rose. Bob sponsored the most prestigious golf tournament in Music City, while at Four Star and Acuff-Rose. Bob loved all sports, particularly walking horse shows. He was the Shelbyville Show's emcee for years. He loved football, too, and liked to bet a little on the ballgames. Sometimes Bob even called Howard from church to get Howard to put a bet down for him on his favorite team.

Not only was Bob Jennings Howard's best friend, but also Chet Atkins' best friend, Eddy Arnold's best friend, and Billy Edd Wheeler's best friend. He probably did more to promote country music than anyone. He did as much for country music golf. That's why the music industry people all cried when Billy Edd wrote, in tribute: *For the birdies, for the pars / For the laughter, for the tears / Thank you, Bob Jennings / For the last fifteen years.*

WLAC was also home to radio pioneer, Big Jeff Bess and his Radio Playboys. The announcer on that show was Charlie Roberts. Big Jeff was a fixture around Nashville, with his very popular radio show, beginning in 1946, and with his personal appearances at the Germantown Inn on the Clarksville Highway for years. He probably started more country musicians on their way than anyone. It was said, in the 1950's, that you really had not "paid your dues" if you didn't have experience with Big Jeff. Sponsored by Purina, *The Radio Playboys* went on the air at 4:45 a.m. Jeff also played at WSIX and at WNOX-Knoxville, but it's his WLAC program for which he is best remembered.

As for interesting characters, at the top of the list is "Scoopie" Bruce Harper. He hung around the fringes of the country music business as long as he lived. Harper really wanted to be a country music reporter or a radio reporter, hence the nickname Scoopie. Once, he really was a sports announcer at WMTS-Murfreesboro in the 1960's. No one ever heard a basketball game given a play-by-play description, like the WMTS "color man," Scoopie Bruce. Listening on radio, we would hear Scoopie saying: "Here he comes, down the field . . . Oh, oh, he was clipped . . . They can't stop him . . . It's a home run!!!" That's basketball?

Harper was Bob Jennings's good friend. He was the lighting man for the strippers at the Rainbow Room in the Alley for a while, and after he was through work, early in the morning, he would go up to Bob's WLAC early morning show. One time, he had just returned from Florida and described to Bob the "little beauty" he brought back with him. Bob said, "How'd you get her to come to Nashville with you, Bruce?" Bruce replied, "Oh, it was easy. I just told her I could get her on the *Grand Ole Opry.*" Bob said later, "You think the Opry isn't powerful!"

Another time we were all at Bob's home playing Charades. Naturally, with a bunch of record and publishing people there, the subject was songs. When it became Scoopie's turn to act out a song, all he did was stand there and point out the window. We all guessed everything from "Window Up Above" to "North To Alaska." Finally we gave up, and Scoopie said, "Man, I thought you'd get it right away, it was so easy. It was 'Kentucky.'" When we looked puzzled, because of his clue, he said by way of explanation, "I was pointing right at Kentucky." (Groan!!!)

In the old days, you could always find Scoopie at the places where musicians hung out, like Tootsie's. He always seemed to know more about the business than anyone. When New York writers and reporters came down to write about the music industry here, somehow they always found Bruce Harper, who gave them the "scoop" on what had happened and what was happening. Maybe none of us took him seriously enough. After all, Scoopie became a self-proclaimed music historian before he died.

In 1949, WMAK's Joe Allison had the highest-rated DJ show in the country. In those days, the DJ played what he wanted to and the only format Joe went by was to vary the songs by the hour of the morning. Joe said, "In the early morning, I'd play Bluegrass and in the late morning, I'd play uptown country artists like Eddy Arnold. It seemed the blue-collar worker got up earlier than the bank president and their tastes in music was different."

Joe remembered that the show became so popular they moved out of the studio on Saturdays to the Princess Theater (then on Church Street), so the kids could come and see it live. One day a fan brought a guitar, so they let him sing, then one after another would come to be on the show. Finally, they hardly played records at all, for they had so many young fans who wanted to play music.

When they outgrew the Princess, they moved to the Ryman Auditorium. One Saturday morning, they gave away two bicycles for box tops. WSM stepped in and got them kicked out, because they couldn't get the Ryman cleaned up before the Opry performance on Saturday night. They were knee deep in box tops.

Joe Allison "got around" and everywhere he went, he had a popular DJ show. In Memphis, he emceed a show for "Eddie Hill And The Boys." "The Boys" happened to be the Louvin Brothers, who became the country duo of the time. Joe was a DJ in Laredo, Texas, when he met Eddy Arnold and Colonel Tom Parker. They talked him into going to WSM at Nashville. Joe was promised his own show, but somehow, WSM could never find the time to slot him in. He was the announcer on such shows as *Noontime Neighbors*, but that wasn't what he wanted, so he left and went to KXLA in California. Joe succeeded Ernie Ford, of "Sixteen Tons" fame. Cliffie Stone took Ford, put overalls on him, blacked out a tooth, and called him "Tennessee Ernie" Ford. When Cliff got him on Capitol Records, Tennessee Ernie became hot and left KXLA to go on the road.

In the early 1950's, Joe had a live TV show on WSIX-Nashville, called *Home Folks*, sponsored by Allis Chalmers. He had a great band on the show: Walter Haynes, fiddle; Ernie Newton, bass; Jerry Byrd, steel; and Harold Bradley and Bobby Sykes, guitars. Allison was a first-rate DJ and emcee, and has been in the DJ Hall Of Fame since 1976. His talents went in so many directions, it's impossible to name them and not leave something out. He was the co-writer of the Grammy Hall of Fame classic "He'll Have To

Go" by RCA's Jim Reeves, and produced a major hit for Roy Clark, "Yesterday, When I Was Young" at Dot-Paramount Records. Howard maintained, "Of all the people I worked for, he, above all, was his own man."

Howard got to know Smilin' Eddie Hill in 1950's Knoxville, where they both worked on the *Mid-Day 'Merry-Go-Round* at WNOX. Eddie had been performing with Johnnie Wright and Kitty Wells as a hayseed comic, playing the part of "Hump Hammer." He entertained at WMPS in Memphis, before joining WSM in 1951. While there, he pioneered an all-night country DJ show, before Ralph Emery's all-night DJ Show at WSM. In the '60's Eddie's *Country Junction Show* on WLAC-TV, sponsored by B. F. Myers Furniture, proved quite popular. Well-known personalities were always welcome on his show, along with regulars like Kitty and Smiley Wilson. He had a good band led by pianist Fred Shoemake.

Eddie Hill died January 18, 1994, after a long illness prompted by a debilitating stroke. His friends, Judd Collins, Owen Bradley, Joe Allison and Howard swapped amazing stories about Eddie after his "wake." Judd Collins, then retired from WSM, said, "One night Eddie had to leave for a show date, when Nashville was in the thick of a bad snow storm. Eddie would not accept the fact that he couldn't make it. Eddie's wife, Jackie, didn't want him to go, but Eddie felt like the show must go on. They started out slipping and sliding. Then the inevitable happened, they slipped into a ditch and couldn't get out. It was early in the morning and a milkman in his truck came by, stopped and help pull them out." Jackie said, "Well, the Lord was with us." Eddie managed to say, "Yeah, and didn't we take Him for a helluva ride!"

WSIX programmed its share of live country music. In the 1940's they had a popular show sponsored by Reuben's Furniture, at 2515 Third Avenue North, proclaiming: "Remember, you can buy it for less at Reuben's, naturally!" The star of the show was James Gilbert Buchanan, known to the entertainment world as just "Goober, The South's Favorite Nut." Goober may never have had a hit record, or a network radio show, but he became a local and regional hillbilly favorite. In 1957, Goober went to work with Porter Wagoner as a comic. He also worked with Audrey Williams, Ernest Tubb and others, but one-nighters didn't pay enough, so in 1962, Goober retired from show business. Ironically, he went to work for H. Brown Furniture on Broadway Street, which happened to be a rival of his first WSIX sponsor, Reubens.

The "good old days" of radio are gone forever. Other media have taken away its dominance. Let us not forget that it was the radio that led silent movies into "talkies." Radio attuned the public to sound dialogue and made them miss it at the silent movies. Radio supplied the technology for the movies to make the switch. Radio was powerful and is what made the country music scene so popular. The radio personalities that were the pioneers are not in the business anymore, or have moved upward to radio heaven. They are the ones that kept country music alive, when all around them there were those who were ready to let it die. They worked through the

195

times when there were the naysayers forecasting, "Rock is taking over! Country music died with Hank Williams! Now it has nowhere to go but down!"

Well, here we go again! They say, "country music just ain't the same." Well, that's true. Not one of those Golden Age radio people could have predicted just how Big the country music stars of today would become. No, it *ain't* the same, but country music, in its own way, lives. Maybe the "good old days" exist only in the hearts of the oldsters. Another generation will have their own good old days in time to come. It will still take powerful DJs, announcers and emcees to create that bridge between the artist and the buying public, by playing the music that modern technology takes us to. Let's hope all the new technology and that to come, will not take the place of radio. The next time you get in your car, turn your radio on. Somewhere out there, there is still a DJ, playing country music for all the friends and neighbors. The new sounds may sound foreign, but one can only hope the sounds of the fiddle and the steel never die. And, that on Saturday nights, the *Grand Ole Opry* carries right on, live, even though the new sounds may seem to be a rockin' and a rollin' on a new stage. Hmm, sometimes the music doesn't sound very low to the ground, boys!

Eddie Hill

24 OTHER MEMORIES

"Fallen leaves lay scattered on the ground,
Birds and flowers that were, cannot be found
All the friends we once knew are not around
They are scattered like leaves upon the ground . . ."

-Louis (Grandpa) Jones.

There is a lot in this book about musicians, their hardships and joys, but let us not forget the stars that pioneered Nashville, turning it into *Music City, USA.* They too, in the old days, rode those two-lane roads in automobiles with their sidemen. These stars are the same ones who gave the road musicians work. Well, this chapter is about a few of these artists. Maybe in reading about them, it will bring sweet memories of others to your mind.

Howard and I were traveling on I-40 to California and he had just said, "Oh, what I'd have given for a highway like this, when I had to travel old U.S. 66," as one of those green road signs caught my eye. It read: "Erick, Oklahoma - Home of Roger Miller." We quickly whipped off the Interstate, thinking, "I thought Roger was from Texas." (Roger was born in Fort Worth, but raised in Erick.) It was hot and windy that day, but it didn't take long to pull into Erick, population one thousand, three hundred and seventy five. We turned left at the corner of Roger Miller Boulevard and Sheb Wooley Avenue (yep, Sheb, too, was from Erick, and wrote the bizarre hit "Purple People Eater"). Not a soul was in sight, as we parked by a small brick building, with a sign identifying it as the Police Station. It was locked. Next door was a sign reading Roger Miller Senior Citizens Center. We went in and were warmly greeted by twelve senior citizens, who were sitting around playing dominos. Ewell Martin, Postmaster retired, introduced himself and gave us a guided tour of a small museum in an adjourning room, dedicated to Roger. "Yes," he assured us, "Roger was born in Texas, but from age one, he was raised by an aunt and uncle, right here in Erick." We felt like we were in another time zone.

There were pictures of Roger as a child and as a young boy in school, a photo of his horse, his high school diploma, and early awards he had been given. The old Postmaster explained that on Saturdays, Roger used to bring his guitar and sit out in front, while the kids gathered around him, and he would sing and they sang with him. Roger was beloved by all the town's people, even if he had been expelled from high school once and had to enter another school.

Mr. Martin and Howard began swapping stories. Howard remembered Roger Miller most when Roger, Mel Tillis and Howard were Minnie Pearl's bandsmen. He played fiddle on that tour, and nobody ever thought he was a songwriting genius. After all, when a picker is riding along singing disjointed phrases like, *"In the summertime / When all the leaves and trees are green / You don't want my love . . . / and you don't care for me . . . , "* you don't hear a hit song in what seems like nonsensical rhyming.

When Roger first came to Nashville, he and "roaring" buddies like Willie Nelson and Hank Cochran used to roam around Nashville, stay up all night (with a little help from their "friends"), pull out their acoustic guitars and write off-beat ditties till the sun came up. These songs were way too far out for contemporary music artists to record. Finally in 1964, Miller got a chance to record, in a loose, informal atmosphere, as he and four other acoustic players went into the studio. Out of this came the hits, "Chug-A-Lug," "Dang Me" and other songs equally off-the-wall. If he forgot the words, he simply did his own form of "scatting," until he could think of a new line. He was way ahead of his time. Even though he continued to write nonsensical songs like "You Can't Roller Skate In a Buffalo Herd," he also wrote his classic song about a tragic hobo who was damn proud of whom he was, "King Of the Road." The DJs at our local country music stations, WENO, called him the "Wild Child." Roger Miller became one of the greats. He was in movies, television, a playwright, and a welcome guest on Johnny Carson's *Tonight Show*.

Studio musicians were known to pull elaborate tricks on each other. Roger Miller was known to come to the studio high on pills. The musicians got Jack Evins, who once played steel for Ray Price, but was now a Federal Marshal, to come to the studio with a warrant for Roger's arrest. Jack got there mid-way into the session, read Roger his rights and told him he was under arrest. For once in his life, Roger was speechless. The musicians were knocking themselves out laughing. It was only after Roger promised he would never take another pill that Jack told Roger he had been had, it was all a joke.

Joe Allison remembered vividly the time Roger got stopped by the police: The officer said, "Can I see your driver's license?" and the most quick-witted of them all, Roger Miller, replied, "OK, can I shoot your gun?"

Roger died October 25, 1992, and was only fifty-six years old. One of a kind, he left us too young to have grown out of being Nashville's very own wild child. Erick is not a town one would think of as being home to not just one, but two stars. As we drove out of town, we stopped to take a picture of Roger Miller Boulevard and Sheb Wooley Avenue, not another car approached. The wind and dust swirled around us. (Wooley, an actor-singer-songwriter, died in 2003, at age eighty-two.)

I told Howard, "Roger didn't die with nothing accomplished, he left great songs for the world to sing." The lines of a Roger Miller song haunted me: *"One dyin' and a buryin' / Some cryin' six carryin' me / I wanna be free . . . "* It was hard to gear our minds back into the traffic flow of I-40.

Aubrey Wilson "Moon" Mullican was born around the piney woods of Corrigan, Polk County, Texas, a wild area near the Louisiana state line. The singer-pianist recorded for some thirty years. He had at least eight hits, but his 1950 number one *Billboard* charting "I'll Sail My Ship Alone," was his signature song. During a 1949 tour in Florida, Hank Williams, Senior, met Moon and recommended Moon to the Opry. Despite already having charted three Top Five tunes, Opry officials were reluctant to invite him to join because he didn't play a stringed instrument. Someone opened up the piano and showed the strings to the uneducated at WSM, so they finally made Moon a member. He stayed at the Opry for six years, and was the first Opry star to both sing and play piano, and he became known as "King of the Hillbilly Piano Players."

At age eight, Moon learned to play blues on a guitar from a black share-cropper on the Mullican farm, Joe Jones. When his father bought an organ, so Moon's sisters could learn to play hymns, Moon promptly taught himself the keyboard for blues and boogie. This did not please his father. At age sixteen, Moon left home for Houston, where he worked in brothels and honky tonks. He acquired the nickname, "Moonshine," which was later shortened to "Moon." He then worked for such notables as Floyd Tillman, Jimmie Davis and others, and became the inspiration for future greats such as Jerry Lee Lewis.

By this time, his lifestyle was pretty well set. It was no secret that he liked to drink. Once he was driving to New York to become the first country artist to play Carnegie Hall. During a stop in Shreveport, Louisiana, he got some old friends who were drinking buddies, and they disappeared into the Bayou country for two weeks. Moon bragged about missing this famous historic date, as long as he lived.

There's no doubt that lives were all enriched by Moon during his six-year sojourn with the Opry. Suds Slayman remembered one night that he and Moon were together and they stopped at Hank Snow's house in Madison. They rolled out the old piano and jammed all night long, Hank on guitar, Moon on piano and Suds on fiddle. Moon loved a good time and as Suds, who worked for him, expressed it best, "Moon was a good ole boy."

One night Moon and the band - Suds Slayman, Jabbo Arrington, Randy Hughes and Buddy Killen - were supposed to work at the Blue Jeans Club in Beaumont, Texas. The troupe was booked to do a show and a dance, the usual thing in Texas . The piano was on a stage, but when Moon went up to it to play a few arpeggios up and down the keyboard, he found the piano was out of tune. But that was the least of the piano's troubles, it had keys missing and broken. "Uh-uh, ain't workin' on that," Moon said. He told the club's owner, "I ain't workin', ain't playin', we're leavin.'" There were a couple of good ole Texas boys standing nearby and they said, "Hey, wait, don't leave now! We wanna hear you play!" Moon and the band waited at the bar. In fifteen minutes, the boys showed up with a piano on the bed of their pick-up truck. Moon tried it out and said, "Well, boys, think we'd better work."

Moon had a "calling card" that anyone who was ever on stage with him remembers. He would play a classical arpeggio (run), up the piano, hold on and sing, "Oh, shit-ton-ya!" then he'd go up a tone, hit another "run" and still louder sing, "Oh, pis-son-ya!" The audiences never caught on to what he was really singing, which made it funnier and the band encouraged him to do it again and again. (Although I'm not sure where he learned this, he was really spoofing an old Russian folk song, "Ochee Tchornya, Ochee Yasbiyah," a comedy bit not unknown among piano players. The Russian tune in English is "Dark Eyes.")

Although Moon spent years boogying in the barrooms, some of his greatest record successes were his sad songs, right from his big, beautiful heart, like "I'll Sail My Ship Alone" and "Sweeter than the Flowers." A lot of people today don't remember Moon, but he was one of our true characters and one helluva entertainer. He was only fifty-seven when he died on New Year's Day, 1967.

A name we all remember as so many country artists fell under his influence, is William Orville "Lefty" Frizzell. He was born March 31, 1928, in Corsicana, Texas, but grew up in Arkansas. He earned his nickname, "Lefty" when he competed as a Golden Gloves boxer in his mid-teens. His boxing career didn't last as long as the name "Lefty," which stuck with him the rest of his life.

In 1950, Lefty cut a demo record for promotion man, Jim Beck of Dallas. It was one of country music's historic sessions, as it produced "If You've Got the Money, I've Got the Time," which Lefty and Beck co-wrote. Columbia Records signed him, released the demo intact and it climbed immediately to the number one chart position. A month later, Columbia released "I Love You A Thousand Ways," the chart-topper's actual B side, also written by Lefty, which became his second number one disc. Who else ever debuted on a label with a two-sided number one disc?

Lefty joined the *Grand Ole Opry* on July 26, 1951. In October of that year, he became the fifth country singer to place four songs in *Billboard* the same week, "Always Late" (number one), "Mom And Dad Waltz" (number four), "I Want To Be With You Always" (number five), and "Travelin' Blues" (number seven). (Eddy Arnold, Hank Williams, Red Foley and Hank Snow were the others to achieve this honor up to this time.) In March 1952, only eight months after joining the Opry, Lefty left, reasoning that he didn't need the *Grand Ole Opry* any longer.

Then the hits seemed to stop coming. As a teenager, Lefty fought hard to stay in the ring and it was always a fight to stay on top in the music business. As he earned more and more money, he developed no business sense and was irresponsible. He and his friends went out roaring for days. He would forget concerts and recording sessions, which no doubt contributed to his downfall. He had the reputation for being a drinker. Suds Slayman was with him one night when Lefty's booker, Jack Starnes, Jr., called and told Suds that Lefty was supposed to be at a date in Texas. He explained that Lefty was drunk. Starnes told Suds, "Get him to the airport and pour him on that plane." Suds delivered Lefty to Berry Field (Nashville); however, he had trouble stopping Lefty from drinking long enough to get him out of the car. Finally, he got him on to the plane and the airplane personnel said they would take care of him.

At one point, in the 1950's, Lefty bought an old Army plane, which could carry five people to his tour dates. One night, they started off with pilot Bob Wyche, Lefty and Suds, and fellow musicians Buford Gentry and Hillous Butrum. The noise from the roar of the engines was so loud that you couldn't hear anything else. Suds looked out and oil was all over the wings, the generator started going out and as they started to land – Boom! The plane jumped five or six feet off the ground. "What was that!," someone asked. "Oh," the pilot said, "That was just a flat tire." As they rolled to a stop and got off the plane, you could see in their eyes that this had been a "kiss the ground" kind of flight.

Lefty was a great singer and stylist. In 1959, after a five-year dry spell, he proved he could still sing and have a hit, with "The Long Black Veil," written by Marijohn Wilkin and Danny Dill. Then five years later, in 1964, he scored his sixth and final number one single, "Saginaw Michigan," co-written by Don Wayne and Bill Anderson. Lefty's fans loved him because his songs were intense and nobody could touch his style. His heart and soul somehow projected onto the vinyl. Unlike today's singers, there was no doubt as to who was singing. Although the Lefty Frizzell imitators are many, there was only one Lefty. Brother David tried carrying on the Frizzell name, chalking up two number ones – "You're the Reason God Made Oklahoma" (a duet with Shelly West) and "I'm Gonna Hire a Wino To Decorate Our Home" – but has never attained the lasting legacy of his brother.

Lefty's lifestyle ran out on him at age forty-seven, when he died on July 19, 1975. MCA recorded one of Lefty's last sessions in the early 1970's. On their record, Lefty almost cries, "I Can't Stand To See A Good Man Go To Waste." We then understood that Lefty was really singing a song about himself. His great talent, his ability to charm an audience and his uncanny knowledge of a good song was finally rewarded in 1982. It was then that he was elected to the Country Music Hall Of Fame. Here's hoping he knows.

One of the greats, Marty Robbins, wrote and sang music for the entire world. His records "crossed over" long before the term "crossover" was coined for the music business vocabulary. Between 1953 and 1976, Marty had sixteen number one records, including his famous "El Paso." From the beginning, Marty was different and did things differently. When growing up, he worked around Glendale, Arizona, doing all kinds of jobs, from ditch digging to boxing to farming and delivering ice. While finding his way into the music business, he walked into a radio station, demanded an audition and earned himself a job there, replacing the Western singer the station already had. He began playing club dates in the Phoenix area and was discovered by Little Jimmy Dickens. He was signed to Columbia Records in 1951.

When "El Paso" was recorded in 1960, it was over five minutes long. All the brains in the music business said it wouldn't be a hit, because it was too long. Marty did it exactly as he wrote it and it was not only a hit, it was a gigantic hit. The DJs loved the length. That five minutes gave them time to go to the rest room and back to their turn-tables with a minute to spare.

In show business, the biggest star always closes the show. Since Marty was one of the superstars on the Opry, he was always given the last spot, 11:30 to midnight. Because he had so much talent, he left the audience standing on their feet wanting more. He was a supreme prankster and he loved to run over his time slot. He kept singing encores, while the audience applauded. This extended his time over into Ernest Tubb's *Midnight Jamboree,* which was scheduled to begin at midnight. It made Tubb angry, so Marty kept right on doing it. It got to be a joke around the Opry.

Marty kept people around who made him laugh: musicians, bookers and office personnel. In addition to music, he had a passion for automobile racing. Once in the 1950's, he decided to build a Micro Midget race-track between LaVergne and Murfreesboro. (A micro midget race-car is a miniature race car built like an Indianapolis racer.) Howard went out and helped build the track, along with Jimmy Fox, a guitar player, and Oakie Jones, a bus driver. Marty really did hold races there for a while. But, he really loved to drive stock cars. He drove a purple stock car he called "Devil Woman," named for a hit song. Howard and I used to watch his racing on a little dirt track at Ridgetop. He raced there with another driver, destined to become a big name in racing, Darrell Waltrip. By 1972, Marty had progressed to NASCAR's Grand National Division and was named "Rookie of the Southern 500." Maybe the reason he wanted the last spot on the Opry was so he could race earlier in the evening on Saturday night.

Record sessions were more relaxed in Marty's time. We were still having fun in Nashville and Marty had more fun than anybody else in the studio. Howard was lucky to get a tape of Marty's out-takes from engineer Mort Thomasson. This tape is a study in the way recordings used to be done. So relaxed! This is the way this session progressed: Marty stopped "take one" because Jerry Byrd, on steel, missed the Intro. Then Jerry missed it again. Marty said "F--- you!" Byrd said, "So I made a mistake!" Marty said, "This is a Master, Jerry." Then they started again. At "take two," they stopped again because Marty said, "I'm singing flat. Sounds like Ernest Tubb ricocheting off a tin roof." So, "take three," and pianist Bill Pursell kept messing up the bridge. After a lot of ha-ha's, and more expletives by Marty and Bill, Marty said, "Go ahead, Pursell, you got one more chance." In the middle of "take four," Marty messed up and amid complete frustration, made up and sang a little nonsense rhyme he thought up on the spot: *"There was a little bird / And he shit a little turd / And he flew to a telephone pole / He stretched out his little neck / And he shit about a peck / Then he closed up his little ass hole."* It was "take six" when drummer Buddy Harman started the beat out with a drum lick Marty liked, Grady Martin's fuzz guitar was turned up, Pursell gave Marty what he wanted to hear, and the band clicked. Marty said to the engineer, *"This one's for you."* And, "take seven" of "One Of These Day's" became history. I have a hunch that if Marty walked among us today, he'd still be doing things exactly his way. Marty sang, *"One of these days, I'll find the courage, I'll be the man I want to be."* Marty really was the man he wanted to be.

It was at the Milbrey Hotel in Houston, Texas in 1951, that a then-unknown young man, in a fringed jacket, walked up to the fiddle player with Moon Mullican and asked, "Fellow, how do you get on the *Grand Ole Opry?*" The fiddle player replied, "Chief, I really can't tell you. I don't even know how I got there." Then Moon's fiddler player asked him about the song he was playing, "What's the name of it?" The young man replied, "Wondering.'" Then the seasoned fiddler asked him what his name was? "Webb Pierce," was the answer.

That next year "Wondering" sold a million records for Decca. It rose rapidly to become the number one song in *Billboard*. By then, not only Moon's fiddle player, but everyone else in the country knew exactly who Webb Pierce was.

Pierce was born August 8, 1921 near West Monroe, Louisiana. He played on local radio when he was a teenager. After he moved to Shreveport, he became one of the KWKH *Louisiana Hayride's* first stars recruited by Nashville. In 1951, he signed with Decca, and had that first hit the following January. By mid-1952 when he joined the *Grand Ole Opry*, he was working his third number one, just behind "That Heart Belongs To Me" and "Back Street Affair." In 1953, when Hank Williams died, Webb Pierce was the most popular singer in country music. Similarly, he sang about honky tonks, drinking, jails and cheatin' hearts, personified on songs like "There Stands The Glass" and "In the Jailhouse Now."

Billy Robinson played steel guitar on "Wondering," Webb's first hit, but it was Webb's "Slowly" in 1954, that gave country a new sound it needed, a pedal steel guitar, played by Bud Isaacs. The year before, when Howard was with Cowboy Copas in Indianapolis, a man came to him at the Lyric Theater and tried to sell him a new type steel guitar that had pedals. Howard said, "I thought it would never work. How could you keep your strings in tune with the pedals pulling them." Well, after Isaacs made such a hit on "Slowly," all the steel players in Nashville (but Jerry Byrd) rushed out to change to pedal steel, including Howard, seeking this soft, sliding pedal steel sound. It was "note bending" at its best. It didn't take long for manufacturers to present this new breed of steel players with an instrument of double necks, pedals and legs, and the so-called "lap steel" was slowly, but surely relegated to museums. (These days the lap steel has been pulled out of closets to become popular again.)

Webb Pierce, with pure country hits that followed like "More And More," packed in audiences everywhere, while another part of the business was going rockabilly wild, to the sounds of Johnny Cash and the like. Webb had not only fame, but wealth. He bought the most outlandish Western suits that money could buy. He had Nudie embed hundreds of silver dollars into his Pontiac convertible, substituted six-shooters for door handles, mounted steer horns on the hood and make saddles out of the seats. (He used to park it in front of the Andrew Jackson Hotel at the DJ Conventions.) He was married to an Arkansas beauty named Audrey Grisham. They had a huge Tudor home with acreage at the best address in Berry Hill. His calling card was his guitar-shaped swimming pool on the estate. Always enterprising, Webb sold his swimming pool water in guitar shaped bottles to tourists who came by the busload to gaze upon "Wandering Acres." Even his mailbox had his name atop it, so you would know you were at the right house. Maybe all this was frowned on by Nashville's Curtiswood Lane standards, but this was Webb's style and he lived up to it every day.

Webb and Howard were friends, but in 1953, when Hubert Long, Webb's booker, asked Howard to join Webb's band, Howard turned down the offer, as he was already working. Sonny Burnette took the job with Webb. After Howard had retired from the road, Webb offered to have Shot Jackson build him a new guitar, if he would just go to work for him. By this time, Howard just wanted to stay in town, but he still loved old Webb.

In the mid-1950's, Webb, Carl Smith and Goldie Hill, Red Sovine, and others, opted to quit the Opry. The Opry required they work twenty-six Saturday nights a year at the Opry. There was a lot more money to be made on the weekends on show dates other than at the Opry. Some artists like Jimmy Dickens came back to the Opry, but Webb never did. He was considered to be the top country star in the mid-1950s. In his career, he had fifty-four top ten singles.

Webb liked to bet on baseball, particularly on his favorite team, the Detroit Tigers. One of Webb's best friends was Frank Strong Lary, of Northport, Alabama, a Tigers' pitcher (1954-1964). Frank was known as the "Yankee Killer" by the broadcasters. One season he hurled seven winning games against the New York Yankees. Webb invited Lary to play in Music City's Four Star Golf Tournament and that's where Howard met Frank Lary.

Lary and Howard used to have great telephone conversations and once we even went to Northport, so that Howard could jam with Lary and friends in Lary's barn. Lary told Howard that when he was pitching, Webb used to call him on the phone in the clubhouse at the stadium before the game began. Webb would say, "Frank, this is Webb. Son, how do ya feel today?" Lary answered, "Fine, Webb." Then Webb would ask, "Do ya think ya can beat 'em?" Lary would answer, "Yeah, I think so." Webb would tell him, "Well, I'm gonna bet three hundred dollars on ya today!"

At the end of his life, Webb was very ill with cancer. Howard wanted to see him but Webb's cohort, Max Powell, discouraged him, saying Webb was too sick right then and to wait until he felt better. Webb didn't get better and Howard didn't get to see him. Webb died February 24, 1991, at age sixty-nine. Faron Young, who was brought to Nashville by Webb, sang about living hard, dying young and leaving beautiful memories, which could've been Webb's anthem. Howard always thought of Webb most from happier times, like at the Acuff-Rose Golf Tournament. He felt sure that Webb was up there laughing, as Webb remembered the night Howard sang at the banquet: *"I saw Webb as he drew back his powerful swing / And the ball rolled right up on the green / It's too bad they were playing number seven at the time / Cause the ball rolled on number thirteen."*

Our friend George Morgan, was an instant hit with his song, "Candy Kisses" (number one, 1949). On the strength of that song, which he wrote, George joined the Opry. He also called his band The Candy Kids, and he and wife, Anna named their first child Candy Kay.

In contrast to the other flashy dressers of that day at the Opry, Morgan wore casual sport clothes, sometimes even daring to show up in a modest business suit. There is an often-told story about George when he arrived in Nashville for his first Opry show in 1948. They say he was standing on the parking lot and asked Chet Atkins where the Ryman Auditorium was. Chet laughed so hard he rolled. As you read on, you'll see why Howard believed that George was only having fun with Chet. It makes a good story anyway!

George Morgan was born in Waverly, Tennessee in 1924, but he moved to Barberton, Ohio with his family and graduated from high school there. He sang over WAKR-Akron, then WWST-Wooster and then the WWVA *Wheeling Jamboree* in West Virginia, before coming to Nashville. He did have a small amount of musical training, which taught him to sing sweeter than country singers of that day. Reporters usually said that George was warm and sincere. His friends knew he was generous to a fault, giving money to his friends, sometimes to his own detriment.

If you said that George was a quiet introverted man, that would be a mistake in judgment. He could have received the award for the biggest all-time practical joker at the Opry. He liked to have those kinds of people around him, like Loosh Marvin and Don Davis. Or, he liked to have those people around him that he and Loosh or Don could play jokes upon, like Suds Slayman, Floyd "Mousie" Robinson and Buddy Killen. Those musicians were in his early band. Slayman stuck with him, while others moved in and out.

Morgan, in those days, went to Springfield, Missouri, after the Opry, to cut transcriptions for Robin Hood Flour. There they would cut a month's shows. Tony (R. L.) Lane, steel player, was usually the regular who went along. On one particular Saturday night, they couldn't find Tony. They looked and looked, but he had just disappeared. Billy Robinson was playing steel with Red Foley on the *Prince Albert Show* at that time. Billy had cut "Candy Kisses" with Morgan, so Morgan asked Foley if Billy could go with them to make the transcriptions. Foley agreed, so Billy went with them. (Incidentally, Foley was one who cut a cover version on Morgan's mega hit "Candy Kisses" as did such as Elton Britt and Cowboy Copas.)

Anyway, Morgan had a recording session set up for when they returned to Nashville at Castle Studios. Since Billy had gone to Springfield, he got to cut the session with Morgan. Out of this session in 1952, came Morgan's hit "Almost," which was written for him by Jack Toombs and Vic McAlpin. Suds Slayman, however, played on a session with George when he recorded duets with pop star Rosemary Clooney. One of their songs was a Floyd Tillman song, "You Love Me Just Enough To Hurt Me (But Not Enough For Us To Get Along)." When time came for the "take," Suds missed a note. They refused to do it over. This mistake on the master bugged Slayman for years. The world has forgotten, but not the fiddle player. Morgan was probably the one that wouldn't let them do another "take," just so that he could bug Suds.

One day in June 1975, George went up on his roof to fix his TV antenna. It was then that he had a heart attack. He was rushed to the hospital, but he went on home. The next Saturday night he played his last show on the Opry. He had to return to the hospital for an operation. It was there, on July 5, 1975, his voice was forever stilled. He left his wife, Anna and five children, Loretta (Lorrie, the Opry star), Candy, Bethany, Liana and Marty.

The Opry gang of Morgan's day will always remember his over generosity and his so-called practical jokes. There's an unending supply to write about as they raise another glass to toast him. Howard believed Morgan died as he lived and as he expressed in the unlikely song about the Butris Bird: *"I won't cheat and I won't steal / And I won't lie and I'll win / 'Cause I don't want to be a bigger asshole than him."*

Red Foley was another great singer. Those that worked for him attested that he was a truly nice guy and there are those who swear to this day they never saw him intoxicated. When he sang or recited, it was truly from the heart. A lot of musicians saw him cry for the dog he had as a child, "Old Shep." Some of Foley's greatest songs may have been written by other writers, but this one he wrote himself, for his beloved pet, "Old Shep." *"If dogs have a Heaven / There's one thing I know / Old Shep has a wonderful home . . ."*

Clyde Julian Foley, known as "Red" since boyhood, was from Berea, Kentucky. He began pickin' out songs on a guitar when very young. In high school, he started taking vocal lessons and at seventeen, he won the Atwater Kent Singing Contest. After high school, Red studied at Georgetown College. There, a talent scout hired him for the WLS-Chicago *National Barn Dance* in 1931. Foley married young, but tragically, his first wife died in childbirth, leaving him with a daughter, Betty, who as a grownup recorded duets with dad.

Red worked WLS for a time with Lulu Belle (Myrtle Eleanor Cooper) as a "boy-friend, girl-friend act." Lulu Belle, born in North Carolina, reportedly was the daughter of convicted moonshiner John Cooper. In 1933, Red married Eva Overstake of the *National Barn Dance's* Three Little Maids vocal trio. Eva insisted that the Red Foley/Lulu Belle act break up, so Lulu Belle began working with Scott Wiseman. They scored as the famed Lulu Belle and Scotty team (and she became Mrs. Wiseman, as well).

The Three Little Maids were sisters Eva, Evelyn and Lucille Overstake. Eva was just thirteen when she began singing professionally and only sixteen when she married Red. Evelyn, the oldest sister, began a solo act and sang at WLS for some twenty years. Lucille became one of country music's foremost female songwriters. In the 1940's as Jenny Lou Carson, she recorded briefly for Decca Records, but wrote such country classics as "Jealous Heart" and "Let Me Go, Lover."

In 1937, John Lair left the WLS *National Barn Dance* with Red Foley and Whitey Ford, (The Duke of Paducah), and went to WLW-Cincinnati to form *The Renfro Valley Barn Dance*. Lair led an exodus of artists from WLS and began broadcasting over the five hundred thousand watt WLW. They were only biding their time, while the rural Kentucky barn dance location was being readied. On November 4, 1939, the first show went on the air from the Valley. Shortly thereafter, Foley left the show and joined another Red, comedian Red Skelton on his popular network radio show *Avalon Time*. In 1941, Foley returned to the *National Barn Dance* and that same year signed with Decca Records. In 1944, he had his first major chart hit, the Zeke Clements' song, "Smoke on the Water" (co-written with Earl Nunn). It stayed at the number one spot thirteen weeks, but also peaked number seven on the pop chart, an early crossover success.

The most important segment of the *Grand Ole Opry* was a segment hosted by Roy Acuff, sponsored by the R. J. Reynolds Company, manufacturers of Prince Albert Smoking Tobacco. *The Prince Albert Show* went on the air October 14. 1939, a thirty-minute segment, first carried by twenty-six NBC stations. By 1952, the NBC Red Network carried it to one hundred and seventy-six stations coast-to-coast. On April 6, 1946, Roy Acuff made a critical mistake when he made the decision to leave the Prince Albert Show over a contractual dispute, and to head to Hollywood.

In the spring of 1946, Red Foley, then thirty-five years old, replaced Acuff on the *Prince Albert Show*. Foley brought with him a guitar player, Chet Atkins. Chet left a few months later when the ad agency eliminated his guitar solo. A few years later, Chet returned with the Carters. Foley always surrounded himself with great musicians such as Zeke Turner, lead guitar; Louis Innis, rhythm guitar; Jerry Byrd, steel guitar; and Ernie Newton, bass. As usual, at the Opry, musicians have a way of moving on. The whole band left over a salary dispute, including Jerry Byrd, steel guitarist. Billy Robinson stepped in to take Jerry's place. Tommy Jackson was added on fiddle and sometimes Jimmy Selph played guitar. Grady Martin replaced Zeke Turner. Jerry Byrd said, 'It didn't take but thirty minutes to replace the band." There were probably others added in that period of time. *The Prince Albert Show* also had guest artists on the show and Foley's band backed up those, who did not have their own bands. Cowboy Copas was a guest and his own band backed him up, including Howard on steel guitar.

Red had huge record hits on Decca, "Peace In the Valley," "Steal Away," "Our Lady Of Fatima," "Tennessee Border" and others. In 1950, Red had that crossover *Billboard* smash, "Chattanoogie Shoe Shine Boy." That same year, Foley had "Birmingham Bounce," "Mississippi," and a duet with Ernest Tubb, "Goodnight Irene," all number ones. According to the trade weekly's year-end survey, "Chattanoogie Shoe Shine Boy" and "Goodnight Irene" were among the Top Ten Selling Singles of the Year. Amazingly, Foley, now all but forgotten, attained sixteen Top Ten singles in one year – 1950!

The following year he had six Top Tens, including the gospel classic "Peace In the Valley" which earned him another Gold Record in sales. Red's

Top Ten's slowed to three in 1952, but he bounced back with "Midnight" which went to number one in January 1953. This made Chet Atkins happy, as he and Boudleaux Bryant co-wrote it. Red also scored five more hits that year including "No Help Wanted, Number Two" with Ernest Tubb.

Billy Robinson remembered that he, Grady Martin, Red and Eva, were flying to Enid, Oklahoma, for a show, in a twin engine Cessna. They were flying through a "humongous" storm, when Grady turned around to say something and kicked the radio out. It was getting dark and raining hard with lightning flashing all around. The pilot began to look for a place to set the plane down. "We can't go through this storm," he said. Finally he spotted a deserted field near Stillwell, Oklahoma. He a made a very rough landing, going through tall prairie grass and over very rough ground.

Billy recalled, "There were no lights and as we sat there, we saw a light in a house way off in the distance. Then we discussed who was going to go there and get help. Red and Eva weren't going, naturally. Grady was too fat to run. The pilot had to stay with the plane, so I was elected. I got out and began running through the tall grass, rain and lightning. I was scared to death. I jumped ditches and once a huge Oklahoma jack rabbit jumped out at me. I finally reached the house, panting, soaked, my hair down in my face. When they opened the door and said, 'What can I do for you,' I couldn't get enough breath to talk. Finally they understood and we went out to bring the others in. We missed the date in Enid."

Red had sixty-five country chartings, nearly all Top Ten, plus thirteen pop hits, Top Twenty or better. It seemed nothing could stop him, but at this point, things began to get out of hand. Frank Kelton, a music publisher, and his wife Sally Sweet (born Esther Swartz), an entertainer and TV singer, arrived in Nashville. It was rumored around WSM that Red and Sally were having an affair. Eva Foley definitely had a heart condition brought on by rheumatic fever when a child. She was recovering at home from by-pass surgery when she committed suicide by taking an overdose of sleeping pills. Events accelerated and one thing led to another. Frank Kelton sued Red for alienation of affections in a nasty lawsuit, prompting Frank and Sally's divorce. In December 1952, thirteen months to the day of Eva's death, Red and Sally eloped.

The Ozark Jubilee on KYTV-Springfield, began in December 1953 and they wanted Red Foley for their first ABC program scheduled July 17, 1954. Si Siman came to Nashville with orders to hire Foley away from the Opry. Red's drinking had increased and he was having trouble at the Opry, so he and Si met at the Andrew Jackson Hotel. They spent a weekend together and emptied quite a few bottles of Jack Daniel's. In the end, Si got the answer he sought. Red agreed to go to Springfield. He was tiring of Nashville and this was a way to go on to something new. After his first *Jubilee*, Red received twenty-five thousand fan letters. "Keep those cards and letters coming in" could have been Red Foley's theme song.

Red's drinking didn't slow down even with his new success. He would go on binges, sometimes not straightening up for days. He continued to record for Decca, but his last Top 10 was "You And Me," a 1956 duet with Kitty Wells, which charted shortly after his 1955 duet with Betty Foley on "A Satisfied Mind." When the *Jubilee* folded, so did Red. He moved back to Nashville, but the heart and soul of the former vigorous *Prince Albert Show* host was gone. He still played some package shows and did one-nighters, but rumors flew that he seldom showed up sober.

Howard was on tour with Wilma Lee and Stoney Cooper when Red was booked on the show, near the end of their tour. They were playing the Louisville Fair & Exposition Center in Kentucky. Wilma Lee tried hard to make sure Red didn't get any whiskey, but they all knew he was getting it somewhere. Then she discovered the source. Red had a hollow walking cane and he was carrying vodka in the cane. He got out on stage on cue and he was supposed to sing "Hello Mama, Hello Papa." He never got beyond "Hello Mama," saying it over and over. The audience booed him off the stage. Howard loved Red's talent so much that he cried for him, knowing this was a low point in Red's life.

By 1964, the newspapers were showing Red no mercy, enjoying his misery. They hadn't been able to print this much sad news since the fall of Hank Williams. There were headlines about Foley and the IRS, drug overdoses, an apartment fire at Foley's and arrests from speeding to drunken driving. For a time, it appeared he was making a comeback, when he landed a recurring role in an ABC network series *Mr. Smith Goes To Washington*, a remake of the classic 1939 Frank Capra movie. That 1962-63 TV series, however, which starred Fess Parker and featured Red as his Uncle Cooter, lasted only two seasons. Nonetheless, the great artist that he was, was officially recognized when Red was inducted in late 1967, into the Country Music Hall Of Fame.

On September 19, 1968, as Foley left for a show date in Fort Wayne, Indiana, he was definitely down-on-his-luck from a health standpoint. Sharing the bill were old friends Jean Shepard, Billy Walker and Hank Williams, Jr., and all could see he was sick. Before retiring to his hotel that night, he told Hank Jr., he was so dreadfully tired and had to go to bed. He closed his performance on that last show, singing, *"Well, I'm tired and so weary, but I must go along / Till the Lord comes and calls me away . . . There will be peace in the valley for me some day / There will be peace in the valley for me, oh, Lord, I pray . . . No more sadness, no sorrow, no trouble I'll see / Now there's peace in the valley for me."* Red's lifetime Decca contract finally ended. That night at age fifty-eight he died.

If there is a lesson to be learned from the lives of these stars, it probably is to try and stay out of the fast lane when possible. It's easy to say, but much harder to do. As popularity soars, there is less and less time to be free. There are show dates, recording sessions, meetings with bookers, promoters, producers, advertisers, songwriters, and dealing with the band, plus those long nights on the road and only short times to spend with families. There just never seems to be enough time, and after all, life is too short at best. Yet, as Howard said, "When I think of our friends, Roger, Moon, Lefty, Marty, Webb, George and Red, I have only sweet memories."

25 SIXTEENTH AVENUE

"We aren't worried about posterity;
We want it to sound good right now!"

- Duke Ellington

The very first song ever recorded was "Mary Had A Little Lamb," by Thomas Alva Edison, the great inventor. He invented the first practical phonograph in 1877. That sound came from a cylinder which had a sheet of tinfoil wrapped around it, which could be rotated. This attempt was only a primitive beginning, but it was a prelude of things to come.

When Edison invented his phonograph, the people of America were ready to somehow preserve the sounds they were creating. Once upon a time these songs were mostly in Southern hills, brought to America by the people settling in Pennsylvania, Virginia, the Carolinas, Tennessee, Georgia and Alabama. They had brought their songs with them from the British Isles, played first on bagpipes. When the violin was invented in Europe, it found its way to Scotland and Ireland. They copied the droning sounds the bagpipes made and began calling the violin the fiddle. When they came to America, the fiddle traveled easily. They used it for jigs and reels, but this folk music became a modern sophisticated music style.

By 1924, Vernon Dalhart had the country's first multi-million seller "The Prisoner's Song." OKeh Records is credited as being the first label to market "Hillbillly" music on a national basis. In December 1923, they released recordings by Fiddlin' John Carson. Then in 1924, Victor released the recording, "It Ain't Gonna Rain No More" by Wendell Hall and also in 1924, Columbia released recordings by Gid Tanner and Riley Puckett.

Early recordings were primitive. The Possum Hunters recorded *"My Wife Died Saturday Night,"* a sad but happy song: *"My wife died Saturday night/She was buried on Sunday/Monday was my courtin' day/And on Tuesday, I got married. . . ."* The musicians on that session were Dr. Humphrey Bate (harmonica), Staley Walton (guitar), Oscar Stone (fiddle), Humphrey "Buster" Bate, Jr. (ukulele), Walter Liggett (banjo), Aaron Albright (bass) and Alcyone Bate (piano and vocals). They, in a sense, were the first sidemen; however, they always remained semi-pro, that is, they kept their regular jobs and worked as musicians on the weekends.

Herman Crook did his only recording in 1928 for Victor. After that, he neither recorded nor toured. He earned his living as a twist roller for the American Tobacco Company and played the Opry on Saturday nights. The musicians seemed to be sensitive to the right way of being in the music business, even then. They wrote the songs, they played and recorded, they played them on the radio and they kept their day jobs.

210

There were other music venues in Nashville back then. There was a symphony orchestra, operas, minstrel shows, Broadway-style shows and vaudeville. Hillbilly music was far from the minds of those who backed the symphony and the finer things of life. Then, radio changed the face of the music business forever. Although the first musicians at WSM had been mostly rural, the quality of the bands gradually got better and better. Then the country music business became a major force in the city's economy, mostly beginning after World War Two.

From the time the first fiddle note echoed at the WSM Studios in 1925, country music gained in popularity. The rise of the then called Hill-billy Music, eventually put Nashville on the map. The radio and record-ing industry changed the face of the music business forever. By the time there was a record industry, old traditional country music had been put into categories that record companies had given them, such as: Old Time Tunes, Familiar Tunes, Old Time Southern Songs, Hill Country Music or Songs From Dixie. Country style music didn't get a general name until 1925, when Ralph Peer recorded a string band in New York. After the ses-sion, he wanted to know what name to give the band on the record label. One of the band members is supposed to have said, "Call us anything you want, we're just hillbillies from North Carolina and Virginia." So, Peer called them "The Hillbillies" and the name stuck. It wasn't until the 1940's that *Billboard* magazine popularized the term "Country Music" or "Country & Western Music," they reasoned that the term Hillbilly was derogatory. (Even as late as the 1960's, the WSM Library still catalogued records as either Hillbilly or Pop.)

In 1928, Victor decided to head South and see what kinds of string bands were in our area. At that time Nashville musicians were going to Atlanta or New York to record. We had no shortage of rural talent in Nash-ville. Victor wound up recording The Possum Hunters, DeFord Bailey, The Crook Brothers, The Binkley Brothers and The Dixie Clodhoppers.

The AFofM Nashville Association of Musicians, Local 257, had begun on December 11, 1902, and by 1927 had one hundred and eighty-two mem-bers. Their members were mostly violinists and pianists, those who could read music. There was not one guitar player on their roster. In those days, the Union didn't accept members that could not read music. The rural string players at the Opry saw no need to learn to read music. They played just fine without it. WSM had not organized at that time. Then, Pee Wee King and the Golden West Cowboys became members of the Opry in 1937. They did read music and Pee Wee saw to it that his band was accepted into the union. Then, when the New York labels became unionized, they wanted to record talent that was union. The Nashville union was forced to let any of the Opry members that desired, join the Union. Finally, it became a requirement that Opry members had to join either the AFofM or AFTRA unions. WLAC and WSIX had no such requirements and musicians like Big Jeff Bess at WLAC and Goober Buchanan at WSIX never joined the union. WSM always kept their professional standards high.

There were five banjo players on the union's original roster but, as former Secretary-Treasurer of Local 257 Vic Willis said, "I give you odds that none of them were five-strings." By 1994, the union boasted four thousand members, including two hundred and fifty-two banjo pickers. Vic said, "I'll give you odds that at least ninety-nine per cent were five-strings." Joe Miles was the first president and before George Cooper there were sixteen presidents. Cooper was the longest reigning president, thirty-six years. Most musicians did not realize there was any other president before "Mr. Cooper."

In the early days of recording at WSM, Castle, Brown Brothers or Thomas Productions, producers used WSM musicians. When Victor and Decca began coming to Nashville, they also used WSM musicians. Things were just happening around WSM. There were good and dependable musicians there, ready and willing to work for Union Scale. Pop hits had come out of Nashville, big sellers like "Near You" by Francis Craig on Bullet, and "Down Yonder" by Del Wood on Tennessee Records. However, the big labels wanted to record country here. They reasoned they could get all the pop music they wanted in New York or Los Angeles.

By the time Owen Bradley began to work at Decca in 1947, and he and his brother Harold built a studio at Lindsley and Second Avenues, Nashville musicians were proving they were equal to the job. After several months, they relocated to a building in Hillsboro Village. It had been a garage and was not satisfactory, but Jack Comer had success with a song recorded there, "Crying In The Chapel." Then in 1954, Owen bought an old house at 804 16th Avenue South for seven thousand, five hundred dollars. The musicians called it "The Barn." To Owen belongs the credit for founding *Music Row*. Then Chet Atkins began heading up RCA in 1957, while Ken Nelson brought Capitol records here in 1950, and Mercury came in 1952. Inevitably, the big labels followed. In 1962, Columbia Records bought Bradley out.

At first, the road musicians who worked with the stars, recorded with them. Then the musicians of the 1960's elected to stay home and just do sessions. They had been road pickers, who had paid their dues and had earned their right to break into the recording business. The musicians are the foundation on which the record business rests. They are the ones that made the noise on Sixteenth Avenue (before they called it Music Square West).

In the late 1950's, Nashville had two full-fledged recording studios. By the 1970's, there were dozens and dozens. A new terminology was born, *The Nashville Sound*. Actually, this sound just evolved. One musician once said, "The Nashville Sound is the result of musicians getting together in the studio and fooling around." In the beginning, most country music pickers were self-taught and they blended together in a melting pot. Their music wasn't structured, there were no musical arrangements to read. Musicians naturally stiffen up when music is sitting in front of them. Their relaxation gave the music a different sound. So *The Nashville Sound* was brought about by the musicians themselves, because from the beginning, they have tried to get that something different that makes a little bit of difference.

Joe Talbot got something different when he got a realistic train whistle sound on his steel guitar for Hank Snow's "I'm Moving On." Grady Martin's amplifier was giving him technical trouble, which created the "Fuzztone" heard on Robbin's "Don't Worry." Howard gave Hank Snow a different sound when he added a muted, plucking sound on "Poor Little Jimmie." Suds Slayman wasn't needed on Robbin's cut of "Maybelline," but, as he was doing nothing, he created a sound they wanted, by picking up some drum brushes and beating them on boxes sitting there.

Even the producers tried to come up with something different. Chet Atkins listened to a demo featuring Don Robertson on piano. Robertson "bent notes" in an imitation of a steel guitar. Chet was to produce Hank Locklin and wanted to copy that style. Floyd Cramer was booked on Locklin's session, so Chet asked Cramer to imitate Robertson's style. Cramer did exactly that on Locklin's "Please Help Me, I'm Falling." That piano style became the most popular ever in Nashville. Cramer even used it on his solo hit record, "Last Date."

It's impossible to list all the sidemen who contributed to the Nashville Sound. Nashville became a floating pool of sidemen. They moved from studio to studio, recording behind anybody and everybody. They had known each other for years, having played together at the Opry, in local clubs and road bands. They just anticipated each other's licks. They improvised quickly, without using written arrangements, using only "Nashville Shorthand," a numbering system for charting songs. Their job was to work out a track that backed the lead singer.

A lot of years have passed since recording in Nashville began. When they were young, full of energy and new ideas, there wasn't time to think of the musicians who would come after you. It's only when the phone doesn't ring and your fellow musicians are in the same boat, that you realize the new producers might be using younger musicians with new ideas to match the new artists who have flocked to Nashville, eager for their own brand of music to take the place of the old.

Country music, as well as Pop, Rock, R&B or Gospel, is always changing, always evolving. It changed from The Possum Hunters to Roy Acuff, from Eddy Arnold to Hank Snow, from George Jones to Garth Brooks. I can remember when there were people in the music business in the 1970's who complained about the use of symphonic violins on Eddy Arnold records, even George Jones records. I always said it just made country music more palatable for the masses. After that, you could hardly hear a record out of Nashville that didn't have the smooth sound of strings. So, now you ask, "What's happened to country music?" And, yes, can you identify it with anything we used to call country?

I've heard people say that it seems that what they call "country" today sounds like what they used to call rock. Maybe it starts in the studio. The Nashville Sound used to be recorded when the musicians all played together. Today, due to new technology, the recordings are done in piecemeal fashion: first recording rhythm, then lead, then add vocals. The engi-

213

neers are responsible for the "mix." All we hear from the finished product is a loud rhythm and screaming guitars. The singer is lost in the mix and the words cannot be distinguished from the music. They may be singing a country song, but who knows. I wish the songwriters and the music makers of today understood that the power of the music is in the emotion it draws out of you. We liked to listen to the lyrics and feel the emotion of the song. It's all about the beat these days.

Country music used to tell a story. You had to listen to the words to understand the song. Sometimes the tunes were old, handed down from generations long past, or a songwriter might have written it yesterday, but the folk song, or hillbilly song, or country song was centered around a story. It could be "Knoxville Girl," "Green, Green Grass Of Home" or "If Tomorrow Never Comes," but the sad song or the happy song was centered around a story, about a child who died, or a girl who was pregnant, or a guy who drinks too much, or the depth of the love of a boy and a girl.

The times they are a'changin'. Trends don't just stand still. The new producers, the artists, the sidemen and songwriters have taken country music to a new level. Understandably, young artists want to work with their own generation. They have innovative ideas and a new course has been set for their idea of what constitutes country music.

There's a new thinking on *Music Row* now. Country music was not always about the money. It seems now the Nashville Sound is all about the sound of money. We old schoolers thought about making music great, not just making money out of the music. Yes, the money is important, but musical appreciation has nothing to do with money. Remember the old song, "Money Is The Root Of All Evil"?

Of course music evolves. It always has since the first notes of Pop Stoneman's "Sinking Of The Titanic," recorded about 1925. The buying public only has the opportunity to listen/purchase/download what is offered to them. These days with the purchase of blocks of radio run by Clear Channel or Cumulus or Sirius, the radio station plays what they are told to play. Apparently the listeners have nothing to do with the play list, on a lot of these stations.

Maybe the music makers on *Music Row* will someday remember the roots of country music. Maybe they should listen to the advice of a great guitar player, Grady Martin, who said, "If you can't hear and understand every word the singer is singing, you're playing too much." Or perhaps they should listen again to the Lacy J. Dalton hit that warns: *"And for a while they'll go in style, on Sixteenth Avenue."*

They are still calling the music "The Nashville Sound" that's being recorded today, but the meaning of the Nashville Sound has been absent for years. Maybe a new "hook" should be coined. Sadly, it hasn't.

As you walk down the streets of *Music Row* today, it's surprising to see what's happened to the buildings that were once alive with music publishers, record labels, booking agencies and promotion companies. New tall condos, even hotels, are replacing the old buildings that for years housed artists, songwriters and music business executives doing business their way. The green, green grass of home is fast moving elsewhere. The news is full of *Music Row* moves to downtown Nashville. Headlines say, "Sony could make move to 1201 Demonbreun in The Gulch," and "RCA Building faces sale, the brainchild of Chet Atkins and Owen Bradley." These were the buildings that at one time anchored *Music Row*. Maybe the music business has really become a "business" instead of just a "happening." When what we knew as *Music Row*, that is, 16th, 17th and 18th Avenues South, has been forgotten, I foresee a large plaque, maybe erected in front of the RCA building, which was sold. It might say, "Here, on this spot, *Music Row* began its journey, for what was the *Nashville Sound*." And maybe country music might move elsewhere. As Bob Wills from Texas might say: *"Ah-h-h, come in Austin, Texas!"*

Music Row R.I.P.
- Photo courtesy Shirley Hutchins.

26 NEVER GIVE UP

"We are such stuff as dreams are made on."

William Shakespeare

The very nature of the music business, with all its extreme ups and downs, is hard on the strongest person. I knew about Howard's early mental problems in the Navy, even before I married him in 1965, but he really never showed any signs of his earlier ordeal. Then in 1974, he had his first re-occurrence of his old mental problems.

A mental problem is not something you discuss with your fellow musicians, only your psychiatrist. In the music business, you always have to appear young and vital. We knew about an Arranger in town who had cancer, but couldn't tell anyone for fear if they found out he wouldn't get any more work. It's sad not to be able to have sympathetic conversations with your contemporaries. It's a cruel business.

The first signs that I noticed, which made me question him was that Howard got so he couldn't get along with people. He stopped being funny. He stopped playing golf. He did what was expected of him with no joy. He wanted to sleep all the time. Finally he agreed that he needed to go back to the VA Hospital; however, he thought he just needed rest. At the hospital, rest was still the main objective, but new tranquilizers and anti-depressants were now on the menu. They had also added Group Therapy. Howard was on 4-B, the mental ward, which was now filled with patients from the Korean and Vietnam conflicts. Howard really believed that the doctors at VA tried to get insight into his problem.

This marked Howard's first VA hospitalization in twenty-nine years. His VA disability had been cut to ten percent long before I knew him. Howard was afraid he was going to be plagued the rest of his life and was scared to death of what people would say in the only business he knew. While still in the hospital, on May 30th he dashed off a crude note to then Congressman Richard Fulton, explaining his condition, asking if he could get his benefits raised. On June 3rd, he received a letter from Fulton, advising him that he had arranged for a representative from the Tennessee Division of Veteran's Affairs to meet with Howard. They met and the outcome was a reinstatement at fifty per cent.

Howard was hospitalized for six weeks. Now he was classified as manic-depressive (these days they call it Bipolar). That didn't worry me, I had worked with too many writers and musicians, who could be classified in the same way had they been diagnosed by doctors.

Even with all the medicines prescribed, Howard was admitted again to the hospital in 1975. This time they added to the diagnosis, "anxiety with depression." Outwardly, he seemed to be responding to treatment. When he was released he was followed up for treatment in the out-patient clinic.

Howard fought going back to the hospital. He really wanted to work, but the music business didn't seem to want him. Although he was interviewed many times, it seemed that no one wanted to hire a fifty-four year old, experienced only in the music business, with a history of mental illness. He remembered the time in the early days when he was with Copas, his condition made it hard to hold up under the rigors expected of a musician. He just wanted to be a part of entertainment, so he survived, in spite of it all, because he knew that show would go on, with or without him.

In 1983, Howard suddenly had no movement in his legs and a terrible headache. However, that condition cleared up, only to be followed in a few days by a total collapse. I guessed that he had a stroke and our daughter, Kat, and I got him admitted into the VA Hospital. He had blurred vision and slurred speech, and was unable to walk. Then the neurological doctors said it didn't concern them, so he was admitted again in Psychiatry. They put him on the drug, Lithium, which caused dizziness, muscle spasms and a lack of coordination. When they put him in a wheelchair, Kat and I insisted he be given tests for a stroke. In fact, we followed a doctor down the hall, arguing with him. They finally agreed to an EEG, which showed a seizure focused in the left front temporal region. A CT Scan was then given, which proved the evidence of a stroke, and also showed signs of an old stroke. He was again discharged as an out-patient. At this point, his mood swings became more pronounced. Of course, I knew that a manic-depressive condition is characterized by drastic mood swings.

By the time Howard turned sixty, he had learned a lot. He could not hold a regular job; the music business was not unkind to him, he just wasn't in any condition to work. He also learned that government hospitals could write medical records exactly like they wanted. He often wondered just how many lives had been messed up as his had. He remembered a note posted on the bulletin board on 4-B at the VA Hospital: "Class of '68 – We will always be remembered as that half-generation of fools turned drug-crazed killers of children."

Howard lamented, "Like this poor veteran, in my class of '45, all I wanted to do was serve my country. So much for flag waving!"

Years continued to roll by. Howard and I kept trying to appeal to the Veteran's Administration to up his disability percentage with no results. Then we went to the Disabled American Veterans (DAV). They tried, but were unable to do anything. They said the VA couldn't do anything because there were no records of Howard's claim regarding the gas experiment. They said all the records had been burned in a fire at St. Louis, site of a military records storage center. We also tried through a new Congressman again, to no avail. Then *60 Minutes*, the CBS-TV show, did a show which included a story about two thousand sailors who had undergone a gas experiment in 1945, and were sworn to secrecy. Our friends and neighbors began calling us about it. We sent for a copy of the show. It seemed that

217

then-Florida Senator Porter Goss had discovered the whole shady affair from a veteran in West Virginia, who had been one of the guinea pigs. Another trip to the DAV still offered us no hope. We still had no official records proving that Howard was one of those thousands of "guinea pigs."

One day in 1990, completely frustrated, I called the U.S. Navy Department at the Pentagon, and got in touch with a young Naval officer, who was sympathetic to my plight. He said, "Mrs. White, I'm going to try and find your husband's records. If I do, I'll call you." I thought, "Well, that's that!" I never expected to hear from him again, but about three weeks later, he called, saying, "I've found your husband's records in a locked file cabinet here at the Pentagon!" Seemingly these vital documents had been "lost" since 1945. He mailed us copies, which finally gave us all the proof needed. These records proved that Howard had been used for experimental purposes, that Mustard and Lewisite gases had been used, giving the dates and number of times he had gone into the gas chamber, and when he was hospitalized. The records also said he was a Schizophrenic, paranoid type. At last we knew!

With those records, we went back to the DAV. The agent again warned Howard he didn't believe they could help us. That triggered Howard's going off! All of a sudden, he stood up, grabbed hold of the desk, and stated, "I'm going to turn this desk over, if you don't try to do something!" The agent turned white, stood up and said, "Calm down, I'll try." Again I thought, "Well that's that!"

Then on April 9, 1998 in the mail, Howard received a notice from the Veteran's Administration that his disability had been reviewed and reclassified at one hundred per cent. Then he received, from the Department of Defense, a "Certificate Of Commendation" in recognition of Special Services, loyalty and contribution to the United States of America during World War II. Backdated to May 9, 1996, it was signed by William J. Perry, Secretary of Defense!

Howard was rightly proud. He even gave the government credit saying, "Since the Iraq War began, I realize that maybe the two thousand of us sailors that were used for gas experimental purposes, served a purpose for a new generation of fighting men, who are now issued special preventative gear, in case of use of weapons like gas by the enemy."

Five years after Howard died, I learned that, for years, the government had covered up their experiments on servicemen. By chance in 2013, I was reading a book, "Simple Truth," and on page 378, I came across a statement made about a certain Army experiment with LSD, using the excuse of testing uniforms against gas. I investigated further, finding that in 1959, a certain Master Sergeant at Fort Knox "volunteered" for a chemical warfare testing program. The testing was done at the Aberdeen Proving Grounds in Maryland. They did not wear special clothing or gas masks. Afterwards, they talked at length to psychologists. In 1975, the Army asked those involved to participate in follow-up exams for members of the Army, who had been given LSD in 1959, as the Army wanted to study long-term effects of the drug given. These Army volunteers were administered LSD under the pretense of testing clothing against gas warfare. They were never told they were given LSD. (Court case: United States v. Stanley, 483 US 669, 1987.) Sound familiar?

From Schizophrenia to Manic Depressive to Bipolar to anxiety with depression, the diagnosis had changed over the years; however it changed, it only meant that the VA could not diagnose Howard's specific problem. After all, the VA hospitals didn't have his records either. There was no doubt in our minds that these days the diagnosis would have been classified PTSD (Post Traumatic Stress Disorder). I guess it doesn't matter now. With apologies to Macdonald Carey, "Like sands through the hourglass, so are the days of our lives." Yet another actor Will Rogers philosophically opined, *"Live your life so that whenever you lose, you're ahead."*

Department of Defense

Awards this
Certificate of Commendation
to
Howard O. White

In recognition of special service, loyalty and contribution to the United States of America during World War II.

May 9, 1996
Date

William J. Perry
Secretary of Defense

27 LITTLE THINGS

"Some people come into
Our lives and quietly go
Others stay for awhile
And leave footprints on our hearts."

- Grandpa Jones.

In the year 2000, Howard White wrote the lines in this chapter, just little things, he thought you'd like to know.

"Many years have passed since my daddy bought me my first Kalamazoo guitar. I've traveled a lot of miles since I left home to begin a career in country music. I have done a few things I'm proud I did. I produced an album, 'The Nashville Sound On Sunday Morning,' on which I used ten of the greatest hymns ever sung, with two Nashville choirs and studio musicians. I produced an album on a legendary Canadian artist, Lucille Starr. I worked in three Nashville-based movies, 'Country Music On Broadway,' 'Second Fiddle To A Steel Guitar' and 'Girl From Tobacco Road.' (None were nominated for an Academy Award.)

"As I look back, I asked myself, 'Was I a success?' so I thought of the events that seem important to me now at age 75:

I was born in Mecklenburg County, North Carolina.

I saw Ted Williams play baseball in Washington, D. C. and Mickey Mantle at New York and Stan Musial in St. Louis.

I met Jack Dempsey at his restaurant in New York City. (He asked about Minnie Pearl.)

I met Satchel Paige in Nashville, on tour with The Globe Trotters. (He asked about the Duke of Paducah.)

I made a movie with Leo Gorcey, and we were friends until he died.

I heard Dr. Norman Vincent Peale speak in Knoxville.

Fred Rose produced records on me in 1953, on Hickory Records.

I met Nat King Cole in 1963 in Syracuse, New York at the Three Rivers Club. Hank Snow played there for one night, Nat opened for two weeks.

I was truly blessed to work with great artists.

My wife, Ruth, and my daughter, Kathleen, and I have led a happy life no matter where we lived, in a home always called 'Picker's Rest.'

And I decided, yes, life has been a success. I only had three set-backs in my life that made me more determined to come out on top: 1) I lost the soapbox derby race in 1938; 2) When in high school, my team didn't win the basketball championship in 1943; 3) Arthur 'Guitar Boogie' Smith turned me down when I auditioned for The Briar Hoppers.

"There are still old fans and musicians out there who remember me and to them I say 'bless you.' I am proudest when a younger musician

Howard White no doubt playing 'Steel Away.'

remembers my work. Lloyd Green told me he thought I was Jerry Byrd playing steel when he heard Snow's 'Beggar To A King.' Russ Hicks said he remembered skipping school to buy a record of mine, then going home and learning to play it like I did. (I did the same thing with Jerry Byrd records when I was learning.) The years that have passed have made hours of my life that's left. Was it all really worth it? All the heart aches, pain and suffering, tears, loves, laughs and time given to this thing called music! Well, if I had it to do all over again, I'd probably play the game just like I did. I've never been a star, I've always been a sideman, but there's satisfaction in a job well done. There are so many people I've loved that are playing at that big arena in the sky and they are waiting for the rest of us to join them, when the curtain goes up for the evening show. That will be a really big show. And no one will worry about how many people they can pull in at the box office, or the standing ovations, or who broke the attendance record.

"One thing for sure, there will always be more musicians, more singers, more songwriters – all coming to Nashville to fulfill their dreams. And the music will play on and on."

Amen . . .

Howard White

28 THE FINAL CURTAIN

"It matters not if you win or lose,
It's how you play the game."

- Grantland Rice.

There's an end to every song, every record and every story. My story ended when Howard went to sleep and never woke up again. On October 19, 2008, Howard came to breakfast and said, "I had a dream last night. I dreamed me and Jerry Byrd were playing our guitars together somewhere. I don't know where it was, but it was the sweetest music I ever heard." Knowing Howard and his dreams, I asked, "Do you think it means anything?" Howard answered, "No, not a thing." But, before the next morning, October 20th, Howard went to sleep, never to wake again. I was reminded that Howard said many times, "Death is perfect tranquility."

Howard's Celebration of Life was held at the Ernest Tubb Troubadour Theater, thanks to owner David McCormick. He didn't have to worry about pulling a crowd; he had a full house. Walt Trott was emcee. He's an author, historian and publisher and bless his heart, he held the "show" together for me. Billy Robinson kicked off with, "Howard called me every morning at 6:30." Lloyd Green followed, saying, "Howard called me every morning at 7." That was Howard, always keeping in touch with those he loved.

Besides myself, those that spoke were:

Harold Bradley, President of AFofM Local 257, Nashville Musicians Association. (Howard was a Lifetime member of the Union); Lloyd Green, steel guitar player. (Howard got him his first job in Nashville with Faron Young.); Billy Robinson, steel guitar player, good friend and neighbor; Henry Strzelecki, bass player, writer, producer, golfing buddy, best friend; Joe Lee, from West ("By God!") Virginia, record shop owner from Maryland, and record and film producer; Les Leverett, retired official WSM photographer, who read a letter from Tom Perryman, a DJ from Tyler, Texas; Joe Johnson, former Four Star Music owner, MCA producer and golfing buddy; Buzz Cason, songwriter, artist and owner of Creative Workshop; and Don Jennings, son of Bob Jennings. (Howard promised Bob to look out for him.)

Personally, I got tons of mail. One was so real, so like Howard, that I read it to the audience, warts and all. It said: "You have lost a husband and a father. I have lost my good friend, Howard and I were in a race to see who could piss the most people off, and at the same time, we helped a lot of people. I will miss Howard. Love, Don Davis." (He, too, played steel.)

News reports came from everywhere, including Peter Cooper and Beverly Keel of *The Tennessean* newspaper in Nashville; *Country Music News*, Canada; *Country Music People*, England; *Bluegrass Unlimited* magazine,

Virginia; and *The Nashville Musician*, Nashville, to name a few. Felix M. Snell, retired Methodist minister and a real friend, wrote, stating, "Be comforted by Porter Wagoner's hymn, 'I Don't Have to Cross Jordan Alone.' Howard didn't cross alone. Lots of fellow musicians were somewhere to meet him. His crossing was peaceful and quiet." Because Howard loved "A Picker's Prayer" by Billy Edd Wheeler, I read it with Billy Edd's permission:

A PICKER'S PRAYER

"When I started picking, I prayed I'd be rich and famous. (I don't have to tell you how that turned out.) I held that Sears and Roebuck guitar, and dreamed you'd make me another Chet Atkins with flying fingers, just oozing music. You gave me three chords and a capo. I said, 'Lord, just don't make me work in clubs!' I've had my axe busted, my strings cut, I've been heckled and jeckled and jacked around, and cheated out of my pay. I've been hooted and tooted and my lungs polluted, been shot at and missed, and spit at and hit. Seems like everything I've asked for you've given me the opposite; but they've been shining times and I thank you for 'em. And figure somehow out of the hype and hope of this business, you've got a plan. So just let me say: I prayed for stardom, so I could move the world, You kept me unknown, then the world moved me. I wanted a big voice, so I could put everything in my music, You gave me big ears so I'd hear music in all things. Now I'm over 80 and I'm still paying dues, but I've quit trying to sing in somebody else's shoes. I got nothing that I asked for, but everything I'd hoped for. Almost despite myself, my unspoken prayers were answered. I am among all people . . . most richly blessed." © 1978 – Billy Edd Wheeler, Sleepy Hollow Music.

Howard was a dreamer, but we all benefit from the dreamers around us. They are the music-makers and the dreamer of dreams, but they are also the movers and shakers. Howard was a kind of a philosopher and he loved to write bits of wisdom. While traveling on the road, he once wrote: "Blessed is the man whose understanding is dulled by the infinite challenge of reality, for wisdom to life is as a drop of water to the perishing." Of course, none of his fellow musicians understood what he was saying, just like none of them thought Roger Miller would ever hit with his nonsense.

I feel Howard accomplished a lot in his life. He had a daughter he loved and a wife that backed him up, no matter what outlandish plan he thought up. He followed his dream of playing steel guitar at the Opry with the stars. He was successful in music publishing, he was a good record producer and he was a songwriter and wrote books. He was able to do all that, despite the difficulties of war time ills. He regretted only one thing, he was never inducted into The Steel Guitar Hall of Fame in St. Louis; however in 2006, his fellow steel guitar players in Nashville gave him the Legend's Award from The Nashville Tennessee Steel Guitar Association. Howard was a winner in life. I hope he knew it. One thing, for sure, he always played the game fairly.

One day I walked into Howard's music room. His guitar, picks and bar were there where he had left them, the day his music died. That day was bright and sunny. I remembered our last words to each other were "Good night." I am not a songwriter, but words suddenly came to me and I hurried to write them down. The following is the only song I ever wrote (with apologies to Eugene Field, The Children's Poet)."

"ODE ON AN OLD STEEL GUITAR"

"THE OLD STEEL GUITAR IS COVERED WITH DUST
BUT STURDY AND STRONG IT STANDS,
AND THE PICKS AND BAR SIT WHERE THEY WERE PUT
AND THE STRINGS STILL WAIT FOR HIS TOUCH.

TIME WAS WHEN THE GUITAR WAS NEW
AND THE PLAYER SURE PLAYED IT RIGHT,
AND THEN ONE NIGHT WHEN HE HAD PLAYED HIS LAST SONG
HE PUT HIS PICKS AND BAR DOWN FOR THE NIGHT.

"THEY WILL STAY THERE 'TIL I COME BACK," HE SAID,
AND THEY WON'T MAKE ANY NOISE,"
SO GOING OFF TO BED WITH HIS DOG IN TOW
HE DREAMED OF HIS PRETTY GUITAR.
AND AS HE WAS DREAMING, AN ANGEL SONG
TOLD HIM HE HAD PAID HIS DUES,
OH, TIME HAS PASSED, THE DAYS GROW LONG
BUT THE PICKS AND BAR STAND TRUE.

FAITHFUL TO THEIR PLAYER THEY STAND
EACH IN THE SAME OLD PLACE
AWAITING THE TOUCH OF HIS MASTERFUL HAND,
THE SMILE ON HIS HAPPY FACE.
AND THEY WONDER WHILE WAITING THE LONG DAYS THROUGH
IN THE DUST TO THAT OLD GUITAR,
WHAT HAS BECOME OF THEIR PLAYER TRUE
SINCE HE PLAYED AND PUT THEM THERE.

Dedicated to Howard White . . . by Ruth White
© 2008, Howard White Music (BMI).

Our lives were totally consumed with the music business and now I was stuck with the pain of learning that sometimes there isn't anymore. No more music, no more hugs, no more special moments to celebrate together, no more phone calls and no more, "Just a minute, dear." Sometimes what we care about the most gets all used up and goes away never to return.

"There is a time for leaving. Some must stay, as one must always remain to weave the threads left in the loom, and gather the harvests in the field."

- THE END -

Ruth White, 2014

IN REMEMBRANCE

By *Jean Shepard*

Country Music Hall of Famer

"Howard never changed. I loved Howard back forty years ago and I love him today. I'm sure every person has his down time, but you know, in all the years I knew Howard, I never knew him to have a down time. It was news to me, really, that he had mental problems stemming back to World War II. Coming to Nashville with mental problems, and getting into the music business, Lord have mercy! That's the worst thing you could ever do. But he handled it well. I'll bet you could talk to a hundred people, and everybody knew Howard, and they wouldn't know that.

"Howard was a very good musician. I met him through my future husband, Hawkshaw Hawkins. He was in Hawk's band. He had a great sense of humor that kept us all on our toes. He was quite a practical joker. Now back years ago, there was no cocaine, but the pickers would take little Benzedrine pills, which were diet pills. When I first came to Nashville I heard everyone talk about "bennies" and I told Hawkshaw, "There's sure a lot of guys around here named Benny." And he looked at me real funny and started laughing. He said, "Are you really that dumb?" I said, "What do you mean?" He said, "They're talking about Benzedrine…" But, I just couldn't believe it.

"Well, we had a boy playing bass for us named Cedric Rainwater. He was one of the original Drifting Cowboys of Hank Williams. He was a real good ol' boy. Once we went into this restaurant and we all ordered coffee. It was Howard White who put one of those little white bennie pills into Cedric's coffee. Oh, Lord have mercy! Needless to say, Cedric like to drove us all crazy for the next five or six hours. I think that broke Howard of doing some of his practical jokes.

"Howard was a character, but he was always on our side. I don't ever remember asking him to do something he wouldn't do. He always wanted what was best for us, and best for the show. He was always there. A lot of times you lose contact with people, but we still maintained contact. It's a good feeling to remain friends with somebody you've known over forty years. Howard really traveled every highway out of Nashville. I traveled quite a few of them with Howard."

Jean Shepard

Hendersonville, TN

February 18, 1990

ABOUT THE AUTHOR . . .

Ruth Bland White, a Nashville native, began playing piano as a teen in a seven-piece band under the baton of Bill Wiseman. Although their families had it annulled, she and the band's drummer Murrey (Buddy) Harman were married briefly (he went on to become one of Nashville's original A Team session musicians). Ruth, a graduate of East High School, worked at Strobel's Music Store and attended Ward-Belmont College, as a music major. In the store, she played sheet music songs for customers. After moving to Chicago with late husband Bob Kirkham, she managed the music department in a major retail store. Upon returning to Nashville, she worked briefly at Strobel's, where she met future husband Howard White, then a steel guitarist for Opry superstar Hank Snow. Moving on to WSM, she managed the station's music library, assisting Opry stage manager Vito Pellettieri, and the TV show's *Waking Crew* band director Marvin Hughes, with their music needs. In 1965, she wed White, working with him in their Locomotive Music publishing firm, and together co-managed Henry Strzelecki's October Records, an independent label sponsored by Pepsi-Cola. Subsequently, Ruth worked on Music Row for Country International Records, Strzelecki Publishing, Reed Music, Inc., and artist Porter Wagoner, running the Opry legend's production, booking and publishing operations. Her specialty, administering music publishing and copyrights, was an expertise sought by such clients as Carmol Taylor, Norro Wilson, Sonny James, Gary Gentry, Charly McClain, Joe Stampley and The Nashville Superpickers (including players Strzelecki, Buddy Spicher, Phil Baugh, Buddy Emmons, Pig Robbins, Terry McMillan, Bill Pursell and Buddy Harman). She was production coordinator on albums involving Canadian vocalist Lucille Starr; White's gospel collection; and a music CD for The Hermitage, a popular tourist site. In 2010, Ruth was the recipient of a SOURCE Award, recognizing her pioneering accomplishments on Music Row. She is mom to Bob Kirkham, Jr., and Kathleen White. A prolific author, Ruth White's books have included: "Every Highway Out Of Nashville" (JM Productions/Picker's Rest, 1990); "Mecklenburg: The Life & Times Of A Proud People" (JM Productions/Picker's Rest, 1992); "The Original Goober" (Nova Books, 2004); "You Can Make It If You Try," the biography of R&B pioneer Ted Jarrett (Hillsboro Press & Country Music Foundation Press, 2005); and "Nashville Steeler," a biography of veteran guitarist Don Davis (Schiffer Books, 2012).

THE LAST RIDE . . .

A Bonneville Pontiac station wagon was the last vehicle Country Music Hall of Famer Hank Snow used to transport his troupers to show dates, equipment and all, prior to purchasing his first tour bus in the early 1960s. The iconic Grand Ole Opry star enjoyed such hits as "I'm Movin' On," "The Last Ride" and "I've Been Everywhere."

(Photo by Kathleen White; Pontiac courtesy Spencer Williams.)

HOWARD WHITE'S DISCOGRAPHY

One Man's Diary of Recordings

"The words change,
But the music endures . . ."

1946 - "Recording work for me began in an East Trade Street studio situated in a Charlotte, North Carolina warehouse. A singer named Eddie Kirkley and I recorded there though nobody ever knew about it but Eddie, the band, the engineer and I. Can't remember the studio name nor the independent recording label. Everybody who records has had this sort of first time experience, as it's part of the learning curve."

1947 - "Simpson's Studio in Charlotte began to call me to do a lot of demo sessions; however, the one I remember most was with Bill Trader, who wrote the song "A Fool Such As I," a major hit for Hank Snow (and later Elvis Presley). When Hank cut this song I learned that great things can come out of demo sessions."

1948 - "Shannon Grayson asked me to record with him and the Golden Valley Boys

after hearing a demo I cut at Simpson's."

Shannon Grayson & His Golden Valley Boys (King Records).

Recorded at King Studios, Cincinnati, Ohio, Syd Nathan, A&R, Howard White (steel), Millard Pressley (mandolin), Harvey Rayborn (bass), E. C. Beatty (rhythm guitar), Shannon Grayson (vocals & banjo).

"I Like the Old Time Way" - 880A

"I'm Gonna Walk" - 880AA

1949 - Shannon Grayson & His Golden Valley Boys (RCA Records). Recorded at a hotel in Atlanta, Georgia, Steve Sholes, A&R, Howard White (steel), Millard Pressley (mandolin), Harvey Rayborn (bass), E. C. Beatty (rhythm guitar), Shannon Grayson (vocals & banjo).

"Sunset of Time" - 20-4304

"Someday in Heaven" - 20-4304

"If You Don't Love Your Neighbor" - 20-4426

"The Secret Weapon" - 20-4426

1951 - "Demo sessions with Don Gibson at radio station WBIR-Knoxville, Tennessee, on Gay Street. Don sent this session's results to Troy Martin in Nashville. Troy then set up a session for Don on Columbia Records, Nashville. Don's band and I did the following master session there in 1952."

1952 - Don Gibson, Columbia Records, Nashville, July 7, 1952. Recorded at Castle Studios in the Tulane Hotel, with Don Law, A&R, Howard White (steel), Grady Martin (lead guitar), Luke Brandon (rhythm guitar), Marion Sumner (fiddle), Joe Zinkan (bass), Marvin Hughes (piano) and Don Gibson (vocals).

"Let Me Stay In Your Arms" - 21060A

"Sample Kisse" - 21060B

"We're Steppin' Out Tonight" - 20999A

"No Shoulder To Cry On" - 20999B

1953 - "I was excited to be working with Cowboy Copas, but was even happier when he took me to Cincinnati to record." Copas, King Records, March 1953. Recorded at King Studios, Cincinnati with Syd Nathan, A&R. Howard White (steel), Louis Innis (rhythm guitar), Zeke Turner (lead guitar), Tommy Jackson (fiddle) and Cowboy Copas (vocals & guitar).

"A Wreath On the Door Of My Heart" - 1200A

"I Can't Go On" - 1200B

"Tennessee Senorita" - 1234A

"If You Will, Let Me Be Your Love" - 1234B

Note: Above tracks later incorporated in LP: "A Heartbreak Ago," Masterpiece Records, MLP-201.

1953: "Cowboy Copas took me to Fred Rose and he produced my records for Hickory, at Rose's Studio, 3621 Rainbow Trail, Nashville." Howard White (Hickory Records, December 22, 1953. A&R Fred Rose, Howard White (steel), Grady Martin (lead guitar), Luke Brandon (rhythm guitar), Strollin' Tom Pritchard (bass).

"The Steel Guitar Swallow" - 45-1032A

"Rosette" - 45-1032B

"The Dove" - 45-1008A

"Ensonata" - 45-1008B

Note: Howard wrote "Rosette" and "Ensonata," while on tour with Cowboy Copas in Rolla, Missouri.

1956 - Dave Rich & The Echoes of Calvary Quartet (RCA Records). Recorded at RCA Studios, Nashville, A&R Chet Atkins, Howard White (steel), Floyd Cramer (piano), Spider Rich (lead guitar), Dave Rich (vocals) and other musicians unknown.

"Where Else Would I Want To Be" - 47-7656A

"Brand New Feeling" - 47-7656B

1956 - Simon Crum a.k.a. Ferlin Husky (Capitol Records). Recorded at Columbia Studios, Nashville, with Nelson King, A&R, Howard White (steel), Randy Hughes (rhythm guitar), Sammy Pruett (lead guitar), Ike Inman (bass), Tommy Vaden (fiddle) and Simon Crum (vocals).

"Little Red Web" - 4966A

"Don't Be Mad" - 4966B

1956 - Al Gannaway Show #86 telecast, filmed at old Bradley's Barn, with Jean Shepard singing "You're Calling Me Sweetheart Again," Hawkshaw Hawkins' "If It Ain't On The Menu," and "Doggone Shame," and Rita Faye singing "Your Cheatin' Heart." Released as *Classic Country* series via TV.

1957 - Wilma Lee & Stoney Cooper (Hickory Records). Recorded at Acuff-Rose Studios, Franklin Road, Nashville, with Johnny Erdelyan, A&R, Howard White (steel), George McCormick (guitar), Jimmy Elrod (banjo), Benny Martin (fiddle), Joe "Flapjack" Phillips (bass) and Wilma Lee & Stoney (vocals).

"Heartbreak Street" - 45-1126A

"This Ole House" - 45-1126B

1958 - Wilma Lee & Stoney Cooper: "Radio Gems" (Hickory Records). "Radio Gems #3," Liner Notes by Joe Lucas. Howard White (steel), George McCormick (guitar), Jimmy Elrod (banjo), Joe "Flapjack" Phillips (bass), Stoney Cooper (fiddle) and Wilma Lee & Stoney (vocals).

Program B: "We Live in Two Different Worlds"

"Poor Ellen Smith"

"Wildwood Flower"

"Is It Right"

"Come Walk With Me"

"Wabash Cannonball"

"Are You Walkin' and A'Talkin' With The Lord."

1960 - Mitchell Torok (Decca), June 30,1960.

Recorded at Bradley's Studio, 804 16th Avenue S., Nashville, with Harold Bradley, A&R, Howard White (steel), Harold Bradley (guitar), Ray Edenton (guitar), Grady Martin (guitar), Lightnin' Chance (bass), Buddy Harman (drums), Floyd Cramer (piano) and Mitchell Torok (vocals). Supporting vocals by Hoyt Hawkins, Millie Kirkham, Neal Matthews, Gordon Stoker, Ray Walker and Marijohn Wilkin.

"Happy Street" - 2040

"Little Boy In Love" - 2040

"King Of Holiday Island" - Unissued

1961 - Hank Snow (RCA), February 8, 1961. Recorded at RCA Studios, Nashville, with Chet Atkins, A&R, Howard White (steel), Gene Martin (guitar), Junior Huskey (bass), Chubby Wise (fiddle), Doug Kirkham (drums), Floyd Cramer (piano), Tompall Glaser, Jim Glaser and Joe Babcock, backup singers, and Clarence E. (Hank) Snow (vocals, guitar & leader).

"Beggar To A King" - 47-7869A

"Poor Little Jimmie" - 47-7869B

"The Restless One" - 47-7933A

"I Know" - 47-7933B

Note: "Beggar To A King" stayed in the *Billboard* charts 20 weeks, peaking at #5, while "Restless One" charted nine weeks, topping out at #11.

1961 - Hank Snow (RCA), June 5, 1961. Recorded at RCA Nashville, with Chet Atkins, A&R, Howard White (steel), Velma Williams Smith (guitar), Junior Huskey (bass), Chubby Wise (fiddle), Doug Kirkham (drums), Tompall Glaser, Jim Glaser (singers), Clarence (Hank) Snow (vocals, guitar, leader) with Bill Porter, engineer.

"A Legend In My Time" - LPM-2458   ACL 0124

"Bury Me Deep" - LPM-2458

"Fraulein" - LPM-2458

"Mansion On The Hill" - LPM-2458

"Send Me The Pillow That You Dream On" - LPM-2458

1961 - Hank Snow (RCA), June 6, 1961. Recorded at RCA Nashville, with Chet Atkins, A&R, Howard White (steel), Velma Williams Smith (guitar), Hank Garland (guitar), Junior Huskey (bass), Chubby Wise (fiddle), Buddy Harman (drums), Marvin Hughes (piano), Tompall Glaser, Jim Glaser and Chuck Glaser (singers), Clarence (Hank) Snow (vocals, guitar, leader, with Bill Porter, engineer.

"Just A Petal From A Faded Rose" - LPM-2458 ACL 0124

"Return To Me" - LPM-2458

"That Heart Belongs To Me" - LPM-2458

"I'll Go On Alone" - LPM-2458

"I Care No More" - LPM-2458

"I Love You Because" - LPM-2458

"Address Unknown" - LPM-2458

Note: Songs recorded June 5-6 included on the LPM-2458 album "Big Country Hits - Songs I Hadn't Recorded Till Now" (also LSP-2458).

1962 - Hank Snow (RCA), January 11, 1962. Recorded at RCA Nashville, with Chet Atkins, A&R, Howard White (steel), Velma Williams Smith (guitar), Junior Huskey (bass), Maybelle Carter (autoharp), Tommy Vaden (fiddle), Chubby Wise (fiddle), Buddy Harman (drums), Marvin Hughes (piano), Tompall Glaser, Jim Glaser and Anita Carter (singers), Clarence (Hank) Snow (vocals, guitar, leader).

"You Take The Future (And I'll Take The Past)" - BCD-15502 478009A

"Dog Bone" - BCD-15502 478009B

"If Today Were Yesterday" - BCD-15502 Unissued

"For Sale" (duet with Anita Carter) - BCD-15502 Unissued

"White Christmas" - BCD-15502 LPM-2579

Note: "You Take The Future" charted 10 weeks, peaking at #15. Hank's duet with Anita Carter appeared on the RCA album - LPM-2580 - titled "Hank Snow & Anita Carter, Together Again" (also LSP-2580).

1962 - Hank Snow (RCA), March 28, 1962. Recorded at RCA Studios, with Chet Atkins, A&R, Howard White (steel), Velma Williams Smith (guitar), Junior Huskey (bass), Maybelle Carter (autoharp), Chubby Wise (fiddle), Louis Dunn (drums), Marvin Hughes (piano), June Carter, Helen Carter, Anita Carter, Tompall Glaser, Jim Glaser and Chuck Glaser (singers), Clarence (Hank) Snow (vocals, guitar, leader).

"Black Diamond" - BCD-15502 LPM-2723 CAS-2443

"What Then" - BCD-15502 LPM-3595

"When Today Is A Long Time Ago" - BCD-15502

"Casey Jones Was His Name" - BCD-15502

1963 - Chubby Wise & The Rainbow Ranch Boys (Starday). Recorded at Hank Snow's Rainbow Ranch Studios, with Hank Snow, A&R, Howard White (steel), Chubby Wise (fiddle), Gene Martin (guitar), Ed Hyde (guitar), and Junior Huskey (bass).

Title: "Tennessee Fiddler - Chubby Wise & The Rainbow Ranch Boys" (SLP-154).

Side One:	Side Two:
"Opry Fiddler's Blues"	"Orange Blossom Fiddle"
"Peacock Rag"	"Smoky Mountain Waltz"
"Memphis Blues"	"Tennessee Blues"
"Shenandoah Waltz"	"Cacklin' Hen"
"Rainbow Breakdown"	"Georgiana Moon"
	"Whistlin' Rufus"

1963 - Jack Boles, Wizard 211, February 1963 . Recorded at Nugget Studios, Goodlettsville,Tennessee. Howard White (steel) and Jack Boles (vocal, guitar, leader), while other musicians unknown. Nugget was founded by Rollin & Johnny Sullivan (of Lonzo & Oscar fame) in 1959 as a family label.

"Walkin' In High Cotton"   211A

"You Turned Out Just As Bad"   211B

1963 - Zeke Clements (Guest Star). Title: "The Man From Music Mountain" G-1443. Recorded at Jay Gower's Studio, Nashville. Howard White (steel), Jerry Chesnut (guitar), Zeke Clements (vocals, guitar, leader) and other musicians unknown.

Side One:	Side Two:
"Me And My Big Loud Mouth"	"Tennessee Skies"
"Texas Swing"	"Poor Man's Paradise"
"Where The Sweet Blue Bonnets Grow"	"I Hear My Love Calling Me"
"Mountain Home Blues"	"Beyond The Border"
"Return To Red River Valley"	"Darlin' Rose Malone"
"Lonesome World"	"God Made It All"

Zeke Clements, who wrote the #1 hits "Smoke On The Water" and "Just a Little Lovin'," died in 1994. Reportedly he was the first singer to wear Western style costumes on WSM's *Grand Ole Opry,* and provided the voice of Bashful in Walt Disney's animated feature film "Snow White & The Seven Dwarfs" (1937).

1964 - Benny Williams (Todd). Recorded at Fame Studios, Muscle Shoals, Alabama. Howard White (steel), Benny Williams (vocals, fiddle, guitar), and other musicians unknown. Benny was another struggling musician residing briefly at Mom Upchurch's boarding house in East Nashville, and found success as a bluegrass picker.

"Ninety Miles From Nashville" - 451099

"I Want To Be A Star (In Hillbilly Heaven)" - 451099

1967 - George (Goober) Lindsey (Columbia Records). Recorded at Columbia Studios, Nashville, with Howard White, and Audie Ashworth, A&R.

Title: "The World's Biggest Whopper" - 4-44215

Howard: "I was working for Hubert Long at Moss Rose Publishing Company when I played straight man for Goober at this session. Ralph Emery was supposed to have done this, but he canceled and I landed the part."

1976 - Howard White (Bear Family Records), released May 1992. Recorded at RCA Studios, Nashville, with Henry Strzelecki, A&R. Remixed at Pete Drake's Studio, Nashville.

Album title: "Howard White, Western Swing & Steel," BCD-15575.

Reissue producer Richard Weize. Engineers at RCA: Bill Vandevort and Chuck Seitz. Players: Howard White (Dobro), Henry Strzelecki (bass),Tommy Williams (fiddle), Buddy Spicher (fiddle), Lisa Silver (fiddle), Pete Wade (guitar), Dave Kirby (guitar), Bobby Thompson (guitar), Buddy Harman (drums), Pete Drake (steel) and David Briggs (piano).

"Jealous Heart"

"San Antonio Rose"

"Blue Eyes Crying In The Rain"

"Faded Love"

"Roly Poly"

"Midnight"

Deep Water"

"Columbus Stockade Blues"

"Rose Of Old Pawnee"

"Before I Met You"

Steel guitar instrumentals also released in above album were recorded December 22, 1953, at Rainbow Trail Studio, produced by Fred Rose and originally released on Hickory Records. Howard White (steel), Grady Martin (guitar), Luke Brandon (guitar) and Strollin' Tom Pritchard (bass).

"The Dove"

"Ensonata"

"The Steel Guitar Swallow"

"Rosette"

2002 - Howard White (Independent), released September 2002. Compact Disc titled:

"Great Hymns We Used To Sing" - HOW-326.

Co-produced by Ruth White and Joe Funderburk, with Joe Funderburk as engineer, and liner notes by Joe Allison. Musicians: Howard White (lap steel), Lloyd Green (pedal steel), Bill Pursell (piano), Grady Martin and Pete Wade (lead guitars), Jerry Shook and Joe Edwards (rhythm guitars), Joe Zinkan (bass) and Kenny Malone (drums). Originally recorded in 1974 at Cowboy Jack Clement's Nashville studio; over-dubbing and mix in 2002 at Creative Workshop, Nashville; digitally mastered at Thunder Audio Productions, Nashville.

"The Last Mile Of The Way"

"Sweet Bye and Bye"

"Leaning On The Everlasting Arms"

"Amazing Grace"

"Near The Cross"

"The Church In The Wildwood"

"Softly And Tenderly"

"Just As I Am"

"Bringing In The Sheaves"

"Above The Hills Of Time" (a.k.a. "Danny Boy" or "Londonderry Air") recorded originally in 1963 at Cinderella Studios, Madison, Tennessee, and digitally mastered at Thunder Audio Productions. Players: Howard White (pedal steel), Grady Martin (lead guitar), Luke Brandon (rhythm guitar) and Strollin' Tom Pritchard (bass).

2006 - Howard White (Steel Works), "Sweet Memories," produced by White, featuring Howard White (steel), Pete Wade (guitar), Buddy Spicher (fiddle) and Millie Kirkham (vocals), with Skip Mitchell and Hal Duncan, engineers.

"Sweet Memories"

"True Love"

"Birmingham Jail"

"Mansion On The Hill"/"Cold, Cold Heart"

"Slowly"

"Over The Waves"

"When I Stop Dreaming"

Also on this tape are the Hickory Records releases on Howard White as previously cited.

INDEX

241